LC
10.15.70

The American Churches in the
Ecumenical Movement: 1900–1968

The American Churches
in the
Ecumenical Movement
1900-1968

SAMUEL McCREA CAVERT

ASSOCIATION PRESS : NEW YORK

THE AMERICAN CHURCHES IN THE
ECUMENICAL MOVEMENT: 1900–1968

Association Press, 291 Broadway, New York, N. Y.   10007

Publisher's stock number 1676
Library of Congress catalog card number 68–17775

TO

DANA S. CREEL,

*who encouraged me to record
and interpret this history.*

Foreword

THE relation of the American churches to one another today is markedly different from what it was at the beginning of this century. In 1900 any other form of church life than separatist denominationalism seemed impossible. Since that time there has been a noteworthy drawing together in mutual understanding and concern, in fraternal accord, in cooperative service, in united activities, in federated structure and even in a measure of union. Nothing comparable has happened before in American history.

Although the development of the ecumenical movement in its worldwide aspect has been recorded in considerable detail, the story of the American churches in their relation to it and to one another has not been told. Important contributions to it have been made, dealing with certain periods and certain areas of interest, but there has been no over-all history of cooperation, federation, and union in American church life as a whole. This book is an attempt to fill the gap.

The story which is narrated here begins with the dawn of the twentieth century. To make this our point of departure may seem arbitrary, since the year 1900 marked no sudden break with the past. Yet the twentieth century has witnessed such an acceleration of the movement toward Christian unity in America, with so many new manifestations of it in the early years of the century, that there is ample justification for taking 1900 as our starting point. There is good historical reason for calling the twentieth century the ecumenical era in America.

Another reason for my concentration on the twentieth century is that this is the period of which I can speak out of considerable firsthand knowledge. For fifty years it has been my happy privilege to be in close contact with the ecumenical movement and to have the "feel" of it as it has developed both here and abroad. Whatever qualification I have for historical writing on this subject is derived from personal experience covering half a century.

The history of any movement can be written in either of two ways—from the inside or from the outside. The facts are the same in both cases but the perspective on the facts may be very different. A man in Abraham Lincoln's situation, for example, is so identified with American democracy that he refers to the Declaration of Independence as resulting in "a new nation, conceived in liberty and dedicated to the proposition that all men are created equal." An English historian, on the other hand, with Olympian detachment, baldly describes the same document as "a resolution which made the colonies independent."

This is decidedly an "inside" story. I cannot pretend to be neutral. However much I try to avoid subjective judgments, my commitment to the ecumenical movement will be everywhere apparent. I may even resemble the Virginian who tried to write "an objective history of the War between the States from a Southern point of view."

I hope, however, that I have avoided the two pitfalls that beset everyone who tries to record the past. One is the pitfall of the mere annalist, who produces a depersonalized and dry-as-dust chronicle of bygone events. The other is the pitfall of the romanticist, who imposes his own enthusiasms upon the historical data.

In the course of my research it became clear that there are alternative methods of dealing with a mass of historical material. One method is to review the situation as a whole, as it develops year after year and decade after decade. This presents broad vistas of the changing scene and of the most significant landmarks on the total horizon. The other method is to examine in much greater detail what has happened in each limited area of special interest. This provides a closer scrutiny of procedures and activities in each particular field. To use a shop-worn metaphor, in one case we see the forest in its comprehensive sweep, and in the other case learn about the individual trees. Since both methods are valuable, each for its own purpose, I plan to employ them both and devote a volume to each.

The American Churches in the Ecumenical Movement: 1900–1968 makes the first approach. It is primarily concerned with historical perspective. It presents a general survey of what has happened in successive periods as the American churches have begun to move forward in overcoming the weaknesses of their divided state. It unfolds a panoramic picture, aiming to help the reader to make a discriminating appraisal of trends in the past and of the situation in which the churches now stand in relation to one another.

The companion volume will look more closely at the same years (1900–1968) from the angle of each of the specific areas of cooperative or unitive concern. In so far as it succeeds, it will be serviceable as a reference work for those interested in greater factual detail. If the reader does not find in the present volume some of the information which he expects, perhaps the second will supply what is lacking. It will review the developments in fifteen specific fields: in religious education, in higher education, in evangelism, in missionary responsibility for America, in world-wide mission, in social tasks, in race relations, in international relations, in works of mercy and relief, in the use of mass media of communication, in research and long-range planning, among church women, among Protestants and Catholics and Jews, in local communities and statewide areas, and, finally, in the quest for organic union.

My indebtedness to those who have made it possible for me to carry this study to completion is much greater than I can possibly express. First of all, I pay tribute to Dana S. Creel, director of the Rockefeller Brothers Fund, whose interest encouraged me to undertake the study, and to Mrs. John D. Rockefeller, Jr., whose generous gift to Union Theological Seminary provided indispensable assistance in research.

To Union Theological Seminary I am grateful for sponsoring the project, and especially for assigning Professor Robert T. Handy as my continuous adviser for three years. By his rich scholarship in the field of American Church History, he has introduced me to important source materials and given me new insights into the period of which I write. If the book stands up under the scrutiny of historical critics, it will be largely due to Dr. Handy's help.

To a far greater degree than appears from the title page, this history is the work of a cooperating group. Some of them have assumed extensive responsibility not only in research and counsel but also in the first drafts of several chapters which will appear in the second volume. Chief among these collaborators are Roswell P. Barnes, Elmer G. Homrighausen, Benson Y. Landis (whose lamented death in the midst of our research was a great loss), Mrs. Erminie H. Lantero, S. Franklin Mack, Hermann N. Morse, and William J. Schmidt. I hope to give adequate recognition to their work in the second volume.

I am further indebted to several friends for helpful suggestions, comments, and criticisms. Among them are Yorke Allen, Jr., R. H. Edwin Espy, Miss Elma L. Greenwood, Edwin C. Foster, H. Conrad Hoyer, Constant H. Jacquet, Jr., Hubert C. Noble, John F. Piper, Jr., and Mrs. William S. Terrell. Acknowledgments to many others are made in footnotes to the text.

When John D. Rockefeller, Jr., was involved in the restoration of Colonial Williamsburg, he expressed his hope that through the project "the future may learn from the past." It is my hope that in some measure something like that may result from this historical study of the American churches. If we are to move forward into some larger pattern of unity, we must understand how we have reached the point where we now are. To help in this understanding is the one purpose of this book.

S. M. C.

Glossary of Terms

In any discussion of unity among the churches there will be confusion unless the terms which are used to designate different types of relationship are carefully distinguished. In the interest of clarity it is important to bear in mind the various nuances of meaning involved in words and phrases that will recur again and again in these pages.

Unity is a general term having to do more with spirit and attitude than with organizational structures.

Undenominational and *nondenominational* describe activities at which Christians work together as individuals, without affecting the churches or their official agencies.

Interboard cooperation refers to the action of denominational boards and societies in working together in their specific fields, but without involving decision by the denomination as a whole.

Interdenominational (or *interchurch*) cooperation goes beyond interboard action in indicating measures taken by denominations as corporate bodies.

Federation goes beyond interdenominational cooperation in implying a permanent and official relationship of denominations as corporate bodies under a constitutional charter.

Federal union goes beyond federation in delegating to a central body a measure of responsibility and authority in certain limited fields, while the denominations retain full autonomy in all functions not thus delegated.

Organic union is a form of corporate structure in which the denominations give up their separate identities and become one united church.

Three other terms, all related to the foregoing, need also to be distinguished from one another:

The conciliar movement describes the present structure of cooperation of churches as churches, at all geographical levels, without any commitment to a relationship beyond cooperation.

The ecumenical movement refers to the whole development within the churches in drawing closer together—whether by fraternal fellowship, cooperation, federation, or union—when viewed in the perspective of the nature and mission of the church as one Body of Christ throughout the world.

The interfaith movement, wider than historical Christianity, embraces the relations of friendly contact, dialogue, and collaboration in certain tasks between Christians and the adherents of other religions of the world.

Contents

Introduction

CHRISTIANITY in North America has been pluralistic from the very beginning. To the many branches of the Christian Church which arrived from Europe over a period of more than three centuries have been added a number of indigenous bodies. Church divisions over theological or sociological matters have added further to the spectrum of American denominations, so that at times it has appeared that Christianity in America, especially in its Protestant forms, would keep on proliferating into an ever-increasing number of bodies.

The ecumenical movement in the twentieth century, however, has contributed dramatically to the increased cooperation of many Christian churches through councils of churches and through other agencies. It has also led to some significant acts of church union, some across confessional lines, so that the integrative aspects of Christian life in America seem now to be gaining on the disintegrative. Though the roots of the ecumenical movement lie deep in history, the twentieth century has seen a remarkable growth in its size and impact. It has emerged as the most significant general development in recent American church history.

When we try to tell the story of this important development, we find ourselves confronting a somewhat different set of problems than historians of some earlier movements have faced. For many earlier enterprises, the documentation is limited and one-sided. For the ecumenical movement, however, especially in its twentieth century manifestations, we are embarrassed by the flood of materials we have for a still-growing, many-sided movement which has flourished in an age of the typewriter and the mimeograph machine, and in a period which has seen a vast increase in the volume of periodicals, pamphlets, and books. To write a coherent account that provides useful interpretations based on such a vast body of materials is itself an important achievement and a significant contribution to twentieth century church historiography.

It would probably be impossible to find a person better qualified to do the particular type of historical work that needed to be done at this moment than the author of this work, Dr. Samuel McCrea Cavert. He has been a perceptive observer of much of the story that unfolds here, and an active participant in many of its most central chapters. In 1918, he became assistant secretary of the General War-Time Commission of the Churches, and then, after service in several other posts, became general secretary of the Federal Council of the Churches of Christ in America in 1921. He held this post through three decades, contributing much to the achievements of the council, and also to its merger with other cooperative church agencies to become the National Council of Churches in 1950. He continued as general secretary of the new council until 1954, when he became an executive secretary of the World Council of Churches until his "retirement" in 1957.

As many historians and philosophers of history have shown, no man can be or should be expected to be fully objective in his interpretation of human events and institutions. The man who knows his own commitments and enthusiasms and who determines to be as fair and balanced as he can to all positions, however, is the best prepared to deal objectively with complex movements in which he has been involved. Dr. Cavert is such a man; he has been able to describe and analyze events in which he has had a part frankly and openly, without ever coming close to over-emphasizing his part or yet falsely denying his own views and role. For over half a century he has been involved in the story he now presents, a story which unfolds against the backdrop of two world wars, of times of depression and of prosperity, and of the emergence of nuclear power and jet transportation. He tells the story clearly, yet without divorcing it from the general setting or hiding its real complexity. This is a book which will be useful for any who wish to understand better the many-sided ecumenical movement of the present century, chiefly in its American aspects—a movement that has broadened notably in recent years through the increasing participation of Eastern Orthodox Churches and through the dramatic entrance into the ecumenical scene by the Roman Catholic Church since the pontificate of Pope John XXIII and the Second Vatican Council.

ROBERT T. HANDY

Union Theological Seminary, New York

1

The Nineteenth-Century Background

In the closing years of the nineteenth century Leonard Woolsey Bacon, completing the first major history of American Christianity, contrasted the "solid political unity" of the nation with the situation in the churches. In them, he pointed out, there was no "coordinating authority," no "common leadership," no "system of mutual counsel and concert." On the horizon, however, he detected a rising concern for "a more manifest union."[1] How that concern took form during the twentieth century is the theme of this book, but in order to understand this development we must first review the nineteenth-century background.

The diversity which has marked American religion is an amazing phenomenon. There are more than 250 separate denominations—some large, some very small—each having its independent organization. The ecclesiastical miscellany resembles a "crazy quilt" such as rural housewives used to make, a patchwork of all sorts of interesting pieces without any over-all pattern.[2]

Most of this fantastic fragmentation took place in the nineteenth century, although it had its beginnings in the colonial period. It was chiefly due to the extreme heterogeneity of the population. Before the end of the century the American people had come to be a cross section of all the peoples of Europe. As the successive waves of immigrants came to the new world, they brought their religious traditions with them. All forms of faith in all the countries of Europe became domesticated within a single nation. In the picturesque phrase of Philip Schaff, the historian and theologian who came to this country from Germany in

---

[1] Leonard Woolsey Bacon, *A History of American Christianity* (New York: The Christian Literature Company, 1897), pp. 398ff.

[2] *The Yearbook of American Churches, 1967,* ed. Benson Y. Landis (New York: National Council of the Churches of Christ in the U.S.A.) presents statistics for 251 denominational bodies, and there were a few others that made no report. Nineteen have more than a million members each; thirty-five enroll fewer than a thousand each. The figure of the "crazy quilt" is suggested by Donald H. Yoder.

1843, the religious picture of America in mid-century was "a motley sampler of all church history."

In Europe the dominant religious group in each area had insisted on ecclesiastical conformity enforced by the civil power. In America, too, prior to the formation of the national government, nine of the thirteen colonies had an established church, with restrictions of various kinds imposed on dissenters. Full freedom and full legal equality for all became the accepted pattern only after the federal constitution was adopted.

A New Relation of Church and State

The development of religious freedom and the separation of church and state in America were due to several interacting factors. It is an oversimplification to assume that the new pattern was the result only of popular demand and moral conviction. The requirements of practical wisdom were a decisive factor. None of the colonial churches could claim a majority of the population of the nation. None was strong enough throughout the country as a whole to be able to dominate. Each wanted freedom for itself, and in order to have it accepted similar freedom for the others.[3]

What developed in America was a more radical innovation than is generally realized. For the first time the principle of complete freedom in religion was established over a vast national territory. As a perceptive historian puts it:

> On the administrative side the two most profound revolutions which have occurred in the entire history of the church have been these: first, the change of the church in the fourth century from a voluntary society, having in its membership only those who were members by their own choice, to a society conceived as necessarily coextensive with the civil community . . . second, the reversal of this change. That reversal was completed in America.[4]

The significance of the type of church life emerging in America was rightly discerned by Philip Schaff, when, after a decade in this country, he interpreted it to his former colleagues in Germany. He was frankly critical of such unpleasant features of the American scene in the 1850's as crude rivalries between Protestant groups, heresy hunts, and anti-Catholicism, but he predicted that "something wholly new will gradually arise." Everything, he reported, "is yet in a chaotic transition state,

---

[3] For a discriminating analysis of the complex factors that contributed to the separation of church and state in the nation, see Robert T. Handy, "The American Tradition of Religious Freedom: An Historical Analysis," *Journal of Public Law*, Atlanta, Vol. XIII, No. 2, 1965.

[4] Winfred E. Garrison, *Annals of the American Academy of Political and Social Science* (March, 1948), p. 17. A similar point of view is expressed by Sidney E. Mead in giving the title of "The Lively Experiment" to his interpretation of "the shaping of Christianity in America" (New York: Harper & Row, 1963).

but organizing energies are already present and the Spirit of God broods over them to speak in time the almighty word: 'Let there be light!' and to call forth from the chaos a beautiful creation."[5]

Throughout the nineteenth century American religion was increasingly pluralistic. It was, however, a pluralism within an almost Protestant circle. At the beginning of the republic, Roman Catholics were hardly 1 per cent of the population, and Jews a small fraction of 1 per cent. Later streams of immigration radically changed the picture, but as late as 1927 a European observer could still conclude that Protestantism was "America's only national religion."[6] The tardiness of Protestants in adjusting to the transition to the wider religious pluralism was responsible for much tension in the later decades of the nineteenth century and the earlier part of the twentieth.

The Denominational Pattern

The denomination, as it evolved in the United States, was a novel form of the church. It had antecedents in Great Britain in the rise of the Free Churches side by side with the established church, but it was only in the new world that there was a complete voluntaryism in the relation of the individual to the church. Religious pluralism such as had never been known before was the end result—with new values and new problems.

The absence of any official interlocking between church and state not only gave all the inherited traditions equal opportunities to develop but also encouraged the rise of new religious groups. The continuous expansion of the young nation westward across a great continent placed a premium on individual initiative and pioneering. This independent spirit was a determinative influence in religion as well as in other aspects of American life. If a man did not feel that his church was on the right track in its doctrine, its moral standards, or its administration, there was nothing to prevent his organizing a church according to his own ideas. If his venture was not welcomed at home, there was plenty of room elsewhere. As a consequence, the nineteenth century saw the formation of many new religious bodies of many types.

All the major churches of Europe were represented in the United States at the beginning of the nineteenth century—Anglican, Congregational, Presbyterian, Baptist, Methodist, Lutheran, Reformed, Quaker, Roman Catholic—as well as other small groups like Moravians, Brethren, Schwenkfelders, Mennonites, and Jews. To these, still others were to

---

[5] Philip Schaff, in *America: A Sketch of Its Political, Social, and Religious Character,* ed. Perry Miller (Cambridge: Harvard University Press, 1961), p. 81.

[6] André Siegfried, *America Comes of Age* (New York: Harcourt, Brace & Company, 1927), p. 33. By "national religion" the French commentator meant a religion that had affinity with the American culture.

be added before the end of the century as the result of later migrations. As each tide of newcomers swept to our shores, it brought its own ethnic and religious heritage with it. Differences in language added to the separateness within some of the denominational families. Among Lutherans, for example, there were German, Swedish, Norwegian, Danish, Slovak, Finnish, and Icelandic. Not until the twentieth century, when linguistic factors had ceased to count, could a movement for Lutheran union make headway.

In the last decades of the nineteenth century an inundation of immigrants from Eastern and Southern Europe, which was to reach its peak in the early years of the twentieth, greatly accentuated religious pluralism in the United States. The earlier immigrants had been predominantly of the same ethnic backgrounds as the colonists—English, Scottish, German, Scandinavian, Dutch, Irish—Protestant except for the last. The new arrivals were mainly Jewish, Roman Catholic, or Eastern Orthodox. There was also a token representation of the non-Christian faiths of Asia. The United States had become a microcosm of almost the whole world of religion.

New religious movements of an indigenous character also took root in the free and fecund soil of America and some of them had a remarkable growth. An early one, especially interesting to students of unity, began to take shape in 1809 under the leadership of Thomas and Alexander Campbell on the frontier of western Pennsylvania. They aimed to effect a union of Christians by persuading them to abandon their denominational names and organizations and come together simply as "Disciples" on the sole basis of the Bible and a return to the practice of the primitive church. Entirely contrary to the intention of the Campbells, a movement which was to eliminate denominations ended as one more denomination. A group with similar views had grown up around Barton W. Stone, the revivalist leader in Kentucky, and in 1832 these "Christians," as they preferred to be called, finally joined forces with the Disciples.[7]

Two other denominations which came to birth at the beginning of the nineteenth century were outgrowths of revivalism among people of German background, the United Brethren in Christ and the Evangelical Association. In the forties the supporters of William Miller's proclamation of Christ's return to earth began to assume permanent form, later becoming the Seventh Day Adventists and the Christian Adventists. At the end of the century the Pentecostal groups, with primary emphasis on the gift of "speaking with tongues," began to have a vigorous growth.

---

[7] Thomas Campbell's views were expounded in his "Declaration and Address" and Barton W. Stone's in the "Last Will and Testament of the Springfield Presbytery." The two documents are printed together in a convenient edition, with an introduction by F. D. Kershner (St. Louis: Bethany Press, 1960).

These are but a few of the bodies that have sprung up in the lush American soil. In addition to this Protestant denominationalism there are various other organized groups which have arisen on its periphery, such as the Latter Day Saints in 1830, the Church of Christ Scientist in 1879, and Jehovah's Witnesses in 1884, though not bearing this name until later.

Still other denominations were formed by splits within existing bodies. As early as 1810 a schism within the Presbyterian family over issues connected with revivalism led to the establishment of a separate Cumberland Presbyterian Church.[8] A division between "Old School" and "New School" Presbyterians began in 1837, but was healed in the next generation. In New England Congregationalism a doctrinal controversy led to the formation of the American Unitarian Association in 1825. Within Methodism a controversy over the role of the laity and a protest against episcopacy resulted in the Methodist Protestant Church in 1830. At a later period the "Holiness Movement," magnifying the doctrine of Christian perfection, led to withdrawals from Methodism and the initiation of several small bodies, some of which came together as the Church of the Nazarene. From the Reformed Church in America a dissenting group of the more conservative Calvinists withdrew to form the Christian Reformed Church in 1857. Among the Lutherans a controversy over a strict versus a liberal interpretation of the confessional standards led nearly half of the General Synod to withdraw and form the rival General Council in 1867. In 1873 the Reformed Episcopal Church was founded by evangelicals in the Protestant Episcopal Church who were opposed to Anglo-Catholic trends. Several Negro denominations were organized because of dissatisfaction with a second-class role in a church predominantly white, including the African Methodist Episcopal, the African Methodist Episcopal Zion, the Colored Methodist Episcopal, and the National Baptist Convention.

More dramatic and more fateful were the divisions occasioned by the national struggle over slavery. The three largest denominations whose members were distributed between North and South all broke apart— the Methodists in 1844, the Baptists in 1845, the Presbyterians in 1857 and 1861. Only in the case of the Methodists has subsequent reunion taken place. The division of these three bodies as the result of a conflict in the political realm is a classic illustration of the large role played by social forces in the development of denominationalism.[9]

---

[8] Revivalism, which was the dominant form of religious activity in the nineteenth century, had a partly favorable, partly unfavorable, influence on unity. The revivals largely ignored denominational differences, emphasizing only what was relevant to conversion and personal holiness, and thereby fostered a common body of Protestant sentiment. On the other hand, conflicting views about revivalistic practices and ideas were sometimes a source of schism.

[9] An indispensable treatment of this aspect of organized religion is H. Richard Niebuhr, *The Social Sources of Denominationalism* (New York: Henry Holt and Company, 1929).

Denominational Barriers Ignored

As the nineteenth century was prolific in bringing denominations to birth, it was likewise fertile in developing ways of surmounting denominational barriers. The American experiment in voluntaryism produced not only a great variety of churches but also many organizations through which members of separated churches could work together in enterprises of common concern. These organizations did not bring the churches into relation with one another but secured the cooperation of Christian people by by-passing the denominations and creating non-ecclesiastical societies. The new agencies were formed in the pragmatic interest of accomplishing certain concrete tasks, not for furthering unity among the churches. Individuals who felt impelled to help circulate the Scriptures or to gather children into Sunday Schools or to initiate missionary projects or to work for some social reform banded together for their specific purpose, without reference to the churches to which they belonged.

There was, however, one outstanding exception to this generalization —the so-called "Plan of Union" which two denominations, the Presbyterian and the Congregational, officially adopted in 1801 and which continued for half a century. It was an agreement for close collaboration in the missionary occupation of the virgin territory opening up in western New York and beyond the Alleghenies. They were to be allies, not rivals, in their westward march. Under the provisions of the compact, Presbyterian and Congregational settlers in a new community combined to form a single parish, with freedom to call a pastor from either denomination. There was unity "at the bottom" while the denominations remained separate "at the top." The American Home Missionary Society, formed in 1826, was committed to the Plan. It worked well in most communities and did much to avoid a competitive planting of churches.

But after a time tensions arose. In the Presbyterian Church the schism of 1837 between "Old School," with its insistence on strict Calvinism, and "New School," with its moderating temper, reflected the strain. The adherents of the Old School, feeling that churches established under the Plan were not truly Presbyterian, began to concentrate their support on agencies of their own. The New School stood by the Plan.[10] On the Congregational side, dissatisfaction with some of the results of the agreement arose. It tended to work to the numerical advantage of the Presbyterians, since they had a more closely knit supervisory structure. In 1852 the Congregationalists followed the Old School Presbyterians in abrogating the Plan.[11]

---

[10] Union Theological Seminary in New York was founded in 1836 by strong upholders of the Plan of Union and had a special interest in training ministers for work under it.

[11] For a brief account see Douglas Horton, "The Plan of Union of 1801 in the United States," *Reformed and Presbyterian World*, Geneva, Vol. XXVI (March, 1961), p. 5. For an

In the beginnings of their foreign missionary service there was also a cooperative arrangement between the Congregationalists and Presbyterians through the American Board of Commissioners for Foreign Missions, initiated in 1810 by Congregationalists. In 1812 the Presbyterian General Assembly recommended to its churches that they aid the enterprises projected by the American Board, and at one time a majority of the members of the Board were Presbyterians. In 1837, however, the Old School Presbyterians decided to support a foreign missionary society of their own. The Dutch Reformed Church had also become related to the American Board in 1815, but as the sense of missionary obligation widened, its General Synod voted that it was "the duty of the Church in her distinctive capacity as such" to be responsible for missions abroad. By 1870 the American Board was only one of many denominational societies.

The quarter-century after 1810 was prolific in new organizations that brought Christians together outside their denominational structures. In 1815 the American Education Society was formed "to aid all pious young men, of suitable talents, who appear to be called to preach Christ, and who belong to any of the denominations."[12] It was soon overshadowed by denominational organizations of similar purpose as concern for the training of the ministry increased. In 1816 the American Bible Society was formed, which still preserves its original character as an independent board acceptably serving all the churches. Indicative of the ecclesiastical temper of the times is the fact that in order to avoid giving offense to any denominational group, the devotional periods at the meetings of the Society's Board of Managers were limited to a passage of Scripture, without comment or prayer.

In 1824 the American Sunday School Union was established by laymen as an undenominational agency with the missionary objective of planting a Sunday School "wherever there is a population." What happened to the Sunday School movement is illuminating. It arose quite outside the denominations, but was gradually taken over by them. The report of the Union in 1833 bluntly said that "as a society we recognize the existence of various evangelical denominations only so far as to avoid their points of difference." But pressures for more denominational emphases were soon to come. As a critic of the undenominational character of the instruction argued, with logical consistency, in 1850, "If the truths and principles that are distinctive to any given denomination are not of enough importance to have them taught to the young . . . then

---

analysis of the reasons for both the breakdown of the Plan of Union and the transition of the American Board to a denominational status, see Williston Walker in *Christian Unity: Its Principles and Possibilities*, by the Committee on the War and the Religious Outlook (New York: Association Press, 1920), pp. 285–295.

12 William Warren Sweet, *The Story of Religion in America*, revised and enlarged edn. (New York: Harper & Brothers, 1950), p. 252.

those truths and principles are not of sufficient importance to justify the *existence* of that denomination."[13] The more self-conscious the denominations became, the more they wanted to control the teaching of their children. As a result, most of the program of religious education passed into denominational hands.

In 1825 the American Tract Society began its program of publishing Christian literature that would appeal to people of any evangelical background, but the major denominations gradually developed publishing houses under their own direction. Other nondenominational agencies arose to promote various reforms, such as the American Society for the Promotion of Temperance in 1826, the American Peace Society in 1828, and the American Anti-Slavery Society in 1833. There was hardly any important challenge of religious or social need that did not evoke a response in the form of a voluntary society that ignored denominational distinctions and theological differences.

These nondenominational organizations, taken together, constituted a movement of large proportions—so much so that they even came to be called, collectively, the evangelical "empire." They represented a praiseworthy outpouring of Protestant energies and commanded the support of influential laymen. Their weakness lay in a feeble sense of churchmanship. They reflected John Locke's conception of the church— widely influential in the America of this era—as only a voluntary association of individuals. The organizations, even though effective in pursuing particular objectives, were unrelated to the church as a living organism with a corporate life. Because of this theological deficiency they could not permanently satisfy many of the thoughtful leaders in the churches.[14]

The denominations finally took over the work that the nondenominational organizations had carried on. The one major area of concern that did not become thus denominationalized was the distribution of the Bible. The transition to denominational responsibility had both a good and a bad aspect. It was good insofar as it represented a deepening sense of the mission of the church itself—a mission which could not be left to a group of individuals. It was bad in the resulting fragmentation of effort due to the lack of any cooperative or coordinating plan among the separated denominations.

Denominational Polemics

None of these expressions of common Christian concern in the first half of the century sought to modify the denominational structure in

---

[13] Quoted in William Bean Kennedy, *The Shaping of Protestant Education* (New York: Association Press, 1966), p. 41.

[14] See Lefferts A. Loetscher, "The Problem of Christian Union in Early Nineteenth Century America," *Church History*, Vol. XXXII (March, 1963), pp. 3–16.

any way. Their focus was not on the churches but on specific tasks that Christians faced.[15] Among the churches a polemical and competitive temper prevailed. The enthusiasm of its followers to extend the denomination was a source of organizational vitality but by overemphasizing minor points of difference the rivalries obscured basic agreements at a deeper level. An observant historian could even offer the wry summary that "the fear that the work of the Gospel might not be done seemed a less effective incitement to activity than the fear that it might be done by others."[16]

A revival of denominational emphases which began about 1840 was reflected in local communities in the kind of situation that Washington Gladden described as characteristic of his boyhood. Writing of his experience in a Presbyterian church in a village of western New York in the middle of the century, he said:

> There were other churches in the village, but they had no more dealings with one another than the Jews had with the Samaritans. Sectarian jealousies were fierce; ministers of the different churches were hardly on speaking terms; an exchange of pulpits was a thing never heard of.[17]

The sectarian mood was strongest in the lusty life of the Western frontier. An interesting reflection of it is seen in some of the religious songs which were a part of the folklore of the era. A Methodist historian records, for example, a Methodist verse which ran as follows:

> The Devil, Calvin, and Tom Paine
> May hate the Methodists in vain;
> Their doctrines shall be downward hurled,
> The Methodists shall rule the world.[18]

More deplorable controversies were occasioned by social and political developments. The massive migrations of Roman Catholics from Ireland and southern Germany, beginning in the thirties and rising to a crescendo in the forties, stimulated detestable reactions among citizens of the older Protestant stocks. A "Native American" movement came into being which was aggressively anti-Catholic and at times even erupted into mob violence. In the fifties it took political form in the Know-Nothing Party. In the same period the issue of slavery was precipitating in-

---

[15] There was, however, one regional development that should be noted. Lutheran and Reformed congregations, both of German background—chiefly in Pennsylvania—began to come together in a local affiliation that provided for the use of a common edifice, often operating a joint Sunday School and sometimes having a joint church council. After some years a reaction against the unionizing tendency set in, with an emphasis on the maintenance of the distinctiveness of the two denominations.

[16] Leonard W. Bacon, *op. cit.*, p. 176.

[17] *Recollections* (Boston: Houghton Mifflin Co., 1909), p. 34.

[18] William Warren Sweet, *Religion in the Development of American Culture* (New York: Charles Scribner's Sons, 1952), pp. 157–159.

tense sectional strife. It divided the churches almost as sharply as it divided the nation, and at an even earlier date, and left a baleful legacy whose effect is still felt.

One development in this period, however, was an augury of a more gracious ecclesiastical climate that was to come. In 1838 Samuel S. Schmucker, the prime mover in founding the Lutheran Theological Seminary at Gettysburg, issued "A Fraternal Appeal to the American Churches, with a Plan for Catholic Union on Apostolic Principles." He proposed a confederation of denominations under the name of "The Apostolic Protestant Church of America," within which the denominational structures would be retained but with a free interchange of ministers and open communion. There was to be a statement of common faith, made up of the Apostles' Creed and selections from the main historic confessions of the Reformation.[19] A short-lived "Society for the Promotion of Christian Union" was formed by sympathetic supporters of the plan in several denominations. In 1845 Dr. Schmucker took the further step of publishing an *Overture for Christian Union,* with a list of forty-five distinguished signers endorsing it, and in 1870 he presented, in *The True Unity of Christ's Church,* a modified form of his original proposal. In spite of his persistent advocacy and the support of some influential churchmen, the project came to nought. It was far ahead of its time, but it was important evidence of a rising discontent with the inadequacies of uncoordinated denominations.

After mid-century the Young Men's Christian Association and the Young Women's Christian Association were a potent influence not only in service to youth but also in introducing Christians to one another across denominational lines. The Associations were lay organizations, entirely under non-ecclesiastical control but intimately allied with the churches, and generally regarding themselves as carrying on a program in behalf of the churches of the community. In their earlier decades the Associations were devoutly evangelical and zealously evangelistic. As they became more community-minded and the social and educational facilities of their buildings attracted young people regardless of religious affiliation, the organizational tie with the churches became more tenuous and relations with agencies of social work much closer.[20]

During the Civil War a beneficent program of cooperation in behalf of the social and religious needs of men in the Union army was administered by an organization known as The United States Christian Com-

---

[19] The best edition of the Appeal, including an extended and informative interpretation of it in the light of its historical setting, is Samuel Simon Schmucker, *Fraternal Appeal to the American Churches,* edited with an introduction by Frederick K. Wentz (Philadelphia: Fortress Press, 1965).

[20] The Story of the Y.M.C.A. is told by C. Howard Hopkins in *History of the Y.M.C.A. in North America* (New York: Association Press, 1951). See also S. Wirt Wiley, *History of Y.M.C.A.-Church Relations in the United States* (New York: Association Press, 1944).

mission, which had its origin in a Y.M.C.A. convention. The program, carried out by unpaid volunteers, included personal religious work and comfort to the sick and dying. The Commission proved so serviceable and enlisted so much support in all the churches that after the war it was reconstituted, under the name of the American Christian Commission, for new forms of undenominational ministry in the growing urban communities. One of its important contributions was to promote interest in the "city mission" as a center of Christian contact with neglected groups. Another was its stimulus to house-to-house visitation for reaching unchurched people in the cities.

The Evangelical Alliance

In the generation after the Civil War the Evangelical Alliance was the greatest force in holding up the ideal of Protestant unity. Though the Evangelical Alliance was founded in London in 1846, the American Branch was not formed till 1867, an earlier attempt to establish it having failed because of difficulties created by British agitation against permitting owners of slaves to be members. A "declaration of principles" interpreted the Alliance as desiring "simply to bring individual Christians into closer fellowship and cooperation on the basis of the spiritual union which already exists in the vital relation of Christ to the members of His body in all ages and all countries." It adopted a doctrinal platform of nine affirmations, which were fairly representative of the conservative evangelical theology of the era. Among the most vigorous activities of the Alliance was its championship of religious liberty for minorities in countries where an established church discriminated against them. This tended to give the public image of the Alliance an anti-Catholic slant. Its most far-reaching action was the inauguration of a world-wide week of prayer for all Christians at the beginning of each new year. In 1873 one of the great international conferences of the Alliance was held in New York and made a deep impression upon the American people.

In the later years of the nineteenth century, after three decades of salutary influence, the Alliance experienced a continuous decline. The reasons seem to have been the lack of an effective central organization, a stiff and rigorous doctrinal basis, and differences over policies and programs. Josiah Strong, who became the general secretary in 1886, was committed to a much stronger emphasis on social action than many of his colleagues were ready to accept. He was especially ardent for cooperation of the churches in the same town or city in dealing with social conditions in the community. When he resigned in 1898, dynamic leadership for the future was not forthcoming and the Alliance gradually became dormant. Its meagre assets were eventually inherited by the Federal Council of the Churches of Christ in America. A few of the state and local units of the Alliance became the foundations on which councils of churches were later built.[21]

The Evangelical Alliance stands out clearly as the most significant organization of the nineteenth century that had the specific purpose of furthering Christian unity. Some of its leaders pointed beyond it to a more adequate embodiment of unity. In 1870 Dr. Schmucker, who had been one of the founders, proposed that it be transformed from an association of individuals into a body representative of the churches themselves. A little later a similar vision captured the imagination of the most influential leader of the Alliance, Philip Schaff. At a meeting held in 1893 in connection with the "Parliament of Religions" at the Chicago World's Fair, he urged a "federal or confederate union," which he precisely defined as

> a voluntary association of different churches in their official capacity, each retaining its freedom and independence in the management of its internal affairs, but all recognizing one another as sisters with equal rights and cooperating in general enterprises such as the spread of the gospel at home and abroad, the defense of the faith against infidelity, the elevation of the poor and neglected classes of society, works of philanthropy and charity and moral reform.[22]

Schmucker and Schaff were lonely prophets in their time, but the next century was to see their vision fulfilled.

New Forms of Christian Cooperation

The late decades of the nineteenth century witnessed the rise of several movements which gave leadership in drawing Christians of different churches together in behalf of the Christian nurture of children and youth. National conventions of Sunday School workers of all denominations had been held at intervals of a few years since 1832, largely under lay leadership. State and county Sunday School associations began to be formed as early as 1856. In 1872 an International Lesson Committee was appointed, and a series of uniform lessons launched, undenominational in character. By this time it was plainly seen that something more continuous was called for than occasional conventions, and the movement evolved into the organization known as the International Sunday School Association. Fifty years later it was to be transformed from an organization of Sunday School workers into a council related to denominational boards.

---

[21] No adequate history of the American branch of the Evangelical Alliance has been published. Most of its records and a manuscript by Wallace N. Jamison entitled "A History of the Evangelical Alliance for the United States of America" are in the library of Union Theological Seminary in New York.

[22] David S. Schaff, *The Life of Philip Schaff—In Part Autobiographical* (New York: Charles Scribner's Sons, 1897). The whole address is printed in *Christianity Practically Applied* (New York: Baker & Taylor, c. 1894), Vol. I, pp. 318ff.

In the interest of strengthening the Christian life of young people, Francis E. Clark founded the Christian Endeavor Society in 1881. It spread rapidly around the world, being simple enough in both purpose and plan to find a welcome in the churches of almost every denomination. Its conventions, gathering young people from churches of many types, ministered to mutual understanding. After its success had led the major denominations to organize their own young people's societies, Christian Endeavor gradually declined. An organization for furthering Christian work "by and for men" also reflected the increasing interdenominational outlook. It was the Brotherhood of Andrew and Philip, established in 1888 by Rufus W. Miller. At first limited to the Reformed Church in the U.S., it later developed chapters in several other denominations.[23]

In the colleges and universities the Student Volunteer Movement enlisted young men and women for missionary service abroad under all of the denominational boards. Founded in 1886 as the outcome of one of Dwight L. Moody's conferences of students for Bible study, it kindled the imagination of Christian students for "the evangelization of the world in this generation." By the end of the century almost every college had a "Volunteer Band" and the great quadrennial conventions of students from all parts of the nation were a powerful force both in securing missionary recruits and furthering missionary education on a supradenominational basis.

The Student Volunteer Movement was the missionary aspect of a far wider Christian Student Movement which, by the end of the nineteenth century, was having a pervasive influence. The Student Movement was less an organization than a general stream of Christian concern and commitment among men and women in the college and university world. It owed much to the Y.M.C.A. and Y.W.C.A., both of which gave major attention to work with students. The annual intercollegiate conferences, which summer after summer exposed thousands of students to the inspiration of leaders like John R. Mott, Robert E. Speer, and Sherwood Eddy, gave vision and guidance to Christian work on all the campuses of the nation. By 1895 the movement had spread so widely that the World's Student Christian Federation was organized, chiefly under the initiative of Dr. Mott. The Federation unconsciously became a great training ground for leadership in the ecumenical movement of the twentieth century. A main reason for this was its stress on a student's loyalty to his own church tradition while appreciating others.

---

[23] There were other nondenominational organizations in the latter part of the nineteenth century which brought Christians together in the pursuit of particular objectives. The local units of the Women's Christian Temperance Union, for example, founded in 1874, were made up mainly of women from different churches.

A Vision of Organic Union

While these varied activities of Christian cooperation were going on, a more frontal approach to the problem of disunity called into question the whole concept of the denomination. As in the first half of the century the Disciples of Christ had sought an organic union of all Christians, so now in the second half certain leaders in the Episcopal Church, notably William Reed Huntington, envisaged a similar goal, though by a different route.[24] Instead of making a break with the historical developments of the centuries and trying to restore a primitive pattern, Huntington proposed union based on Christian tradition.

In 1870 he put forward four principles as a basis for uniting the churches: the Holy Scriptures as the Word of God, the Apostles' and the Nicene Creeds, the two sacraments of baptism and the Lord's Supper, and the historic episcopate. In 1886 the Episcopal House of Bishops, meeting in Chicago, adopted the four points, and in 1888 the Lambeth Conference reaffirmed them in slightly modified form. This Chicago-Lambeth Quadrilateral was highly influential in all subsequent discussions of union involving the Episcopal Church.

Many non-Episcopalians, however, felt that the proposal was hardly more than a gracious way of inviting them all to become Episcopalians. It was, of course, the fourth point, the historic episcopate, that created the greatest difficulty. The nub of the problem was how to resolve the impasse between churches unwilling to accept reordination of their ministers and a church unready to accept unambiguously the non-Episcopal ministries.[25]

Response to the Social Challenge

The sweeping changes in the social, economic, and industrial life of the nation after the Civil War presented a sharp challenge to the churches and affected their relation to one another. Gone was the time when a simple rural economy would dominate the nation. A phenomenal growth of great cities and urban industry was under way. Prosperity was booming. Business ethics sank to a low ebb, as the unscrupulous manipulations of financial buccaneers like Daniel Drew, Jay Gould, and James Fiske amply testified. Political corruption was at high tide. Floods of immigrants from Southern and Eastern Europe provided cheap labor for operating mills and factories and building railroads. Wretched city

---

[24] William Reed Huntington, *The Church Idea: An Essay Towards Unity* (New York: Hurd and Houghton, 1870). Also *The Peace of the Church* (New York: Charles Scribner's Sons, 1891) and *A National Church* (New York: Charles Scribner's Sons, 1897).

[25] Huntington hoped that the Quadrilateral might serve to bridge the gap not only between Anglicans and Protestants but also between Anglicans and Roman Catholics. In 1896, however, Pope Leo XIII rejected the validity of Anglican orders.

slums existed side by side with ostentatious displays of new wealth. Industrial strife became rife, as labor found the way of organizing for collective action. Conflicts of unprecedented bitterness broke out: the railroad strikes in 1877, the Haymarket riot in Chicago in 1886, the steel strike in Homestead, Pa., in 1892, the Pullman Company strike in 1894—all marked by violence that shocked the nation.

During the 1870's and 1880's there was little evidence that the churches understood the nature of the Industrial Revolution or were prepared to wrestle with its problems. They did, indeed, try to cope with the new situation by expanding their charitable and philanthropic work for needy individuals.[26] But it was not until the nineties that there came to be any significant appreciation of the need for bringing a Christian social ethic to bear upon the structures of society. The ruling assumptions of *laissez-faire* individualism were taken for granted in the churches as well as in the market place. There was little sympathy with efforts of the workers to better their lot by organizing into unions, and slight awareness of the conditions that made unions necessary. An intensive student of the era even summarizes by saying that on the eve of the calamitous series of strikes, "Protestantism presented a massive, almost unbroken, front in its defense of the social *status quo.*"[27]

An "almost unbroken front"—but not completely so. There were a few men who discerned the signs of the times and tried to reorient the churches to the realities of the new industrialized society. As early as 1875, Washington Gladden had begun to discuss the issues of justice for wage-earners.[28] "In view of the stupendous combinations of capital," he concluded a few years later, "the refusal to permit the combination of laborers is a gross injustice."[29] With his interest in the social significance of Christianity he combined an enthusiasm for cooperation among the churches as essential to making their influence felt on society. His little book, *The Christian League of Connecticut,* described in fictional form what he felt could be accomplished by united efforts of the churches in a factory town.[30] The awakening conscience of the churches

---

[26] The effort of the churches to adapt to the new urban conditions is appreciatively described, with much commendable detail, by Aaron I. Abell, *The Urban Impact on American Protestantism: 1865–1900* (Cambridge: Harvard University Press, 1943). For an analysis of both the intellectual and the social changes that were affecting the life and thought of the churches in the last decades of the nineteenth century, see Arthur M. Schlesinger, "A Critical Period in American Religion 1875–1900," *Proceedings of the Massachusetts Historical Society,* Vol. LXIV, pp. 523–546.

[27] Henry F. May, *Protestant Churches and Industrial America* (New York: Harper & Brothers, 1949), p. 39.

[28] In his *Working People and Their Employers* (Boston: Lockwood, Brooks, 1876), pp. 137–138.

[29] In his *Social Facts and Forces* (New York: G. P. Putnam's Sons, 1897).

[30] *The Christian League of Connecticut* (New York: Century Company, 1883).

was further stimulated by scholars like Professor Richard T. Ely, founder of the American Economic Association, who called *laissez-faire* economics into question on both social and Christian grounds.

Organizationally, the rising social concern found partial expression
in the Evangelical Alliance after Josiah Strong became its general secretary in 1886. In 1887 it held a national congress in Washington which
focused attention on "perils and opportunities of the nation" and the
need for cooperation of the churches in meeting them. The "perils and
opportunities" included immigration, the issues between capital and
labor, and the misuse of wealth. The president of the Alliance at this
time, a distinguished layman, William E. Dodge, predicted that "many
things will be found which can only be successfully met by a cordial
cooperation of all the churches." Several local branches of the Alliance
were formed which had an orientation toward social action.

An informal association which came into being in 1892, unimportant in size but exerting considerable indirect influence, was the
Brotherhood of the Kingdom. Originating in the late eighties in the
personal friendships of a group of Baptist ministers for whom the
goal of the Kingdom of God on earth was all-controlling, including
Leighton Williams and Walter Rauschenbusch, it later embraced members of other denominations.[31]

In the last decade of the century the movement of Christian social
concern found expression in what was called the "institutional church."
This was an experiment in reaching the unchurched masses in the
swarming cities. The adjective "institutional" (hardly a felicitous one)
was intended to convey the picture of a church not limited to worship
and "religious" activities but engaged in meeting all sorts of human
needs. Edward Judson, a pioneer in the institutional church, defined
it as simply "a system of organized kindness" supplementing the "ordinary methods of the Gospel." The activities varied from church to
church, the guiding principle being to adapt the program to the needs
of the neighborhood—physical, social, educational, spiritual. In 1894
an organization known as "The Open and Institutional Church League"
was established to promote the development and coordinate the interests
of the increasing number of institutional churches in the major denominations. The platform of the League declared that it stood for
"open church doors every day and all the day, free seats, a plurality
of Christian workers, the personal activity of all church members, a
ministry to all the community through educational, reformatory, and
philanthropic channels to the end that men may be won to Christ and

---

[31] Charles Howard Hopkins, *The Rise of the Social Gospel in American Protestantism: 1865–1915* (New Haven: Yale University Press, 1940), pp. 131–132. The volume is indispensable for understanding Christian social thought and action in the period after the Civil War.

His service."[32] The secretary of the League was Elias B. Sanford, who in the first decade of the next century was to become the moving spirit in church federation.

In the last decade of the nineteenth century the churches were becoming more sensitive to the problems of an industrialized society. The complacent attitude of the seventies and eighties was dissolving, even though there was still little in the way of social education and action. Sizing up the status of the new social concern in the churches, the historian Leonard W. Bacon cautiously observed just at the end of the century, "Thus far there is not much of history to be written under this head, but somewhat of prophecy."[33] In the next century the new social orientation was to be an important factor in furthering interchurch cooperation.

Denominations Under Self-Criticism

When James Bryce wrote *The American Commonwealth* in the late eighties, he was impressed by the religious harmony he found in the United States. He reported that in spite of the great diversity, "there are no quarrels of churches and sects."[34] This favorable picture probably reflected the British statesman's comparison of the American condition with the unhappy conflicts that had been so characteristic of Europe. It would not have been difficult for him to discover plenty of illustrations of denominational asperities in America. His observation, however, accurately pointed to the main trend at the end of the nineteenth century. The jealous rivalries and sharp polemics of the earlier period were giving way to a spirit of accommodation and mutual acceptance. In the changing situation some of the original sources of separation were no longer as important as they once had seemed. There was less claim to possession of the whole truth, more interaction and reciprocal goodwill.

The denominational system in America had served the Christian movement well. It had afforded each group full opportunity to develop its distinctive tradition. It had provided freedom for new groups to take institutional form around fresh insights. It had stimulated the churches to occupy a constantly enlarging territory and to plant congregations and schools and colleges across the nation. Through voluntary religious activity the nineteenth century in America had been a period of extraordinary expansion and the record of the churches a great "success story."

---

[32] The pamphlet giving the full text of the platform is in the archives of the National Council of Churches.

[33] *Op. cit.,* pp. 385–386.

[34] *The American Commonwealth* (New York: The Macmillan Company, 1910), p. 779.

But by the end of the century the deficiencies of unpatterned denominationalism were only too plain. In both the sparsely populated rural areas and the chaotic cities, overchurching, side by side with underchurching, had become a scandal. In 1883 a Congregational home missionary had to report: "We know of one western town with a population of 1,000, including Roman Catholics, where there are five evangelical churches having their edifices and drawing from their respective missionary boards an aggregate of $1,500 a year."[35] This was an extreme case but it indicated the general problem arising from the lack of comity agreements among the denominations. As late as 1897 an influential Baptist could remark, on reading the report of his missionary society: "I could not discover that any home mission work was being done except by Baptists. I found no hint of cooperation in either counsel or work."[36]

Worse than the waste of resources was the divisive effect of competing churches on the life of the community. Instead of being a force for understanding and reconciliation at the deepest level, they sometimes seemed to be adding one more fragmenting factor to the separations caused by race and class and culture. As the sense of Christian responsibility not merely for individuals but for society as a whole increased, the weakness of denominationalism became more and more apparent. Local churches in the same community had no connection with one another and the national bodies had no common planning. Discerning leaders in many denominations were concluding that this was far from an adequate embodiment of the Church of Christ. They were coming to realize that, since their freedom was now secure, they might use it to cooperate or even to unite. A conspicuous illustration of the changing temper was a resolution of the National Council of Congregational Churches in 1898, proposing a national conference of representatives of interested denominations to consider questions of unity.

The limitations of denominationalism had been partly overcome in the nineteenth century by the numerous organizations which members of separated churches had created for the pursuit of various common objectives. Many of these nondenominational associations had achieved marked effectiveness. This very fact, however, raised the question why the churches should not themselves work together in common tasks.

From dissatisfaction with an anarchical denominationalism two movements in the direction of "a more manifest union" were due to get under way early in the twentieth century. One would pursue the path

---

[35] Cited by Winfred E. Garrison, *The March of Faith* (New York: Harper & Brothers, 1933), p. 128.

[36] Quoted in Robert T. Handy, *We Witness Together* (New York: Friendship Press, 1956), p. 13.

of interdenominational cooperation on the federal principle, following the lead given in the nineteenth century by Samuel S. Schmucker and Philip Schaff. The other movement would focus on the more radical vision, glimpsed by William Reed Huntington, of a union in which the denominations would merge their separate existences into one corporate body. We shall follow both these developments in the succeeding chapters, discovering how the century of expansion was followed by a century of increasing unity.

2

The Churches Begin to Work Together

(1900–1907)

A DISTINGUISHED American historian describes the last decade of the nineteenth century as a "watershed" of our national life.[1] The United States was no longer a land in which a man could stake out a homestead for himself on an expanding frontier. It was rapidly becoming a land of industrialized cities and factories more than of villages and farms. Although 60 per cent of the people at the turn of the century still lived in rural areas, the shift was under way that was to find 70 per cent in urban centers.

There was also a historical watershed in American religious life around the turn of the century.[2] It was a time of decisive transition in the churches. This was especially noteworthy in two movements, both affected by the changing character of the national life. One was the quest for a greater unity. The other was the effort to face up to the unprecedented social challenge of an urban society.

A Quest for National Unity

Although the lines of demarcation between historical eras are seldom sharply drawn, the beginning of the twentieth century is clearly marked as a time when a new movement toward unity was arising in the churches. Throughout the nineteenth century Christians of separated denominations had often joined hands in projects of common interest, but they had done so by working outside the churches. This experience, however, had resulted in by-products of mutual acquaintance and fellowship that cut across ecclesiastical lines and paved the way for future cooperation by the denominations themselves.

An ecclesiastical map of America at the beginning of this century would show a bewildering array of churches, separated from one

---

[1] Henry Steele Commager, *The American Mind* (New Haven: Yale University Press, 1950), pp. 41–54.

[2] The comparison of the two watersheds is suggested by Winthrop S. Hudson, *The Great Tradition of the American Churches* (New York: Harper & Brothers, 1953), p. 158.

another both by confessional inheritance and by ethnic, social, and racial backgrounds. With rare exceptions, these denominations went their independent and isolated ways, each preoccupied with its own affairs, and having little knowledge or concern about what the others were doing.

But there was a cumulative discontent with this orderless situation. The most overt and explicit manifestation of it came from the National Council of the Congregational Churches, at its last triennial session in the nineteenth century. Proposing a national convocation of denominations looking toward federation, William Hayes Ward moved and the Congregationalists voted[3]

> that a representative council or conference of the Protestant churches in the United States and Canada be called to meet in the city of Washington in May, 1900, for the purpose of organizing an interdenominational union, which shall meet at regular periods, and which shall serve as a visible expression of the unity of the churches and as a common bond in their fellowship with each other and their service of the Lord Jesus Christ.[4]

This action by the Congregationalists has the distinction of being the first formal overture by any American denomination in behalf of an official association of churches. Although it bore no obvious fruit, it encouraged an undenominational organization that was to be formed two years later, called the National Federation of Churches and Christian Workers, to plan for a conference of denominational representatives to consider how the churches might come more closely together.

A major impulse toward unity at this time was the deepening concern in the churches for a stronger influence in relation to the baffling problems of an urban industrial society. This concern, voiced by a few prophetic spirits in the last quarter, and especially the last decade, of the nineteenth century, was now finding organized expression. In 1901 the General Convention of the Episcopal Church and the National Council of the Congregational Churches both appointed commissions on the relation of capital and labor. In 1903 the Presbyterian (U.S.A.) Board of Home Missions established a Department of Church and Labor, with Charles Stelzle in charge, the first employed executive of any official church agency in this field.[5] Other denominations began to

---

[3] WILLIAM HAYES WARD (1835–1916), Congregational minister, archeologist, and editor, after a brief pastorate in rural Kansas, was a professor of Latin in Beloit College. Beginning in 1870 he was the long-time editor of *The Independent*. In 1884–1885 he was director of the Wolfe expedition to Babylonia.

[4] *Minutes of the National Council of the Congregational Churches of the United States, 1898* (Boston: Congregational Sunday School and Publishing Society, 1898), pp. 36–37.

[5] CHARLES STELZLE (1869–1941), Presbyterian pastor in Minneapolis, New York, and St. Louis, 1895–1903, was superintendent of the Presbyterian Department of Church and Labor, 1903–1913, and field secretary for special service, Federal Council of Churches, 1916–1918. In subsequent years, he was publicity director, World Alliance for International Friendship through the Churches.

make provision in various ways for dealing with social and industrial conditions.

The problems of the social order, however, had no denominational aspect and the need for concerted action for any effective approach to them was too plain to be ignored. The trend toward greater social responsibility and the trend toward a cooperative unity gradually converged, leading in 1908 to the organization of the Federal Council of the Churches of Christ in America, the first national structure officially yoking denominations together as corporate bodies.

The "Social Gospel" movement of this era is sometimes portrayed by its critics as a substitute for the evangelical heritage of the American churches. This is a superficial interpretation. The evangelical tradition was the basic stock on which the new social interest was grafted. In the historical development of church federation three concerns were fused—the evangelical, the unitive, and the social. All three of them were clearly reflected in the Constitution of the Federal Council.[6]

A Quest for Local Unity

During these years when progressive denominational leaders were becoming sensitive to the need for a greater solidarity among the churches, an impetus in the same direction was coming from local communities. This was especially true in the great cities, confronted with baffling social conditions in the face of which a single parish, standing alone, felt powerless. As early as 1886, Josiah Strong, when general secretary of the Evangelical Alliance, had begun to promote the idea of local organization of the churches for joint action in behalf of moral standards and social welfare.[7] "If now," he said, "the churches of each city or town were organized for cooperation, constituting what might be called the collective Church of the community, and these collective Churches were knit together into county and state organizations—all of which is entirely practicable—the Christian public opinion of the state could quickly and emphatically utter itself."[8]

The conviction that local churches could be "organized for cooperation, constituting what might be called the collective church of the community," began to find expression in a few places before the end of the nineteenth century. The first official organization of this character

---

[6] The evangelical note was seen in the commitment to "Jesus Christ as divine Lord and Saviour"; the unitive, in the declared objective of expressing "the fellowship and catholic unity of the Christian Church"; the social, in the purpose "to secure a larger combined influence for the Churches of Christ in all matters affecting the moral and social condition of the people."

[7] JOSIAH STRONG (1847–1916), Congregational minister, was a pastor in Sandusky, Ohio, 1876–1881, and in Cincinnati, Ohio, 1884–1886; secretary of the Ohio Home Missionary Society, 1881–1884; secretary of the Evangelical Alliance, 1886–1898; and thereafter president of the American Institute of Social Service.

[8] *The New Era* (New York: Baker and Taylor, 1893), pp. 312–313.

seems to have been The Christian League of Methuen, Mass., formed in 1888 by five congregations under the guidance of the youthful E. Tallmadge Root.[9] He had been inspired by reading Washington Gladden's imaginative story, "The Christian League of Connecticut."[10] In 1895 the New York "Federation of Churches and Christian Workers" came into being, the first structure of its kind in a metropolitan area. It included about 150 congregations and various other interested groups. It was, however, not an official federation but an association of church-men who were far-seeing enough to face together citywide problems that could not be handled on either the parish or the denominational level. Its most important contribution at this early stage was its statistical studies, the first of their kind, aiming to furnish to the churches "a scientific basis for accomplishing their social mission." In fulfilling this function the Federation organized a district-by-district canvass for information not only about church attendance but also about educational opportunities and social and economic conditions.

A few city federations, of at least a semi-official character, were organized around the turn of the century. Sometimes a local branch of the Evangelical Alliance was transformed into a federation of churches as in Pittsburgh, Pa., in 1899. Occasionally a Bible Society took the lead in stimulating local churches to become associated for cooperation, as in Hartford, Conn. Sometimes a ministerial alliance or an enthusiastic individual provided the initiative, as in Cambridge, Mass., where the Dean of the Episcopal Theological School gave the needed impulse. In a few large cities—including Detroit, Albany, Jersey City, Portland (Me.), Rochester, Syracuse, and Toledo—federations were reported as "organized" but in most cases did not secure sufficient support to assure a continuous life. Generally, however, after lapsing for a time for lack of leadership or finance, they were reorganized and took on fresh life.

The absence of any arrangements for comity or consultation among local churches meant that there was no more common planning in the burgeoning cities than had earlier been the case in rural America. Overchurching in some areas and underchurching in others was an inevitable result. As a highly informed student of the urban church had to conclude a generation later:

> All the machinery of the church visible, as it exists in the American city, has come to pass according to no general plan and no unity of

---

[9] E. TALLMADGE ROOT (1865–1948), Congregational pastor in Baltimore, Md., 1891–1896, and Providence, R.I., 1896–1904; secretary of Rhode Island Federation of Churches, 1903–1912, and of Massachusetts Federation of Churches, 1904–1930.

[10] The story of the founding of the Christian League of Methuen is told by Dr. Root in *Federal Council of the Churches of Christ in America: Report of the First Meeting, 1908* (New York: Fleming H. Revell Co., 1909), p. 131.

Protestant purpose. . . . What the city presents is a vast spectacle of churches and allied agencies accidentally founded as to numbers, location, and distribution.[11]

The emergence of city councils of churches represented, in large part, an attempt to replace such chaos with some measure of order and system.

Statewide organization of the churches for cooperation had also made a small beginning by the time the twentieth century arrived. The pioneer was the Interdenominational Commission of Maine, inspired by William DeWitt Hyde.[12] It was constituted by five denominations—Baptist, Christian, Congregational, Free Baptist, and Methodist—with the intention of avoiding wasteful competition by reciprocal exchanges of exclusive responsibility for the churching of the smaller communities. Just after the century began, embryonic federations of churches came to birth in the states of New York, Ohio, Rhode Island and Massachusetts. The Massachusetts Federation proved to be the pace-setter.

Antecedents of Federation

On the national level there was one area of concern in which a type of cooperation had begun before the twentieth century that had gone somewhat beyond joint action by individuals. The new development involved the relation of the denominational boards and societies for foreign missions to one another. As early as 1893 the officers and other representatives of twenty-three of them came together in an informal meeting for exchange of information and discussion of common problems, methods, and policies. The suggestion for such a consultation had been made in the previous year by the Council of the Presbyterian and Reformed Alliance. There was no proposal for a continuing organization but the mutual counsel proved so profitable that it was decided to meet again a year later. At the end of their session in 1894 they agreed to meet once again in 1895. Out of these annual gatherings emerged the agency of cooperation known as the Foreign Missions Conference of North America.

In 1900 a great "Ecumenical Missionary Conference" was held in New York, prepared for by the committee that was responsible for the annual conferences of the missionary boards.[13] It came at a time when

---

[11] H. Paul Douglass, *Protestant Cooperation in American Cities* (New York: Institute of Social and Religious Research, 1930), p. 41.

[12] WILLIAM DeWITT HYDE (1858–1917), Congregational minister, president of Bowdoin College, and professor of mental and moral philosophy from 1885 until his death.

[13] It is interesting to note this early use of the adjective "ecumenical." The word was used, it was explained, "because the plan of the campaign which it proposes covers the whole area of the inhabited globe." Some criticism of the term was voiced as "savoring of ecclesiasticism." See *Report of the Fifth Conference of the Officers and Representatives of the Foreign Mission Boards and Societies in the United States and Canada* (New York, 1897), p. 100.

the heightened American participation in international affairs after the war with Spain and the new American role in the Philippines and the Caribbean were kindling public interest in foreign missions. President William McKinley gave the opening address, and the total attendance at the various sessions was estimated as exceeding 150,000. The conference was, however, primarily promotional and contributed only indirectly to policies of cooperation.[14] More important from this standpoint was the founding of the Young People's Missionary Movement in 1902, which later broadened into the Missionary Education Movement with a united program of publications and conferences.

After fourteen years of annual consultations, the Foreign Missions Conference in 1907 created a Committee of Reference and Counsel to perform certain tasks between conferences. The need for acting together in contacts with governments was a major factor that made a continuous committee seem important. The formation of this simple Committee of Reference and Counsel signalized a new development in the functional cooperation of denominational agencies.

The interest in a federated structure of the denominations as corporate national bodies, which the Congregationalists had voiced in a lonely way in 1898, gained wider expression just as the twentieth century dawned. On February 12, 1900, a conference was convened in New York under the joint auspices of the Open and Institutional Church League and the New York Federation of Churches and Christian Workers, to consider the practicability of some kind of national association that would draw the denominations more closely together. Its primary purpose, as then conceived, was to serve as a clearing house of communication between local and state groups trying to develop patterns of cooperation.[15] There was, however, a clearly expressed hope that a federation of national denominations would eventuate. The call to the conference said of the contemplated structure:

> It has thus far, and could have at first, no official relation with any denominational body. But it is desired that it may be the forerunner of an official Federation of Churches to which it shall give place.[16]

At a second conference, held in Philadelphia a year later, the organization of a "National Federation of Churches and Christian Workers" was completed.

The central figure in this development was Elias B. Sanford, who

---

[14] The full report was published as *Ecumenical Missionary Conference* (New York: American Tract Society, 2 vols., 1900). For a summary, see William Richey Hogg, *Ecumenical Foundations* (New York: Harper & Brothers, 1952).

[15] Elias B. Sanford, *Origin and History of the Federal Council of the Churches of Christ in America* (Hartford, Conn.: S. S. Scranton Co., 1916), p. 113.

[16] "Call to a National Conference on Federation of Churches, 1900." The document is in the archives of the National Council of the Churches of Christ in the U.S.A.

since 1895 had been the corresponding secretary of the Open and Institutional Church League.[17] More than anyone else, he did the patient day-by-day spadework for the new movement of federation and enlisted in its advocacy both denominational leaders and forward-looking laymen. While still a small-town pastor in Connecticut, he had been an early spokesman for federation. After becoming the executive of the Open and Institutional Church League he began to think of it as an organizational John-the-Baptist preparing the way for something greater. At the first annual conference of the League in 1895 he had predicted:

> The indications multiply on every side that Protestantism in its historic development has passed beyond its divisive age and is now to fulfill and prove its power, as a divinely guided movement, in gathering its forces into closer unity of spirit in thought and action. . . . Organic ecclesiastical unity we can hold as a dream of the future, or dismiss with the interrogation, Is it desirable? But Christian unity as a spiritual reality and as a practical factor bringing the denominations into federative relations through which they can work out the problems of Christian service in city, country, and abroad without the present waste of forces . . . is coming.[18]

The Philadelphia conference of 1901 was attended by a small and rather miscellaneous group of pioneers in cooperative action. There were delegates from thirteen local or state organizations—embryonic federations of churches in a few cities, branches of the Evangelical Alliance in Pennsylvania and Boston, the Connecticut Bible Society, and the Interdenominational Commission of Maine. None of the participants represented a denomination, but they were all men of influence in their churches.

The new organization sent out a letter addressed to all those "who are troubled at the failure of our churches to reach a considerable part of our population and who believe that much more might be accomplished by united effort intelligently directed." After offering help to local communities desiring to establish federations and urging a federation in each state, the organization avowed its intention to give way as soon as possible to an official structure of national denominations. In making this avowal the signers of the latter reiterated that "the present organization of the National Federation is only temporary," and recorded the expectation "that it may be the forerunner of an official Federation of Churches."[19]

---

17 ELIAS B. SANFORD (1843–1932), Congregational minister, pastor in Cornwall, Thomaston, and Westbrook, Conn., 1869–1895; corresponding secretary, Open and Institutional Church League, 1895–1900; secretary, National Federation of Churches and Christian Workers, 1900–1908; corresponding secretary, Federal Council of the Churches of Christ in America, 1908–1912.

18 Sanford, *op. cit.*, p. 38.

19 A copy of the letter, with full list of the signers, is in the archives of the National Council of Churches.

This letter of the National Federation of Churches and Christian Workers may fairly be regarded as the first formal and deliberate step in the creation of the interdenominational structure that came to be known as the Federal Council of the Churches of Christ in America. The letter bore the signatures of twenty-five well-recognized leaders, both clerical and lay, of nine denominations—Baptist (North), Congregational, Disciples, Lutheran (General Synod), Methodist Episcopal, Methodist Episcopal South, Presbyterian (U.S.A.), Protestant Episcopal, and Reformed. Among the signers were J. Cleveland Cady, the architect who designed New York's Metropolitan Opera House; W. H. P. Faunce, president of Brown University; Charles E. Hughes, later to be Chief Justice of the Supreme Court of the United States; John H. Converse, president of the Baldwin Locomotive Works; William Hayes Ward, author of the Congregational resolution on federation in 1898; Bishop John H. Vincent, Bishop Eugene R. Hendrix, Frank Mason North, Charles L. Thompson, and Rufus W. Miller.

The members of the National Federation of Churches and Christian Workers took this step entirely on their own personal responsibility. None of them had any authority to act for his denomination. Their coming together had been stimulated chiefly by a concern for cooperation in local areas, but they were convinced that some national structure which enlisted the officialdom of the denominations was urgently required.

Prospecting for a Federated Structure

At their next annual meeting in Washington, D.C., in 1902, Dr. Sanford proposed that plans should be laid for a national conference of delegates appointed directly by the denominations. He ventured the judgment that "that which but a few years ago seemed a dream of the future is today in our thoughts as a possible realization at the very beginning of the twentieth century."[20] The proposal was duly approved and a Committee on Correspondence appointed.

The burden of preparing for such an unprecedented gathering fell on Dr. Sanford. The record of his itinerary for the spring of 1902 is an illustration of his indefatigable promotion of the project. In the six weeks between mid-April and the end of May, he was in Syracuse, N.Y., Rochester, N.Y., Buffalo, N.Y., Detroit, Mich., Lansing, Mich., Chicago, Ill., Milwaukee, Wisc., St. Paul and Minneapolis, Minn., Huron, S.D., Omaha, Neb., Lincoln, Neb., Council Bluffs, Iowa, Des Moines, Iowa, Kansas City, Mo., Dallas, Tex., Muskegee, Okla. (then still known

---

[20] Sanford, *op. cit.,* p. 17.

as "Indian Territory"), St. Louis, Mo., Indianapolis, Ind., Columbus, Ohio, and Pittsburgh, Pa. All in the days before the airplane![21]

Through such incessant labors of interpretation and consultation over a period of three years, enough support was enlisted in influential denominational circles to warrant the calling of an "Interchurch Conference on Federation," to be held in the fall of 1905. In 1903 a "Letter Missive" was sent to denominations "already in fraternal relations and in substantial agreement as to fundamental Christian doctrine," inviting them to appoint delegates to such a gathering. The letter not only contemplated the establishment of an official federation but boldly outlined some of its prospective tasks, including weighty social responsibilities:

> We believe that the great Christian bodies in our country should stand together and lead in the discussion of, and give impetus to, all great movements that "make for righteousness." We believe that all questions like that of the saloon, marriage and divorce, Sabbath desecration, the social evil, child labor, relation of labor to capital, the bettering of conditions of the laboring classes, the moral and religious training of the young, the problem created by foreign immigration, and international arbitration—indeed, all great questions in which the voice of the Churches should be heard—concern Christians of every name and demand their united and concerted actions if the Church is to lead effectively in the conquest of the world for Christ.[22]

In the Letter Missive the objective of the conference was explicitly defined as the formation of a permanent interdenominational body representative of the churches as corporate entities. At the same time it was made clear that the new body would have no authority over the denominations and that "its basis would not be one of credal statement or governmental form but of cooperative work and effort."

The General Conference of the Methodist Episcopal Church South, meeting in Dallas in 1902, was the first official body to decide to appoint delegates to the projected conference. It did so even before the formal invitation was issued. In two denominations the invitation precipitated a sharp difference of judgment. This was conspicuously so among the Disciples of Christ. In their origin nearly a century earlier the plea for unity through a "restoration of the New Testament Church" had been one of their chief notes, but now they were divided over the question whether the proposal for federation was in line with that goal.

---

[21] In a personal letter to me dated August 16, 1922, Dr. Sanford records that during the entire decade from 1895 to 1905, his salary was only $2,500 a year. "I was looked upon," he commented, "by those outside the little circle who stood by me, as a man with a wild vision trying to earn a salary to keep him alive."

[22] Sanford, *op. cit.*, p. 455. The text of the communication appears in full in *Church Federation: Interchurch Conference on Federation, 1905*, ed. Elias B. Sanford (New York: Fleming H. Revell Co., 1906), pp. 29–31. The signers were J. Cleveland Cady as chairman, Elias B. Sanford as secretary, and William Hayes Ward (Congregational), William H. Roberts

Under the influence of J. H. Garrison, editor of *The Christian Evangelist,* and a few other progressive spirits, an affirmative answer was made to the invitation. In the Protestant Episcopal Church there were enough misgivings about the nature of the proposal to prevent official approval, but authorization was given to its Commission on Christian Unity to cooperate in limited ways.

The Committee on Arrangements for the Conference had as its chairman a staunch Presbyterian, William H. Roberts, whose role in the federative movement was to be important during the next decade.[23] The vice-chairman was Frank Mason North, who as executive of the New York City Church Extension and Missionary Society of the Methodist Church had become deeply sensitive to the forces of social change and to the social responsibility of the church.[24] His hymn, "Where Cross the Crowded Ways of Life"—a memorable expression of Christian social insight—appeared at this time (1903). For a quarter of a century he was to be a tower of strength in the growing movement of federation.

Dr. Sanford, as corresponding secretary, was at the center of all the preparatory work for the conference, with a volunteer assistant in Melatiah E. Dwight.[25] A New York broker, Alfred R. Kimball, served as treasurer; and a prominent banker, Stephen Baker, as chairman of a finance committee, raised about $20,000 for the expenses of the conference. William Hayes Ward, editor of *The Independent,* was chairman of the committee on program.

Planning the Federated Structure

When the conference finally convened at Carnegie Hall in New York, November 15–21, 1905, twenty-nine national denominations were represented by duly appointed delegates. They included most—though by no means all—of the bodies which might be described as constituting the

---

and Charles L. Thompson (Presbyterian, U.S.A.), John B. Calvert and Henry L. Morehouse (Baptist), Frank Mason North and William I. Haven (Methodist), Joachim Elmendorf (Reformed in America), George U. Wenner (Lutheran—General Synod), and Rivington D. Lord (Free Baptist).

[23] WILLIAM H. ROBERTS (1844–1921), Presbyterian minister, pastor at Cranford, N.J., 1873–1877; librarian, Princeton Theological Seminary, 1878–1886; professor of practical theology, Lane Theological Seminary, 1886–1893; stated clerk of General Assembly, Presbyterian Church (U.S.A.), 1888–1920; Moderator of the Assembly, 1907.

[24] FRANK MASON NORTH (1850–1935), Methodist Episcopal minister, pastor in Florida, N.Y., Amenia, N.Y., Cold Spring, N.Y., White Plains, N.Y., New York City, and Middletown, Conn., 1873–1891; corresponding secretary, New York City Church Extension and Missionary Society of the M.E. Church, 1892–1912, and of the Board of Foreign Missions, 1912–1924; president, Federal Council of Churches, 1916–1920. See Creighton Lacy, *Frank Mason North: His Social and Ecumenical Mission* (New York: Abingdon Press, 1967).

[25] A daughter of Mr. Dwight once explained to me why her father was deeply interested in the Conference on Church Federation. As a young man he had gone as a missionary to a small Illinois town in which he found six other churches all struggling to survive. He wrote home, "I came out here to be a missionary of Christ, but I found myself only a missionary of Congregationalism."

"main-line" of American Protestantism—Presbyterian, Reformed, Lutheran, Methodist, Baptist, Congregational, Disciples, United Brethren, Evangelical, Moravian, Friends. Some of them had memberships running into the millions; others, like the Primitive Methodists and the Free Baptists and the Reformed Episcopal, numbered only a few thousand. Two large Negro denominations, African Methodist Episcopal and African Methodist Episcopal Zion, were among the participants.[26]

In the case of the Protestant Episcopal Church no authorization for participation had been given by its General Convention, when it met in Boston in 1904. Its Commission on Christian Unity, however, had been instructed "to seek the cooperation of the other Christian bodies of this land in the observance of the Lord's Day, in the preservation of the sanctity of marriage, in the religious education of children, and in other like matters of mutual interest, so as to bring about closer relations and better understanding between us than now exists." On the strength of this resolution, the Commission on Christian Unity appointed delegates to the Interchurch Conference on Federation, though with the clear understanding that they had no authority to commit the Episcopal Church.

The most conspicuous absentees were the Southern Baptists, the Southern Presbyterians, and the Lutherans other than those of the General Synod.

No one can read the voluminous record of the Carnegie Hall Conference without being impressed by the range of concerns that were finding interdenominational expression. The evangelistic and missionary and educational interests held the major place, but social and international problems also received attention. Justice David J. Brewer of the U.S. Supreme Court appealed to the churchmen to make it plain that war and getting ready for war must be ended. President William Jewett Tucker of Dartmouth College stressed the duty of the churches in the area of citizenship. Woodrow Wilson, then president of Princeton University, addressed a supplementary assembly of young people. There

---

[26] The full list of participating denominations was as follows: Northern Baptist Convention, General Conference of Free Baptists, General Conference of Seventh Day Baptists, American Christian Convention, National Council of the Congregational Churches, Disciples of Christ, Evangelical Association, Evangelical Synod of North America, Society of Friends, General Synod of the Lutheran Church, General Conference of the Mennonite Church, General Conference of the Methodist Episcopal Church, General Conference of the Methodist Episcopal Church South, General Conference of the African Methodist Episcopal Church, General Conference of the African Methodist Episcopal Zion Church, Protestant Episcopal Commission on Christian Unity, Primitive Methodist Church, General Conference of the Methodist Protestant Church, Executive Board of the Moravian Church, General Assembly of the Presbyterian Church in the U.S.A., General Assembly of the Cumberland Presbyterian Church, General Assembly of the United Presbyterian Church of North America, General Synod of the Reformed Presbyterian Church, Reformed Episcopal Church, General Synod of the Reformed Church in America, General Synod of the Reformed Church in the U.S., United Evangelical Church, General Conference of United Brethren in Christ, Welsh Presbyterian Church (Calvinistic Methodist).

were presentations of the relations of capital and labor and of problems of family life. The latter included some uncomplimentary remarks about woman suffrage!

The conference, though called for the specific purpose of creating an interdenominational structure, did not hesitate to express its judgment on certain matters of public policy. On the motion of Washington Gladden, venerable spokesman for the rising social conscience in the churches and author of the hymn, "O Master, let me walk with Thee," a protest was voiced against the persecution of Jews in Russia.[27] Another resolution called for an "international inquiry" into the wrongs which were being perpetrated on the people of the Belgian Congo.

The organizational business of the conference centered in the "Plan of Federation," which called for the formation of a "Federal Council of the Churches of Christ in America" and presented a draft of its constitution for submission to the denominations. Its chief architects seem to have been (though formal record is lacking) Dr. Ward and Dr. Roberts. Theologically, these two men represented divergent types—Roberts being essentially conservative both in temper and doctrine, Ward being liberal in viewpoint—but they were equally devoted to the movement of federation.

Very little attention was given to theological differences, except at the one point of the centrality of Christ. It was apparently assumed that the differences were not great, and the invitation had been sent to denominations which were believed to be (as the Letter Missive said) "in substantial agreement as to fundamental Christian doctrine." There was a further assumption that since each denomination was to continue to exercise full authority in matters of doctrine, the Council should not enter this field further than to set forth a simple evangelical commitment. This was done through a preamble which declared that "the time has come when it seems fitting more fully to manifest the essential oneness of the Christian Churches of America in Jesus Christ as their Divine Lord and Saviour."

The Theological Basis

The theological issue involved in this brief preamble came to a concrete testing even before the conference met. The Unitarians, having received the general invitation, designated three delegates to attend the conference, one of whom was the highly esteemed preacher-author, Edward Everett Hale. When word of their appointment was sent to Dr. Sanford, he replied that the invitation had gone to the Unitarian Asso-

---

[27] WASHINGTON GLADDEN (1836–1918), Congregational pastor in Brooklyn, N.Y., Morrisania, N.Y., and North Adams, Mass., 1860–1871; North Congregational Church, Springfield, Mass., 1875–1882; First Congregational Church, Columbus, Ohio, 1882–1918; moderator of National Council of Congregational Churches, 1904–1907.

ciation through an error in the office of the Committee on Correspondence. The Unitarians, accordingly, did not attend.[28]

On the floor of the conference the theological issue came to the fore as soon as the draft of the constitution was submitted. In its first form the preamble referred to Christ as "Lord and Saviour."[29] Samuel J. Niccolls, pastor of the Second Presbyterian Church in St. Louis, moved to amend by inserting the word "Divine" before "Lord and Saviour." In advocacy of his motion, he said:

> Any extended doctrinal statement is not desirable, even were it possible; but there must be some definite center of unity or the plan will have no cohesion. . . . We all know what that center is; it is none other than the Person of Christ and His supreme position as the Lord and Saviour of men.

Dr. Niccolls then went on:

> There is one word left out of this Plan of Federation which should be in it, so that our position and testimony may be known clearly and unequivocally before the world. . . . The word "Divine" should be writtten before "Lord and Saviour," not for the purpose of shutting anyone out of the Federation, or to pass judgment upon the character of anyone because of his intellectual belief, or to deny to any party the Christian name, but simply because fidelity to the truth as we see it and hold it, and as the truth has been entrusted to us, demands it.[30]

The amendment was adopted with only a single dissenting vote.

The same theological issue came before the conference in connection with an article in the proposed constitution having to do with the future admission of other denominations to the Council. A delegate from Rhode Island desired an amendment which would leave open the possibility of admitting new members on a basis as broad as that which prevailed in the Rhode Island Federation of Churches and Christian Workers. In the Rhode Island organization there was no doctrinal reference, and its membership included both Unitarian congregations and other interests not ecclesiastically constituted. The proposed amendment, which received little support, elicited a reply from Bishop E. R. Hendrix as chairman of the Business Committee:

> The question has been raised: Is this plan on a Trinitarian basis? On behalf of the forty men representing every Church in this great Federation of Christians, and after prayer and much careful consideration, I most emphatically in their name say, "Yes." It was called on that basis.

---

[28] For the Unitarian version of the incident, see a memorandum by Samuel A. Eliot, president of the American Unitarian Association, quoted by Charles S. Macfarland, *Christian Unity in the Making* (New York: Federal Council of the Churches of Christ in America, 1948), p. 32.

[29] See *Church Federation*, p. 76.

[30] *Ibid.*, p. 85

Its whole proceeedings have been conducted on that basis, and on that basis it voted this morning with only one dissenting vote, to adopt the words, "Our Divine Lord and Saviour."[31]

A perplexing issue had to do with the relation of the new national body to local areas. During the preceding years there had been a few, notably Josiah Strong, who urged that a federation based on local councils of churches would be more effective than one based on national denominations. The fear was voiced that the latter would always have to move at the slow pace of the most conservative denomination. It was urged, too, that the churches in the same community "have much more in common with each other than with churches hundreds of thousands of miles away." Strong accordingly kept pressing for what he called "federation at the bottom" in preference to "federation at the top." The conference was committed to federation "at the top" but it had to define some kind of relationship to local communities.

The Plan of Federation, as presented to the conference, tried to meet the problem by declaring that one of the objectives would be "to assist in the organization of local branches of the Federal Council to promote its aims in their communities." But if local councils were to be "branches" of the Federal Council, would they not be expected to draw their members from the same denominations as constituted the Federal Council? This raised the objection that the churches of a community ought to be free to determine their own cooperative structure. Motions both to amend and to delete the reference to "branches" were made, but did not carry. What was involved in the word "branches" was left in uncertainty. All agreed that there must be effective channels of communication and mutual aid between the local and the national agencies of cooperation. But on what basis? Were local councils to be wholly autonomous in their policies or were they to conform to national standards defined by the Federal Council? Or was there some middle ground?

To complicate the issue further, there was the question whether local councils should have official representation in the Federal Council. Against this it was argued that to provide for a dual basis of representation—geographical as well as denominational—would weaken the sense of denominational authority and responsibility. On the other hand, it was insisted that the national body would have little vitality apart from the activity of local councils and that it was therefore essential that they should be represented in it. The arguments pro and con were so inconclusive that the question was referred to the constituent

---

[31] *Ibid.*, p. 98. EUGENE R. HENDRIX (1847–1927), Methodist Episcopal Church, South, pastor in Leavenworth, Kan., Macon, Mo., St. Joseph, Mo., Glasgow, Mo., 1869–1878; president of Central College, 1878–1886, bishop, 1886–1927; president, Federal Council of the Churches of Christ, 1908–1912.

bodies for further study and to the first meeting of the future Federal Council for decision.

When the Plan of Federation was finally adopted with only one negative vote, the delegates spontaneously sang the doxology. The draft of an official communication to the churches, reporting what had been done and submitting the proposed constitution of a Federal Council for their ratification, was approved. In his closing remarks the presiding officer, Dr. Roberts, summarized that "the chief work of the organization we have approved is to bring salvation from sin to the lost race of man through Jesus Christ, our Divine Lord and Saviour." He then added that "we are ready to cooperate as an organization with good men of all creeds and races for the moral uplift of mankind."[32] His words were apparently designed to give assurance that the proposed Council would work in friendly concert with others outside its own circle while at the same time maintaining its own evangelical witness.

Before the conference adjourned Dr. Roberts was elected chairman of an executive committee which was to assume interim responsibility until the new federated structure should come into official existence. This was to take place when two-thirds of the denominations represented at the conference should have ratified the plan. As the man who had been the most continuous exponent of church federation, Dr. Sanford was asked to become the corresponding secretary of the organization now in process of formation. During the next three years he was in constant consultation with key leaders in the denominations that were already involved, and in still others that were becoming interested. Before the end of 1908 thirty-two had approved the constitution, three more than had been represented at the Carnegie Hall Conference. In the General Convention of the Protestant Episcopal Church there was sufficient difference of judgment to stand in the way of ratification, but provision was made for a measure of support by authorizing its Commission on Christian Unity to cooperate at appropriate points.[33]

The Plan of Federation conceived the Council, in broad terms, as created "for the prosecution of work that can better be done in union than in separation." Its objectives, also very broadly outlined, were declared to be:

I. To express the fellowship and catholic unity of the Christian Church.[34]

---

[32] *Ibid.*, p. 117.

[33] Later, the Episcopal Commission on Social Service also was authorized to cooperate. Still later, in 1925, the National Council of the Episcopal Church became the agency for maintaining contacts with the Federal Council's activities. In 1940 the General Convention of the Episcopal Church voted to become an official member.

[34] It is interesting to note the use of the adjective "catholic." Though undefined, it indicated what we would today call an "ecumenical" outlook.

II. To bring the Christian bodies of America into united service for Christ and the world.

III. To encourage devotional fellowship and mutual counsel concerning the spiritual life and religious activities of the churches.

IV. To secure a larger combined influence for the churches of Christ in all matters affecting the moral and social condition of the people, so as to promote the application of the law of Christ in every relation of human life.

V. To assist in the organization of local branches of the Federal Council to promote its aims in their communities.[35]

Attitudes Toward the Denomination

In structure the Council was designed to be a strictly delegated body, with all its members appointed by the constituent denominations. Each denomination was entitled to four representatives, the larger bodies having additional members according to their size. There was an explicit delimitation of its ecclesiastical status, doubtless for the sake of allaying fears of too much centralization. "This Federal Council," it was declared, "shall have no authority over the constituent bodies adhering to it; but its province shall be limited to the expression of its counsel and the recommending of a course of action in matters of common interest to the churches, local councils, and individual Christians." More explicitly still, there was the additional clause: "It has no authority to draw up a common creed or form of government or of worship or in any way to limit the full autonomy of the Christian bodies adhering to it."[36]

In the course of time the Council developed functions that went far beyond "the recommending of a course of action in matters of common interest." It gradually found itself acting as much as "recommending." It could not fulfill what was expected of it without doing so. In justification of its procedures it could point to the general clause in the constitution which affirmed that the Council was brought into being "for the prosecution of work that can better be done in union than in separation." Even while the Council was still in process of formation, it was moving into action in more than one realm of public affairs.

During the three years after the Carnegie Hall Conference a considerable discussion of the prospects for federation went on in the religious press. Most of it was favorable, but not all. *The Christian Standard,* organ of the conservative wing of the Disciples of Christ, was an outspoken opponent. It protested that a federation of denominations could not be a substitute for "the free undenominational Church of Christ." It stoutly held that "for Churches of Christ to go into such arrangements

---

[35] Although the constitution thus provides for "local branches" there never were any "branches" in any formal sense. Instead, the Federal Council assisted in developing autonomous city and state councils.

[36] *Church Federation,* pp. 34–35.

. . . is to surrender the grand plea for Christian unity on the New Testament platform."[37]

The main problem facing the pioneering movement, however, was not opposition but preoccupation with established denominational interests. In his first report, at the end of 1906, Dr. Sanford made the plaintive comment that sectarianism and ever-so-busy denominational officials and pastors were the major "hindrances." He foresaw the danger of only a "fluctuating" and "sporadic" support, unless denominational leaders could give more time to the Council and ensure a sound financial base.[38]

In contrast to an occasional realistic note like this was the roseate optimism of many church leaders as to what the coming federation could accomplish. Some of the more enthusiastic were almost utopian in their expectations. Josiah Strong and A. B. Leonard foresaw church federation closing saloons and gambling houses and "other evil resorts," and reforming business and politics.[39] A Presbyterian journal even thought that federation might be "the morning star of the millennium!"[40]

In their underlying attitude toward the denominational system the spokesmen for federation were conservative. There were differences in viewpoint but not much radical criticism. What was criticized was not the denominations as such but a sectarian or separatist spirit within them. The denomination was thought of as a useful instrument for the Kingdom of God if it lived and worked in reasonable concord with others. It was popular to quote what President Theodore Roosevelt had said to the delegates at the meeting of the National Federation of Churches and Christian Workers in 1902: "There are plenty of targets we need to hit without firing into each other." Beyond this general mood of mutual consideration for one another, the representatives of the denominations at Carnegie Hall also hoped to see a great increase in active cooperation all along the line.

Some of the supporters of the movement regarded federation as the beginning of a process that could lead to the goal of a more complete form of unity.[41] The majority, however, regarded organic union as

---

[37] *Christian Standard,* February 3, 1906, p. 8. Among the religious journals that gave editorial support to the Plan of Federation were *The Congregationalist, The Christian Advocate* (Methodist), *The Christian Evangelist* (Disciples), *The Reformed Church Messenger, The Interior* (Presbyterian), and *The Churchman* (Episcopal).

[38] *Church Federation: Interchurch Conference on Federation, 1905,* ed. Elias B. Sanford (New York: Fleming H. Revell Co., 1906), p. 20.

[39] In an article on "Essential Unity," *The Churchman,* Nov. 25, 1905.

[40] *The Interior,* quoted in *Church Federation,* p. 678.

[41] In the same year in which the Federal Council of Churches was organized, Newman Smyth, distinguished pastor of the First Congregational Church of New Haven, Conn., published *Passing Protestantism and Coming Catholicism* (New York: Charles Scribner's Sons, 1908). He regarded church federation as only a temporary measure and boldly envisioned a reunited Christianity which would even heal the breach caused by the Reformation. He was encouraged by the modernist movement in Roman Catholicism which he hoped might democratize the church.

visionary. For them John M. Buckley, editor of *The Christian Advocate* (Methodist), was a spokesman when he concluded that "the only kind of union that can ever exist in this world among the Christian Churches will be of the nature of a federation."[42] Whatever differences there might be in the conception of the ultimate goal, there was a general agreement that at least for that time the right word was federation.

A marked characteristic of the whole movement was its pragmatic approach and practical temper. An existing spiritual unity within the household of faith was taken for granted, and this was regarded as the foundation on which the federated structure was to be built. The prevailing assumption was that the theological differences among the evangelical denominations were not significant enough to keep them from working together. There was, accordingly, little concern to define doctrinal agreement except at the one crucial point of insisting that Jesus Christ is "Divine Lord and Saviour." The Person of Christ was the sufficient center of unity.[43] Bishop John H. Vincent, in the closing address of the Carnegie Hall Conference, summed up the general viewpoint:[44]

> The Federation is a public declaration of virtual unity in faith, in doctrine, and in spirit. In ecclesiastical theories and policies we may still differ widely; in detailed doctrinal definitions we may not perfectly agree. But we are one in Christ Jesus, in our recognition of Him, in our love of Him, in our loyalty to Him.[45]

---

[42] *The Christian Advocate,* April 19, 1906.

[43] It is interesting to note that there was nothing in the Plan of Federation which precluded membership of either the Eastern Orthodox or the Roman Catholic Church in the Federal Council. Although all the charter members of the Council were Protestant bodies, there is no use of the adjective "Protestant" in the constitution or by-laws. The way was left open for non-Protestant bodies to become members, as the Eastern Orthodox began to do three decades later.

[44] JOHN H. VINCENT (1832–1920), Methodist Episcopal pastor in Joliet, Mount Morris, Galena, and Rockford, Ill., 1857–1865; editor of Methodist Sunday School publications, 1868–1888. In the latter year he was elected a bishop. He was the founder of the Chatauqua Institution.

[45] *Church Federation,* p. 613.

3

The Churches Federate

(1908–1914)

ON December 2–8, 1908, there was a gathering in Philadelphia which was without precedent in American history. For the first time thirty-three denominations became visibly linked together in an interdenominational structure which had been authorized by their most representative bodies. The Federal Council of the Churches of Christ in America was holding its inaugural session, its constitution having been duly ratified by all the denominations that three years earlier had officially participated in the drafting.[1] In addition, there were now five others: National Baptist Convention, Congregational Methodist, Colored Methodist Episcopal, Presbyterian in the U.S. (Southern), and Swedish Lutheran Augustana Synod.

The sessions were pervaded with a high hopefulness that a new era in the relations of the churches was beginning. As William H. Roberts put it, in welcoming Bishop Eugene R. Hendrix of the Methodist Episcopal Church South as the first president:

> There was a church in the days of old before which an open door was set, and it bore the name of Philadelphia; and we here in this city of Philadelphia set before you, as the leader of the Council, an open door for cooperation in Christian work in this great Republic, which should be the beginning of the thorough Christianization of the whole land.[2]

In his response Bishop Hendrix contrasted the new "federal union of great Christian Churches, aggregating in number of communicants nearly eighteen millions," with the feeble political union of thirteen small colonies that had been formed in Philadelphia somewhat more than a century earlier.

---

[1] The Cumberland Presbyterian Church does not appear in the roster of denominations sending delegates, for in 1906 it had effected an organic union with the Presbyterian Church in the United States of America. The Protestant Episcopal Church continued to be represented only by its Commission on Christian Unity.

[2] *Federal Council of the Churches of Christ in America: Report of the First Meeting*, ed. Elias B. Sanford (New York: Fleming H. Revell Co., 1909), p. 21.

An Unprecedented Gathering

During six days the Council surveyed the need for cooperation in all important areas except worship and doctrine. These two received only incidental attention, presumably because it was especially stressed in the constitution that the Council had "no authority to draw up a common creed or form of government or of worship." In evangelism, home missions, foreign missions, Sunday School work, higher education, temperance, family life, Sunday observance, and still other fields of concern, there were forceful presentations of the urgency for greater and more coordinated effort. There was, however, very little projection of concrete activities. The existence of the Council was an official endorsement of interdenominational cohesion and cooperation as a general policy, but was it to be more than a glorified symbol? What specific tasks was it to undertake?

The answer to this question was complicated not only by the long-established programs of the denominations but also by the more recent development of other than denominational organizations operating in various fields. Some of them were undenominational, like the International Sunday School Association and the Y.M.C.A., made up of members from all the churches but having organizational ties with none. Others were representative of denominational boards with specialized functions, like the Foreign Missions Conference, though without official relation to any denomination as a whole. The Federal Council had a distinctive character as representing a new principle—the drawing together of the denominations as total entities. Unlike the agencies of cooperation which had grown out of the interests of either boards and societies or individuals, it had come into being to "manifest the essential oneness" of the churches in their corporate life. It thus gave additional sanction to all organizations that were contributing to unity of effort under any banner, but its generalized objective did not outline particular programs. It had to learn experimentally what its functions were to be as distinguished from those of existing agencies.

The Foreign Missions Conference of North America had created a Committee of Reference and Counsel—the first step toward becoming more than an annual consultation—in the year before the Federal Council met. In the early part of 1908 the boards of home missions had formed the Home Missions Council in the interest of bringing about harmonious adjustments in their work.[3] The missionary leaders who were most active in the Foreign Missions Conference and the Home Missions Council were also identified with the Federal Council and sup-

---

[3] The early development of cooperation in missions is recounted in the following chapter. There will be a fuller treatment of these and other fields of cooperative activity in another volume.

ported its general objective, but saw no reason for turning over their specialized responsibilities to it.

In other areas than missions there were as yet no cooperative structures of denominational boards but there were voluntary societies of Christians which were rendering valuable service. Conspicuous among them was the International Sunday School Association, largely under lay leadership, which had for several decades been vigorously promoting religious education in all the churches. With these and other undenominational agencies, as well as with the interboard structures for missionary coordination, the Federal Council, committed in principle to cooperation in every field, was in warm accord. But there were complex problems of relationships and functions that could be solved only by patient exploration.

Accent on Social Tasks

There was, however, one unoccupied field that was wide open for cooperative leadership and into this the Federal Council promptly entered. This was the responsibility of the churches in the social and industrial scene. It was a direct engagement with this challenge which, more than anything else, gave vitality to the Council in the years of its infancy and established it as an important factor in American Christianity.[4]

At first thought, it appears surprising that the official instrument of the denominations should have ventured into territory as uncharted as that of the relation of the church to the new industrial society. It would seem to have been more prudent for those primarily interested in unity to avoid a field that was bound to have many controversial aspects. As it turned out, however, the boldness of the Council in grappling with critical social issues gave it a program of concrete action that appealed to progressive spirits in most of the denominations. If the Council had not become deeply involved in the problems presented to an uneasy social conscience, it is doubtful whether it would have commanded enough support to survive the testing times that lay ahead.

The outstanding feature of the first meeting of the Council was the Report on the Church and Modern Industry, presented by Frank Mason North. No one can read the document without recognizing its prophetic quality. It brought to a sharp focus the Christian social concern that had been developing during the two preceding decades. It reflected the general viewpoint which had found its fullest exposition in Walter Rauschenbusch's epochal *Christianity and the Social Crisis,* published

---

[4] This thesis is developed at considerable length by John A. Hutchison in *We Are Not Divided* (New York: Round Table Press, 1941).

a year earlier.[5] The Report was a forthright defense of the labor movement, and especially of the right to organize. At a time when there was still widespread antagonism to labor unions the Report unqualifiedly said:

> That workingmen should organize for social and industrial betterment belongs to the natural order. . . . It is their right as it is the right of men everywhere, within the law, to combine for common ends. Both Church and society should cease to talk of "conceding" this right. It exists in the nature of things. We do not confer it. But we welcome its exercise. . . . Despite the errors of individuals and groups, the faults of spirit, the imperfection of methods, and, in some instances, most deplorable results, organized labor is to be regarded as an influence not hostile to our institutions but potent in beneficence.[6]

If taken out of context, these sentences seem more sociological than religious, but the Report as a whole is clearly a blending of evangelical conviction and sensitive social outlook. At the outset it takes "the supreme authority of Jesus Christ" as the keynote and presents this authority as final "in the social as in the individual life."

Earlier in 1908 the General Conference of the Methodist Episcopal Church had adopted a statement of social objectives, which, with slight modifications, was incorporated into the Council's Report on the Church and Modern Industry. Endorsed by major denominations, and also by the Y.M.C.A. and the Y.W.C.A. during the next few years, it became an almost classic document. Some of its proposals which are today taken for granted as accepted standards sounded radical in 1908. As adopted in Philadelphia and subsequently known as "The Social Ideals of the Churches," it declared that "the Churches must stand"

> For equal rights and complete justice for all men in all stations of life.
> For the right of all men to the opportunity for self-maintenance, a right ever to be wisely and strongly safeguarded against encroachments of every kind.
> For the principle of conciliation and arbitration in industrial discussions.
> For the protection of the worker from dangerous machinery, occupational disease, injuries and mortality.
> For the abolition of child labor.
> For such regulation of the conditions of toil for women as shall safeguard the physical and moral health of the community.
> For the suppression of the "sweating system."

---

[5] WALTER RAUSCHENBUSCH (1861–1918), Baptist minister and theologian, pastor of Second German Baptist Church in New York's "Hell's Kitchen," 1886–1897; teacher at German Baptist Theological Seminary, 1897–1902; professor of church history at Rochester Theological Seminary, 1903–1918.

[6] *Federal Council of the Churches of Christ in America: Report of the First Meeting,* p. 234.

For the gradual and reasonable reduction of the hours of labor to the lowest practicable point, and for that degree of leisure which is a condition of the highest human life.

For a release from employment one day in seven.

For a living wage as a minimum in every industry and for the highest wage that industry can afford.

For the most equitable division of the products of industry that can ultimately be devised.

For suitable provision for the old age of the workers and for those incapacitated by injury.

For the abatement of poverty.[7]

The adoption of this statement of social commitment was charged with strong evangelical feeling. The delegates felt that they were moving out into frontier territory to be occupied in the name of Christ. One of them, looking back on the occasion after nearly sixty years, described it in these words:

> Most vivid in my memory is our singing of Frank Mason North's hymn, "Where cross the crowded ways of life," after the presentation of his report. Most of us had tears running down our cheeks.[8]

The term "Social Creed," which was sometimes applied to the statement, was hardly a felicitous one. It lent itself too easily to the erroneous inference that a humanitarian platform was taking the place of religious conviction. Yet there was a sound impulse behind the use of the term, for it implied that in addition to a doctrinal confession the full witness of the church in the modern world required a testimony to the relevance of Christian faith to society.

There is no ground for supposing that church members generally were committed to all the goals outlined in the "Social Ideals" or prepared to work for them. Their formulation and adoption by the Council, however, plainly indicated that thoughtful leaders in many denominations were moving toward such a consensus. The statement at least showed the direction which Christian social concern was taking. A discriminating observer, writing from the perspective of the next generation, rightly appraised the significance of this and various subsequent declarations of the Council by saying that "they are probably to be interpreted as outposts held by more advanced persons rather than . . .

---

[7] *Ibid.*, pp. 238–239. The statement was somewhat expanded in 1912, and in 1932 substantially revised in order to update it in the light of experience during the Depression. For an illuminating analysis of the connection between the Methodist statement of 1908 and the Federal Council's statement later in the same year, see Creighton Lacy, *Frank Mason North: His Social and Ecumenical Mission* (New York: Abingdon Press, 1967).

[8] From a personal letter to the author, October 21, 1965, by Rockwell Harmon Potter, of Hartford, Conn., former moderator of the National Council of Congregational Churches, the last surviving delegate to the Federal Council's first meeting. He lived until 1967.

the opinion of the majority" and as having "an educational value" rather than a "direct effect" upon public policy.[9]

The new insight into the social significance of Christianity led some enthusiasts into a one-sided emphasis—so much so that in later years it became the fashion to criticize the "social gospel" as lacking in spiritual depth. That it was naïvely optimistic and assumed that men could "bring in the Kingdom" by their own efforts was a common charge. But if there were some who reduced the Kingdom of God to a kingdom of man, they did not reflect the real genius of the movement. It represented an enlargement, not a reduction, in the understanding of the Gospel, a reaching out to relate Christian faith to all of man's relationships and institutions. In its earlier years the movement was over-idealistic in its expectations; a more realistic estimate of the possibilities of human nature and society began to prevail after the First World War and the Depression of the thirties.

The Church and Labor

After adopting the Social Ideals, the Federal Council issued a message to working people which was obviously aimed at lessening their estrangement from the churches. It said:

> To the toilers of America and to those who by organized effort are seeking to lift the crushing burdens of the poor, and to reduce the hardships and uphold the dignity of labor, this Council sends the greetings of human brotherhood and the pledge of sympathy and help in a cause which belongs to all who follow Christ.[10]

On the Sunday afternoon before the Council adjourned, there was a public meeting on the theme, "The Church and Labor." The chairman on this occasion was a well-known union leader, D. A. Hayes, vice-president of the American Federation of Labor. After reading the Social Ideals of the Churches, he commented:

> Had we been told a few years ago that a convention of prominent ministers and laymen would have adopted such declarations, we would have doubted it, because—and we may as well speak frankly about it—many working people have felt that the churches were unsympathetic, if not indifferent, to the desires and aspirations of labor for more justice and for better opportunities to realize and enjoy the standard of life which the very teaching of Christianity inspires in the minds of men.[11]

In the report on the Church and Modern Industry there was an appeal to theological seminaries to help prospective ministers understand social

---

[9] Willard L. Sperry, *Religion in America* (Cambridge: Harvard University Press, 1945), p. 64.

[10] *Federal Council of the Churches of Christ in America: Report of the First Meeting*, p. 239.

[11] *Ibid.*, p. 444.

problems. This prompted Charles Stelzle, the representative of the Presbyterian (U.S.A.) Board of Home Missions responsible for reaching out to industrial workers—who had himself been a machinist before entering the ministry—to make this pungent remark:

> When our young men go to the theological seminary, they study about the social life of the Israelites and the Jebusites and the Hittites and the Hivites and the suburbanites . . . but when a man studies into the social life of the Chicagoites or the Buffaloites or the Pittsburghites and preaches about it in precisely the same way that he would talk about the social life of the Amalekites, some good brother will calmly remind him that he might better preach the "simple Gospel," whatever that may mean.[12]

Against this background, the Council appointed a permanent Commission on the Church and Social Service. It was instructed "to study social conditions and ascertain the essential facts . . . and, in general, to afford by its action and utterance an expression of the purpose of the Churches of Christ in the United States to recognize the import of present social movements and industrial conditions, and to cooperate in all practical ways to promote in the churches the development of the spirit and practice of social service and especially to secure a better understanding and a more natural relationship between workingmen and the Church."[13] The first chairman of the Commission, as anyone could have predicted, was Dr. North. Among its first members were Professor Walter Rauschenbusch of the Rochester Theological Seminary, Professor Shailer Mathews of the Divinity School of the University of Chicago, President Herbert Welch of Ohio Wesleyan University, President Robert L. Kelly of Earlham College, President George C. Chase of Bates College, Josiah Strong, Graham Taylor, John Howard Melish, and Charles Stelzle.

Another report which reflected a pioneering interest had to do with international relations. Presented by the dean of Yale University's Law School, Harry Wade Rogers, it expressed a buoyant hopefulness for an era of peace. There was no inkling of the war clouds that were gathering in Europe. "The hour is soon to strike," he predicted, "when the death knell of militarism will be sounded throughout the world." There was a spirited appeal to the churches to "make plain to all mankind" that they support "the effort now being made in all countries to abolish war and to put a stop to the increasing expenditures for armaments."[14] Arbitration was held up as a practicable alternative to war in adjudicating all international disputes that could not be settled by diplomacy.

---

12 *Ibid.,* p. 71.
13 *Ibid.,* p. 242.
14 *Ibid.,* pp. 139, 141, 310.

Concern for Evangelism and Missions

Although the note of Christian responsibility in social life was strongly sounded at the Philadelphia meeting, it would be wholly erroneous to assume that this was regarded as a substitute for Christian evangelism and Christian nurture. The men who created the Federal Council were fully committed to the primary need for conversion to personal faith and discipleship. They were men of evangelical conviction and evangelistic ardor but they had moved beyond the pietistic outlook which limited Christ's redeeming work to souls in isolation.[15] From the beginning of its life the Federal Council had a Committee on Evangelism, and its status was soon raised to that of a Department. It found itself looking for some way to provide for constructive guidance in a changing situation. After the death of Dwight L. Moody, there were no evangelists who offered a comparable leadership. A stereotyped appeal, usually with high-pressure methods, was characteristic of much post-Moody revivalism. It also had little grasp of the relevance of the Gospel for modern society. After some unfruitful efforts to exert an influence in the field of professional revivalism the Council put its emphasis on the continuous role of every pastor in evangelism.

In home missions the main emphasis of the Philadelphia meeting was on the need for comity in the location of churches. The report on this subject was sharply critical of the lack of common planning and the resulting competition between denominations. "We often imagine," its spokesman bluntly said, that "we are winning victories for the Kingdom when in fact we are simply making it uncomfortable for some other regiment of our own army."[16] There was a special plea for cooperation in the cities, where the influx of industrial workers from the rural areas and the hosts of immigrants from overseas presented a challenge that was overwhelming.

A resolution which seemed hardly more than incidental at the time but proved to be important for the future had to do with a religious ministry to the men in the armed forces. Calling attention to the fact that there were only five chaplains for the sailors on sixteen battleships in the Atlantic fleet, the Council urged the President and the Congress to make "such provision for the increase of chaplains as shall adequately provide for the spiritual needs of the Navy."

Other subjects on which reports were presented to the Council at its first meeting were temperance, Sunday observance, and family life.

---

[15] A careful study of Walter Rauschenbusch, who, though not prominent in the organization of the Federal Council, was an inspiration to its early leaders, will show that he never ceased to believe that the primary contribution to the transformation of society was a transformation of persons. See Robert T. Handy, *The Social Gospel in America, 1870-1920* (New York: Oxford University Press, 1966).

[16] *Federal Council of the Churches of Christ in America: Report of the First Meeting*, p. 57.

These had long been active concerns of the churches and no new ground was broken in Philadelphia. The report on family life, drafted by a venerable Episcopal bishop, at one point makes rather strange reading today. He saw the family as threatened by a declining birth rate and an "alarming increase of restriction about the bearing of children."[17] The "population explosion" had not yet been heard of!

A report on weekday religious instruction sparked the lengthiest debate of the entire meeting. "Has the Church," it asked, "a right to any part of the time of week-days for the purpose of exercising the legitimate function of religious education?" The answer was an unqualified Yes, recommending that public schools "be closed on Wednesday or some other afternoon, for the purpose of allowing children to attend religious instruction in their own churches." A substantial number of delegates, however, feared the proposal might prove to be an entering wedge for breaking down the separation of church and state. The Council accordingly felt the need for further study of the issue and limited itself to saying that the state should recognize the need for "more time during the week for religious instruction."[18] The issue remained a clouded one for many years, and was not finally settled until the U.S. Supreme Court, more than forty years later, upheld the constitutionality of "released time."

Divergent Views of Denominations

A long-range issue which evoked a brisk exchange of views had to do with church union on mission fields. In a forward-looking address Robert E. Speer made an out-and-out commitment to the principle of union:[19]

> I have not the slightest zeal in seeking to have the Presbyterian Church extended over the non-Christian world. I believe in one Church of Christ in each land. I believe that it is far more important that the Presbyterians of Japan should relate themselves to the Methodists of Japan than that either of those bodies should retain any connection whatever with any ecclesiastical organization in the United States.[20]

In the same general spirit the Committee on Foreign Missions, in a report presented by James L. Barton, recommended

---

17 *Ibid.,* p. 313.

18 *Ibid.,* pp. 115–124; 135–139; 278–286.

19 ROBERT E. SPEER (1867–1947), Presbyterian layman, secretary of the Board of Foreign Missions of the Presbyterian Church in the U.S.A., 1891–1937; president of the Federal Council of the Churches of Christ in America, 1920–1924; moderator of Presbyterian General Assembly, 1927. See W. Reginald Wheeler, *A Man Sent from God: The Biography of Robert E. Speer* (New York: Fleming H. Revell Co., 1956).

20 *Federal Council of the Churches of Christ in America: Report of the First Meeting,* p. 352.

That we favor the closest possible federation of all Christian Churches in foreign mission fields and the elimination so far as possible of denominational distinctions.[21]

In interpreting this recommendation Dr. Barton likened denominational lines to "fossilized bird tracks" which he had seen in an archeological museum. A Methodist bishop objected to such a comparison. "I do not believe," he said, "in the utter abolition of denominationalism even as an ideal for the future."[22] Another Methodist, however, Dr. Levi Gilbert, editor of the *Western Christian Advocate,* was less ready to defend the permanent validity of the denominational system and suggested that in the churches coming to birth in Asia and Africa there was an opportunity for a new pattern which would magnify the unifying convictions and not call attention to historical differences that had arisen in the West.[23] The recommendation of the Committee was finally softened by an amendment which omitted the reference to "the elimination . . . of denominational distinctions."

This debate reveals how much difference of opinion there was as to the ultimate goal of the federation which had been created. The delegates were of one mind in supporting mutual recognition and increasing cooperation. They were divided as to whether this should lead to eventual union and the disappearance of denominations—a cleavage of judgment which still remains.

Relation of National and Local Agencies

The knottiest problem on the organizational side had to do with the relation of the Federal Council to local and state federations. Many, but not all, of the delegates seem to have assumed that the Federal Council would largely depend for its practical effectiveness on state federations and that their chief function, in turn, would be to stimulate federations in cities and counties of their respective areas. Encouraging accounts were given of accomplishment in certain communities in which organization for cooperative efforts had begun. Eleven states were reported as already having some kind of official (or at least semi-official) structure for cooperation, sometimes called "federation," sometimes "interdenominational commission." They were, in chronological order, Maine (1891), Wisconsin (1898), Vermont (1899), New York (1900), Rhode Island (1901), Massachusetts (1901), Ohio (1901), New Hamp-

---

[21] JAMES L. BARTON (1855–1936), Congregational missionary in Turkey, 1885–1892; secretary of American Board of Commissioners for Foreign Missions, 1894–1927; chairman of Near East Relief, 1914–1936.

[22] *Federal Council of the Churches of Christ in America: Report of the First Meeting,* pp. 32, 33.

[23] *Ibid.,* p. 34.

shire (1903), South Dakota (1905), Connecticut (1906), and Montana (1906). In Pennsylvania a branch of the Evangelical Alliance had begun to function as a federation of churches.

In the main, however, these emerging interchurch agencies reflected experiments and hopes more than achievements. There was no clear picture of what they were to do. Some were trying to promote comity agreements in church extension. Some were feeling their way in investigating social conditions as a basis for reform. Most of them had to depend on the volunteer work of men who were busy with their own parish or denominational responsibilities. Changing personnel in leadership often resulted in a discontinuance of previous support. Experience was beginning to demonstrate that if cooperation was to be effectively sustained in a community, it would require the appointment of employed executives.

The relation of local and state federations (or "councils" as they later came to be called) to the national body was left in a hazy state. Although the constitution of the Federal Council referred to "local branches," it was becoming clear that conditions in communities varied so widely that local councils could not be standardized in a national format but must have their own autonomy. The question whether they might not have some kind of official representation in the Federal Council evoked such sharp difference of judgment—as had been the case when the constitution was being framed three years earlier—that it was bypassed and left for future experience to answer.

The operations anticipated for the newly created Federal Council were exceedingly modest, contemplating a budget of $30,000, to which each member-denomination was to contribute in proportion to its numerical strength. There was, however, an ambitious organizational pattern, calling for four regional offices in addition to the central headquarters. These district offices were expected to be (but did not turn out to be) the chief means both for developing cooperation at the "grass-roots" and also for building up nationwide support for the Federal Council.

The Philadelphia meeting ended on an almost lyrical note, when a St. Louis pastor portrayed the prospects for the future:

> I do not mean to say that all bigotry and all intense sectionalism or denominationalism have passed away. They linger like the belated snow-drifts which lie upon our western mountains in June. The song of the birds is in the trees, and the flowers are blooming; the frozen drift is slowly yielding to the genial spirit in the air. . . Soon where it lay the grass will be green and the violets and anemones bloom.[24]

The ecclesiastical climate was to prove much less balmy than this poetic peroration implied. Chilling frosts were soon to come that would

---

[24] *Ibid.*, p. 150.

almost kill the budding plans. But the federative movement survived and in the perspective of history it is not too much to say that the year 1908 marked a real turning point in the relation of the American Churches to one another. It had witnessed the first official and corporate avowal by a large group of diverse denominations that they had so much in common by reason of their relation to one Lord that they would come together and stay together in a common witness and a common service.[25]

A Struggle for Federated Survival

Denominational leaders welcomed the newly born Federal Council as public testimony to harmonious relations among the churches but for some time active support of it was hardly more than marginal. Many were only dimly aware of the changes that were called for. Some seem to have naïvely assumed that just the fact of its existence had ushered in a new day. The *Western Christian Advocate* could even editorialize:

> We Protestants can now sing without any mental reservation, "We are not divided, all one body we." The hour is considerably past when we need to argue for unity. We have unity and need not plead for it.[26]

Among the leaders of the Council there seems to have been a surprising lack of realism about the resistance to change to be expected from entrenched denominational interests. One of Dr. Sanford's documents, entitled "Enlargement of Work in 1910," was so sanguine about the prospect of increasing comity that it made this wishful prophecy of an early end of overchurching:

> The habit of crowding a few choicer towns with too many churches, to the neglect of the many more needy communities, will soon be displaced by a cooperative and balanced missionary policy.[27]

The contrast between this rosy expectation and the thorny realities can be illustrated by reference to a concrete local situation in the Far West at this time. When Robert L. Paddock in 1907 was elected Missionary Bishop of the Episcopal Church in eastern Oregon, he was determined not to encourage the building of Episcopal edifices in small communities where other churches had already been established. Instead he urged Episcopalians to identify themselves with the churches already there, at the same time making due provision for the Holy Communion according to the Episcopal rite. This policy did not commend itself to those who were more narrowly concerned with the institu-

---

[25] The French Protestant Federation, consisting of five denominations, was being formed at the same time. Its first meeting was held a year before that of the American Federal Council. Its constitution was formally adopted in 1909.

[26] *First Annual Report of the Executive Committee of the Federal Council of the Churches of Christ in America.* New York, 1909, p. 41.

[27] Pamphlet in archives of National Council of Churches.

tional growth of the Episcopal Church. After an unsuccessful struggle Bishop Paddock resigned in 1922. The denominational pattern of church extension was still too strong to be overcome even in new missionary territory.[28]

The most serious difficulty in the development of cooperation was not opposition but absorption in established denominational activities. Most denominational officials were sympathetic with the Federal Council and the Home Missions Council but too weighted down with denominational commitments to give more than incidental attention to anything else. Cooperation was accepted as right in principle but it had no priority in practice. As for the rank-and-file members of local churches, they did not know that either Council existed, or if they did were too occupied with parochial affairs to be greatly concerned.

As a general summary, it appears that in the first years of its life the Federal Council faced "a continuous struggle against obscurity and bankruptcy."[29] With neither precedents nor mandates, its approaches to a program were fumbling. Its first major effort, directed toward organizing state and local councils of churches across the nation, was far from successful. Regional offices were established—one in Denver for the West, one in Chicago for the central area, one in Trenton, N.J., for the East—with an executive secretary for each district. The plan further contemplated a regional office for the South, but before it could be established the whole districting plan had to be abandoned for lack of financial support.

Even if the financial factor had not been decisive, it is doubtful whether the plan could have produced the results that had been foreseen as on the near horizon. It assumed that with a little stimulus the ecclesiastical jurisdictions—synods, conferences, associations—in state-wide areas would soon come together in a federated organization, which in turn would encourage the formation of cooperative agencies in cities and counties. Some progress was reported from the district offices, and several of the larger city councils of today go back to this period before the First World War, including Chicago, Philadelphia, St. Louis, Baltimore, Boston, Louisville, Cleveland, and Indianapolis. But it was not long before it became evident that the establishment of stable structures at the grass roots would call for a persistent process of cultivation and continuous building. The task could not be accomplished by preaching the ideal of cooperation, holding occasional consultations, and offering a model constitution drafted in a national headquarters.

In 1912 the plan for district offices of the Federal Council was

---

[28] The story of Bishop Paddock's struggle is told in detail in his biography, *Portrait of a Rebel*, by Maria Minor (New York: Seabury Press, 1965).

[29] John A. Hutchison, *op. cit.*, p. 59.

dropped. Stimulating and strengthening state and local councils, however, remained a major concern. A substantial impulse to it was imparted by an independent nationwide campaign in the major cities, known as "The Men and Religion Forward Movement," for eight months in 1911–1912. Initiated by a layman, Fred B. Smith, who was intent on rallying churchmen for more active Christian leadership in community life, it combined an evangelistic with a social service thrust, and prepared the way for councils of churches in several cities. The director of the movement, Roy B. Guild, three years later became the Federal Council's executive for its long-term service to local and state councils.[30]

The Threat of Insolvency

The annual meetings of the Federal Council's executive committee in 1909, 1910, and 1911 heard no such buoyant note as had resounded at its inauguration in 1908. The financial aspect of its affairs made everything else uncertain. In 1909 the member denominations contributed only $9,000, instead of the $16,500 that had been apportioned among them. In 1910 the amount contributed was $10,000, toward expenditures of $16,000. To close the gap, appeals were made to interested individuals.[31] In 1911 the denominational payments were a little more than $12,000 and the total of contributions from individuals somewhat over $5,000.

Although the amounts contributed directly by the denominations seem miniscule judged by today's standards, they represented a noteworthy development. The significant thing was not their size but the establishment of the principle of making official ecclesiastical appropriations to an interdenominational body. As Frank Mason North remarked a decade later, in a semi-humorous and semi-serious vein, "When the General Conference of the Methodist Episcopal Church first voted to give $2,000 of our good Methodist money to the Federal Council, it was one of the most remarkable changes in the history of Methodism!"[32]

On its precarious financial foundation the Council obviously could not project any extensive program of activities. Bishop Hendrix voiced what seemed to be the general view of the Council's future role when he said that it "aspires less to be an organization than an influence." Dr. Sanford, in a similar vein, conceived its mission to be "one of testi-

---

[30] ROY B. GUILD (1871–1945), Congregational minister, pastor in Woodstock, Chicago, Ill., 1897–1906; executive for Congregational home missions, 1906–1910; director of "Men and Religion Forward Movement," 1911–1912; pastor in Topeka, Kan., 1912–1915; executive of Federal Council's Commission on Councils of Churches, 1915–1925; pastor in New Bedford, Mass., 1925–1929; associate general secretary of Federal Council, 1929–1937.

[31] The report of the treasurer for 1910 lists 124 individual contributions. The two largest ($500 each) came from Cleveland H. Dodge and John D. Rockefeller. See *Second Annual Report of the Executive Committee.* New York, 1911, pp. 83–86.

[32] A personal remark to the author, quoted from memory.

mony, guidance and inspiration."[33] An objective observer summarized the situation by describing the Council at this time as "mainly a state of mind." Moreover, the "state of mind" appears to have been limited chiefly to the more prophetic denominational leaders and not yet to have been widely pervasive.

At the national headquarters of the Council, Dr. Sanford, its main guiding spirit up to this time, was in declining health and approaching the age of retirement.[34] In 1911 a step was taken that was destined to give the Council the leadership it needed for the future. On May 1, Charles S. Macfarland became the first employed secretary of its Commission on the Church and Social Service.[35] There were no adequate financial resources for its program but the Commission had been granted authority to move ahead if it could enlist supplementary support designated for this purpose. As a young pastor Macfarland had become deeply interested in the relation of the churches to social and industrial issues. In spite of the problematical outlook for the Federal Council he was willing to run the personal risk of embarking on its uncharted course.

By this time five denominations had established departments, in varying organizational forms, for education and action in the area of social responsibilities. They were Baptist, Congregational, Methodist Episcopal, Presbyterian (U.S.A.), and Protestant Episcopal. The five secretaries of these agencies agreed to coordinate their pioneering efforts through the Federal Council.[36] This aided its first major venture into a national program of a specialized character on a continuous basis under salaried leadership.

Later in the same year Dr. Sanford's failing health made it necessary for his new colleague to assume responsibility not only for the Commission on the Church and Social Service but also for the general interests of the Council. The two men—Sanford and Macfarland—were about as different in temperament and personality as could be imagined. The contrast is highlighted by a comment made by one who knew both men well: "Sanford was a dreamer, not an organizer, but he found an organizer at the moment of his need for one."[37] In 1912 Macfarland was

---

33 *First Annual Report,* 1909.

34 On his eightieth birthday in 1923, then retired in Rockfall, Conn., Dr. Sanford was the recipient of a host of congratulatory and appreciative messages, including greetings from Charles E. Hughes, Secretary of State, and Woodrow Wilson, both of whom had supported him in his work.

35 CHARLES S. MACFARLAND (1866–1956), Congregational minister, pastor in Malden, Mass., 1900–1906, and South Norwalk, Conn., 1906-1911. General secretary, Federal Council of Churches, 1912–1930. See his autobiography, *Across the Years* (New York: The Macmillan Company, 1936).

36 They were Henry A. Atkinson (Congregational), Samuel Z. Batten (Baptist), Frank M. Crouch (Episcopal), Charles Stelzle (Presbyterian), Harry F. Ward, (Methodist).

37 Rockwell Harmon Potter, in a personal letter to the author, October 21, 1965.

elected "a secretary" of the Council (later general secretary), and until his retirement after eighteen years of service was the central figure in a steadily growing program. He brought to the Council a capacity for vigorous promotion and audacious action which were essential for its survival at a critical juncture, when accumulating deficits raised the specter of insolvency. He was sometimes criticized for being "aggressive" but without his bold initiatives the Council would probably never have developed enough of a program to command attention and enlist increasing support.

In his autobiography Dr. Macfarland gives a realistic picture of the situation as it looked to him when he came to the Council in 1911:

> Administratively speaking, the institution consisted of little more than a constitution, a small office, and a typist. . . . The denominations were paying only a little over $10,000 and the movement had not yet secured the cognizance of more than a few individuals. . . . I visited nearly twenty of the New York banks, asking for a loan. Presidents and other officers listened kindly, agreed that the Federal Council was a charming proposition, but all concluded by saying, "It is not a banking proposition," or using words to that effect.[38]

Surmounting Obstacles

In general, the first four years after the inauguration of the Federal Council were so beset with difficulties that when Shailer Mathews, dean of the Divinity School of the University of Chicago, was invited to become its president in 1912, he hesitated to accept the office.[39] He wondered whether the Council might not already be moribund.[40] It had committees on evangelism, foreign missions, home missions, religious education, Sunday observance, temperance, and family life, but their activity went little further than reporting on conditions and problems and making suggestions for future procedures and progress. The one field in which the Council was engaging denominational agencies in a program of active cooperation was that of Christian social responsibility —which was virtually virgin territory. Even before its Commission on the Church and Social Service had an employed secretary, the Council had sent fraternal delegates to conventions of the American Federation of Labor, promoted the observance of Labor Sunday, made an investi-

---

[38] Charles S. Macfarland, *Across the Years,* p. 90. To this record I add the personal reminiscence that Dr. Macfarland once remarked that in his effort to raise funds his first group of "prospects" was his wife's list of their wedding guests!

[39] SHAILER MATHEWS (1863–1941), Baptist minister, professor of historical and comparative theology in the Divinity School of the University of Chicago, 1906–1933, and dean of the School, 1908–1933; president of the Federal Council of Churches, 1912–1916; president of Northern Baptist Convention, 1915.

[40] When, in later years, he recalled his first visit to the Federal Council's headquarters in 1912, he described it as consisting of "one large room, broken into three parts, with a small mailing and stock room adjoining." *Federal Council Bulletin* (December, 1928), p. 15.

gation of an industrial conflict in the steel mills of South Bethlehem, Pa., and established contacts of mutual helpfulness with many agencies of social welfare, such as the National Child Labor Committee, the American Prison Association, and the National Conference of Charities and Correction.

The second unoccupied field into which the Council entered in this early period was Christian witness in international affairs. The time was ripe for it after the Spanish-American War had catapulted the United States into world politics. In 1912 the Council created a Commission on Peace and Arbitration (later to be renamed International Justice and Goodwill) with Frederick Lynch, editor of *Christian Work and Evangelist,* as volunteer secretary. The name seems to have been chosen because of current interest in proposed treaties of unlimited arbitration with England and France. This was the beginning of a program that became of central importance in the Federal Council after the world war which was soon to burst on the horizon.

Like the early work in the field of social affairs, this new project was made financially possible less by the denominations than by concerned individuals. The two undertakings demonstrated that although at this stage the process of securing adequate appropriations from denominational treasuries for uncharted programs might be so slow as to be stultifying, it was possible—granted initiative and ingenuity on the part of officers and staff—to discover supporting friends for interdenominational work in exploring new fields of service. The fact that extra-denominational resources could thus be enlisted gave the Council considerable freedom of action, as well as enabling it to move ahead without long periods of waiting for denominational financing.

By the end of 1912 more than half the total income of the Federal Council was provided by individuals. They were contributing $18,500, while the denominations were appropriating $14,500. The evolving pattern was one in which central administrative expenses would be met by denominational grants while programs in specialized fields of operation would be sustained in large part by interested friends or foundations.

As a matter of strict principle and logic, it could well be argued that an official body of the denominations ought to keep its expenditures within the limits of the resources that they officially supply. In practice, however, denominational budgets are planned so long in advance and are subject to so many pressures that to be entirely dependent on them for new projects would often result in missing a day of opportunity. From a theoretical angle, it was a weakness in the Federal Council that its financial nexus with the denominations was never very strong. From a practical angle, however, its ability to secure extra-denominational support gave it a flexibility which was valuable, especially in connection with new projects and emergency needs. When criticized in later years for following "opportunistic" policies, including policies in financing, Dr. Macfarland took the criticism as an unintended compliment. He was convinced that during the first two decades of its life the Council had made headway "not by the promulgation of clear-cut plans and schemes but by attempts to meet needs and opportunities as they arose and to gather the forces which the hour demanded."[41]

An important illustration of meeting "needs and opportunities as they arose" occurred in 1913, when a group of missionaries in Japan, gravely disturbed by proposed legislation in California discriminating against Japanese laborers and by its effect on friendly relations between Japan and America, appealed to the Federal Council to do something about it. A request was promptly made to the American Board of Commissioners for Foreign Missions to release Sidney L. Gulick temporarily for leadership in dealing with the issue. This was the beginning of what was to prove a long-range program for fostering justice and goodwill between the United States and the peoples of Asia. Dr. Gulick was at this time one of the outstanding missionaries in Japan, and a scholarly student of Japanese culture.[42] When he came to the Federal Council a Committee on Relations with Japan was formed, later expanded into a Commission on Relations with the Orient, and still later merged into a Department of International Justice and Goodwill. Its earliest measures were to provide for an objective study of conditions affecting Japanese on the Pacific Coast and to send Dean Mathews and Dr. Gulick on a special mission of friendship to Japan in 1914.[43]

Another concern began to find a place in the Federal Council's program in 1913—the problems of the rural church, accentuated by the steady drift of population from the country to the cities. The general condition had been pointed out by President Theodore Roosevelt's Country Life Commission, headed by Gifford Pinchot. His report had included a picture of the declining influence of religious leadership in rural areas and had declared that "the spirit of cooperation among churches, the diminution of sectarian strife, the attempt to reach the entire community, must become the guiding principles everywhere if the rural church is long to retain its hold." In an effort to improve conditions, and greatly aided by Mr. Pinchot, the Federal Council created a Committee on the Church and Country Life, with Charles O. Gill, a rural pastor with sociological experience, as its secretary, and established its headquarters

---

[41] *Christian Unity in the Making* (New York: Federal Council of the Churches of Christ in America, 1948), p. 348.

[42] SIDNEY L. GULICK (1860–1945), Congregational missionary in Japan for twenty-six years, professor of theology in Doshisha University, secretary of Federal Council of Churches for international interests, 1913-1934.

[43] The study of conditions on the Pacific coast was made by H. A. Millis, a professor of sociology in the University of Kansas, and the results published in the volume, *The Japanese Problem in the United States* (New York: The Macmillan Company, 1915).

in Columbus, Ohio. A handbook written by Messrs. Pinchot and Gill, *The Country Church: The Decline of its Influence and the Remedy*, was issued in 1913, and a few years later their *Six Thousand Country Churches* appeared, an intensive first-hand survey of the rural churches of Ohio.[44]

The pioneering of the Council in controversial areas of social change did not commend itself to all of its lay constituency. The experience of Peter Ainslie, one of the progressive spirits in the Disciples of Christ, was doubtless extreme but it illustrates the gap that existed between the leadership in the Council and the rank and file in the churches on Main Street.[45] He once confessed that when he began to attend meetings of the Council's executive committee he did not tell his congregation where he was going lest his participation be regarded as ground for firing him.[46] Especially in some of the smaller denominations, with pietistic traditions and no educational program in Christian social responsibility, much of the activity of the Council seemed off-center and questionable. By 1913 the Primitive Methodist Church, the Congregational Methodist Church, the Reformed Presbyterian, and the Augustana Synod of the Swedish Lutheran Church had dropped out of its membership.[47] In the Southern Presbyterian Church the issue of remaining or withdrawing was continuously debated for several years.[48]

In the main, however, the membership of the Council was surprisingly stable, year after year. Of the thirty-three denominations that were charter members in 1908 all but five small ones were still associated with the Council when it merged with the other interdenominational agencies in 1950 to constitute the National Council of the Churches of Christ in the U.S.A. None of the larger denominations had ever withdrawn, and several additional bodies, including four of the Eastern Orthodox family, had entered the fellowship. The Council might take positions that evoked critical reactions from the most conservative elements within its diverse constituency, but the thoughtful leadership of most of the denominations valued its service in dealing with frontier situations in their behalf.

---

[44] (New York: The Macmillan Company, 1919).

[45] PETER AINSLIE (1867–1934), minister of the Disciples of Christ, pastor of the Christian Temple, Baltimore, Md., 1891–1934; editor of *Christian Union Quarterly*, which he founded, 1911–1934; president of the Association for Promoting Christian Unity, 1910–1925.

[46] In a personal remark to the author.

[47] In 1917 the Mennonite General Conference withdrew for a different reason, finding that there was a "strongly marked variance" between it and most of the other member denominations on the issue of supporting American participation in the First World War. Other small denominations that withdrew in later years were the Christian Reformed Church (1924), the General Eldership of the Churches of God (1933), and the Reformed Episcopal Church (1945).

[48] In the early period it withdrew from the Council for a year but then returned. In 1931 it withdrew again, once more returning in 1941.

The example of the American churches in forming the Federal Council was widely followed in other lands. Essentially the same type of federated structure was adopted by other national councils, and also by the World Council of Churches when its constitution was drafted thirty years later. In the words of a seasoned observer, the conciliar development in the United States pointed to "a new form of church life."[49]

---

[49] The descriptive phrase is Henry P. Van Dusen's, in an unpublished manuscript, *The National Council of Churches, U.S.A.: An Appraisal,* in the library of the Union Theological Seminary. In his *One Great Ground of Hope* (Philadelphia: Westminster Press, 1961), p. 61, he refers to the Federal Council as having "projected the pathway and pioneered the pattern for all types of interchurch cooperation, that have been achieved in this century."

4

Forward on All Fronts

(1908–1914, continued)

In the half-dozen years before the First World War there were three different movements within the churches which gave expression in three different ways to the rising concern for unity. There was the movement of *practical cooperation* among denominational boards and agencies operating in a particular field of service. There was also the movement of *federation,* seeking to draw the churches as corporate bodies into closer fellowship. Beyond both of these was a movement that cherished the hope of *union* in one church by resolving the differences among the denominations. All three of these movements received organizational embodiment within the decade before the First World War. From the standpoint of interest in unity, it was a uniquely creative time. The two previous chapters have dealt mainly with the rise of church federation. We now consider the other two movements of this period.

Early Cooperation in Home Missions

Until the end of the nineteenth century home missions had been conceived primarily as the task of "winning the West" as the national territory kept expanding toward the Pacific. Now the geographical frontier had vanished but there were new social frontiers which called for "new home missions."[1] The growth of the great cities, the tremendous influx of immigrants, the industrialization of the economy, the changing character of rural life, the alienation of the working masses from the Protestant churches, all presented tremendous problems. And they were problems which did not lend themselves to fragmented denominational approaches but called for unified effort.

Some of the denominational leaders who had taken the lead in creating a federation of churches were at the same time feeling their way toward a more cooperative functioning in home missions. Foremost

---

[1] This was the title of an influential volume by H. Paul Douglass (New York: Missionary Education Movement, 1914), which strongly stressed the social responsibility of home missions.

among them was Charles L. Thompson, the general secretary of the Presbyterian (U.S.A.) Board of Home Missions.[2] In the late nineties he and Dr. Sanford had been closely associated in the Open and Institutional Church League, which had helped to pave the way for the Federal Council of Churches. Just at the turn of the century, the two men decided to invite the executives of the major missionary boards to a friendly dinner to discuss their common interests. The group found the occasion so helpful that they continued to meet in informal fashion at least once a year.

In his autobiography Dr. Thompson recounts an incident which illustrates what significant results could be accomplished simply by this kind of consultation. In 1899, when missionary enthusiasm was high for opening up work in Puerto Rico after the Spanish-American War, the secretaries of four boards (Baptist, Congregational, Methodist, Presbyterian) met in his office to share their plans and hopes with one another.[3] Here is his summary of what happened:

> We agreed to moderate denominational zeal, to go into the island as a band of brethren. . . . We divided the island into four sections, each board taking responsibility for one of the sections. . . . Since that first year several other denominations have gone to the island. But the ideals of comity and cooperation have never been forgotten.[4]

After several years of meeting occasionally for consultation, the executives of the boards organized officially as the Home Missions Council on March 6, 1908. The declared purpose was "to promote fellowship, conference, and consultation among Christian organizations doing missionary work in the United States and its dependencies."[5] Nine boards were charter members—Baptist (Northern), Congregational, Evangelical Lutheran, Methodist, Presbyterian U.S.A., Presbyterian U.S. (Southern), Reformed in America, Reformed in U.S., United Presbyterian.

For several years the Home Missions Council carried on without developing an administrative staff. When the denominational executives saw a cooperative task that required more than volunteer leadership, they decided among themselves to whom to assign it or arranged for the

---

[2] CHARLES L. THOMPSON (1839–1924), Presbyterian pastor in Juneau, Wis., Janesville, Wis., Cincinnati, Chicago, Pittsburgh, Kansas City, 1861–1888, and Madison Avenue Presbyterian, New York, 1888–1898; general secretary, Presbyterian Board of Home Missions, 1898–1914; moderator of Presbyterian General Assembly, 1888; president of Home Missions Council, 1908–1924.

[3] *Charles Lemuel Thompson: An Autobiography* (New York: Fleming H. Revell Co., 1924), pp. 139–140.

[4] This proved to be too optimistic a picture of subsequent developments. The simple comity agreement did not provide an adequate form of cooperation after the transition from a rural to a more industrialized economy began. The situation was further complicated by the entrance of other denominational boards into the island, some of which did not recognize the principle of comity.

[5] William R. King, *History of Home Missions Council, with Introductory Outline of Home Missions* (New York: Home Missions Council, 1930), p. 13. See also Handy, *op. cit.*, pp. 22–27.

temporary loan of a staff member of one of the boards. Not until 1918 did the Council acquire a full-time executive.

In the same year in which the Home Missions Council was established, the women's societies also effected an organization of their own for united action. Its antecedents were two-fold. One was the movement for mission study in local churches, which led in 1903 to the Interdenominational Committee on Home Mission Study. The other was the chain of regional summer conferences, beginning in 1906, which provided a joint program for promoting popular interest in home missions. The two streams of interest converged in November, 1908, to create the Council of Women for Home Missions, representing eight denominational societies at the outset. Its circulation of educational literature was extensive enough to go far toward financing its program. At this stage the women's societies were committed to maintaining their independence, chiefly because the general boards of the churches made so little place for leadership by women. The two missionary councils worked closely together but not till 1940 did they unite their forces.

The dominant concern of the Home Missions Council at the beginning was comity in the locating of churches. So long as the national territory was still enlarging, the problem of competition among the denominations in the occupation of it did not appear serious. There was room enough for all. By the end of the nineteenth century, however, the consequences of uncoordinated activities in church extension were too grave to be ignored. Each denomination had naturally been eager to serve the places that offered the promise of greatest growth, but it was less intent on ministering to the small community with an uncertain future. The result was a great deal of "overlapping and overlooking."

The overlooking was more serious than the overlapping. When the Home Missions Council, as one of its first concrete projects, joined with the Federal Council in 1910 in a survey of the distribution of religious forces in the state of Colorado, it was found that only 11.2 per cent of the financial assistance given by the boards went to churches where there was any conspicuous duplication of effort. Eleven per cent, however, was far too much when there were many communities with a population of a thousand with no church whatever.[6]

In the following year the cooperative survey was extended to cover fifteen states in the Far West, and fifteen statewide consultations were held that brought together the denominational missionary superintendents of the several areas to face the problems of overlapping and overlooking. This combination of survey and conference has been discerningly described as "the first large-scale attempt in American Protestant history realistically to get at the problem of neglect on the one hand and

---

[6] Charles S. Macfarland, *The Progress of Church Federation* (New York: Fleming H. Revell Co., 1917), pp. 110–112.

duplication on the other."[7] The most important result of the survey was the impetus that was given to the formation of several statewide inter-denominational commissions or councils of home missions which, though feeble in their influence at first, later developed into useful councils of churches.

A second major concern of the Home Missions Council in its early years was a more specialized ministry to both rural and urban churches facing changing social conditions and also to neglected minority groups in the population—Indians, Negroes, Spanish-speaking peoples, Orientals, Alaskans, immigrants. These specialized ministries called for specialized knowledge. This in turn called for surveys and investigations. Since the knowledge that one denomination needed was the same as the others needed, a cooperative technique began to be developed. In several cases there was also need for public efforts to protect the interest of neglected groups or to secure needed reforms, and this necessitated contacts with governmental agencies. To facilitate such contacts as these, and also to serve as a clearing house for the appointment of chaplains in the Army and the Navy, the Home Missions Council and the Federal Council of Churches established a joint office in Washington in 1914.[8]

One of the best illustrations of a cooperative approach to the ministry to minority groups was found in the Committee on Indian Affairs, which the Home Missions Council appointed in its first year. It had considerable success in securing comity among the denominational boards in their evangelistic and educational work for the various tribes, and it also improved the relationship of the boards with the U.S. Bureau of Indian Affairs.

Although the Home Missions Council and the Federal Council of Churches were organizationally independent of each other—one representing denominational boards and the other representing denominations as total entities—they worked in harmonious association. The Federal Council regarded the Home Missions Council as virtually, though unofficially, its agent in the field of home missions.

Closely related to the Home Missions Councils was the Missionary Education Movement of the United States and Canada, which represented the denominational boards, both home and foreign, in educational and publishing interests. At first study books were issued over the joint imprint of the Council of Women for Home Missions and the Missionary Education Movement. After several years of exploring how a more unified program of education could be projected, which would satisfactorily serve the interests of both home and foreign missions and

---

[7] Robert T. Handy, *op. cit.,* p. 46.

[8] By mutual agreement the Federal Council assumed full responsibility for the Washington office after a brief period of joint administration.

also of both the general boards and the women's boards, the Missionary Education Movement became their well-recognized common agent.

In all of this cooperative activity in missions there was no challenge to the denominational system as such. There was a clear criticism both of the sectarian spirit and of complacency with the *status quo*, but it was coordination of denominational efforts, not union, that was the objective in view.

Early Cooperation in Religious Education

In the first decades of the twentieth century enthusiasm for the Sunday School was at its peak. Revivalism was ceasing to be the dynamic influence that it had been during the period of the expanding frontier. The death of Dwight L. Moody in the last days of the nineteenth century (December 22, 1899) was symbolic of the end of an era.[9] With the decline of the revival the teaching of the Bible in the Sunday School came to be increasingly looked upon as the great way of winning and holding members of the churches. This trend was reinforced by the national interest in education in general and the growing conviction that the Christian teacher had more to offer than the revivalist.

Leadership in the Sunday School movement at this time was largely in the hands of laymen. It commanded the personal devotion as well as the financial support of business leaders like John Wanamaker and H. J. Heinz. Although organized outside the denominational structures, it had a pervasive influence in bringing about a common outlook within them. This was due in considerable part to the nationwide use of the uniform lesson plan, as a result of which those in all denominations who studied the same passage of Scripture at the same time were numbered by the millions.

Another unifying factor was the system of conventions of Sunday School workers, beginning in the county, moving up to the state level, and culminating in great national gatherings held triennially. An outgrowth of the national conventions was the International Sunday School Association organized in 1872. Later in the nineteenth century the Sunday School movement, at first concerned only with children, began to embrace adults also and "organized Bible classes," loosely related to the churches, began to be popular. In 1905 the Association established an adult department.

Dissatisfaction with the plan of uniform lessons, however, was growing, due to a rising awareness of its educational deficiencies. Along with this there was coming to be a stronger sense of the responsibility of the church itself for the religious education of both its children and its adult members. It was a combination of these two influences that in

---

[9] See Winthrop S. Hudson, *op. cit.*, p. 137.

1910 produced a new national structure, the Sunday School Council of Evangelical Denominations. The Council was an official agency of denominational boards and reflected their decision that the time had come when they could no longer leave the educational program to an "outside" agency.

For several years there was serious tension between the International Sunday School Association and the Sunday School Council of Evangelical Denominations. The Association had a vigorous organization and an honored history of service during decades when the churches themselves had not been alert to their responsibility for children and youth. The Council represented a mounting desire within the churches for control of the educational program. It was also an expression of a deepening insight that a curriculum with a sound philosophy of education would provide a completely graded series of lessons and would not be limited to exclusively Biblical material. The leaders in the Council felt that "while the Bible is the chief source book of religious education, an adequate religious education should introduce the growing person to a richer and wider range of the Christian tradition, including the history of the church, the biographies of its saints and heroes, its missionary enterprise, and God's creative work in nature."[10]

For a time it looked as if there would continue to be two competing organizations, each trying to secure the allegiance of those who were concerned for unity in the program of religious education. Fortunately, this did not harden into a continuing pattern. The first step in reconciling the differences was taken in the International Sunday School Lesson Committee, which up to this time had been answerable to the Association. In 1914 a reorganization of the Lesson Committee was effected which provided for representation of the denominational boards and their Council. From this point on there were patient negotiations looking toward a complete union of the Association and the Council. This was eventually accomplished by their merger in 1922, thereby creating the International Council of Religious Education.

This new development in religious education presented no threat to the denominational system. On the contrary, it tended to strengthen denominational authority by transferring leadership from an undenominational to an interdenominational body. In this process there was an implicit criticism of the denominations for having so long left the responsibility for religious education to non-church agencies. There was also a decisive recognition that the denominational boards could now assume this responsibility only by well organized cooperation and joint

---

10 William Clayton Bower and Percy Roy Hayward, *Protestantism Faces Its Educational Task Together* (Appleton, Wis., C. C. Nelson Publishing Co., 1949), p. 11. This is an important record of the history and philosophy of the International Council of Religious Education.

action. A gauntlet was thrown down to denominational separatism but not to the denomination itself.

Early Cooperation in Higher Education

At the beginning of the twentieth century the relation of the churches to higher education was in a state of confusion. Up to this time they had concentrated their attention on the church-related college. During the latter part of the nineteenth century, however, a pronounced shift had taken place in the college and university world. As a result of the phenomenal growth of tax-supported institutions, the church-related college was no longer dominant. As late as 1890 there were only thirty institutions under state or municipal control, but within two decades the number had increased to eighty-nine, and in the first decade of the century the enrollment in them increased twice as fast as in the privately supported institutions.[11] It was obvious that the churches could no longer fulfill their mission to the student world solely by supporting the colleges they had founded in an earlier era.

Another factor making for change and confusion in the situation was a mounting conviction within the churches that they ought themselves to follow their students with a religious ministry instead of leaving this task to non-church agencies like the Y.M.C.A. and Y.W.C.A. Prior to 1900 the only full-time religious workers among students were the Association secretaries, usually without theological or pastoral training. They effectively stressed the devotional life and personal evangelism and for this the churches were grateful. But they had begun to raise questions about the adequacy of the Associations' program. They felt that it was not sufficiently church-oriented and did not keep students in touch with the church during their college years. Out of this situation arose a new type of campus ministry, paralleling the Y.M.C.A. and the Y.W.C.A., centered in a university pastorate.

This development began around 1905, when a few of the major denominations appointed their first pastors for work with students. By 1910 there were, for example, Presbyterian pastors at the Universities of Michigan, Kansas, Illinois, Wisconsin, Colorado, Arkansas, and Nebraska. The Baptists, the Congregationalists, the Episcopalians, the Lutherans, and the Methodists were making similar experiments.[12] By 1912 there were twenty-six pastors devoting full-time service exclusively

---

[11] Clarence P. Shedd, *The Church Follows Its Students* (New Haven: Yale University Press, 1938), pp. 6–8. This is a mine of information about church work in the universities.

[12] The Disciples followed a variant pattern, emphasizing the teaching of religion at the academic level, and establishing "Bible Chairs." The Roman Catholics developed Newman Clubs, stimulated by an encyclical of Pope Pius X in 1905. The Jews began to establish Hillel Foundations two decades later.

to state university students.[13] As these experimental steps met with favor, denominational student centers, usually called "foundations," began to be established close to the campus as a base for the religious and social programs of the churches. The first of these was the Wesley Foundation (Methodist) at the University of Illinois, organized in 1913. It was soon followed by other denominational foundations for work with students.

The proliferation of denominational pastors and denominational student centers would obviously result in serious embarrassment for all if they carried on their work with any sectarian accent or in a competitive spirit. They accordingly lost little time in drawing together in informal association for the sharing of experience, the discussion of methods, and the presentation of something like a common front to the university administration. This was already happening at the University of Michigan and the University of Wisconsin in the years 1905 to 1908.

The personal contacts soon flowered into a more official relationship. The organizational pattern for such cooperation varied from campus to campus. At the University of Pennsylvania, beginning in 1914, the Y.M.C.A. provided the administrative center for a group of denominationally appointed pastors. At Cornell University a similar plan evolved into an interfaith set-up, in which Catholic and Jewish workers share, and in which there is a measure of specialization in tasks within the total personnel. The more common arrangement was a simple coordinating council. The first national conference of university pastors serving different denominations was held in 1908, and within two years it had organized on a permanent basis as the Association of Church Workers in State Universities.

As the university pastorate took on more definite shape, considerable tension arose between it and the student Y.M.C.A.-Y.W.C.A. This necessitated a good many years of patient consultation and experiment in developing an over-all program that represented a united approach to the university.[14]

While these developments were taking place on the campus, the denominational boards of education were having a parallel experience of coming together to deal with the increasingly complex problems. In fact, what could be done by local initiative was quite limited until national policy could be clarified and financial support made available from national sources. The first consultation among the executives of the denominational boards of education looking toward some form of continuous cooperation occurred in 1911, in response to an initiative

---

13 Shedd, *op. cit.*, p. 63.

14 For a description of different types of united work, see Shedd, *op. cit.*, Chapter V.

from Thomas Nicholson, secretary of the Methodist Board.[15] The six boards that were represented at this initial stage were Congregational, Lutheran, Methodist, Southern Methodist, Presbyterian U.S.A., and Southern Presbyterian. On January 17, 1912, the Council of Church Boards of Education was officially organized. At first it depended for its administrative leadership on the voluntary service of its officers, but in 1917 Robert L. Kelly, president of Earlham College, became its executive, serving also the Association of American Colleges at the same time. This Association came into being in 1915, largely on the initiative of the new Council of Church Boards of Education, as a central clearing house for private and church-related institutions.

In its origin the Council of Church Boards of Education had as its primary concern the strengthening of the church-related colleges, which were being overshadowed by the public institutions. In the words of its first chairman, its purpose was "to awaken the American church conscience to a new conception of the value and vital necessity of distinctively Christian schools . . . and to create a spirit of liberality toward them."[16] Soon, however, it assumed a role of interdenominational leadership also in relation to the tax-supported institutions, and in 1915 appointed a special University Committee to concentrate on this aspect of the task.[17]

As in the case of home missions and religious education, the impulse to work together in the college and university world had come from the concern to be effective in a common enterprise. Those who were involved in it were not thinking much about the nature of the church and its unity but they discovered that something more than segmented and self-sufficient denominationalism was a practical necessity.

World-wide Cooperation in Foreign Missions

It was in the area of foreign missionary responsibility, as we have earlier noted, that cooperation among denominational boards and agencies began. A tremendous impetus to the first exploratory steps in this direction was given by the World Missionary Conference held in

---

[15] THOMAS NICHOLSON (1862–1944), Methodist pastor in Michigan, 1884–1894; professor of philosophy at Cornell College (Iowa), 1894–1903; president of Dakota Wesleyan University, 1903–1908; general secretary, Methodist Episcopal Board of Education, 1908–1916; bishop, 1916–1932.

[16] *First Annual Report*, 1912, p. 14.

[17] There was no instrument of cooperation in theological education and the training of the ministry until 1918. In that year representatives of fifty-three seminaries met for the first time to consider common problems. Two years later the Conference of Theological Seminaries and Colleges in the United States and Canada was organized, which developed into the American Association of Theological Schools in 1936.

Edinburgh in the summer of 1910.[18] Unlike previous international conclaves this was not an assembly of interested individuals but a delegated body of representatives of missionary boards and societies.

In the initiation of the Conference, the preparation for it, and the leadership of it, the American contribution was noteworthy. The initial overture came from the conference of North American missionary boards, which had been held annually since 1893. At first it was apparently assumed that the 1910 gathering would be on the same general pattern as the Ecumenical Missionary Conference in New York in 1900, but as early as 1906 John R. Mott was suggesting that "the missionary enterprise at the present time would be much more helped by a thorough unhurried conference of the leaders of the Boards of North America and Europe than by a great popular convention."[19]

In the preliminary preparation for the Conference two joint sub-committees, one British and the other American, were set up in 1907. A little later the Standing Committee of German Protestant Missions assumed a similar role. The American group had Arthur J. Brown as its chairman.[20] Many of the arrangements which gave a distinctive character to Edinburgh, 1910, were suggested by this group, including the provision for officially delegated representatives of the boards and for intensive preparatory studies.

In 1908 eight topics were selected for study and commissions appointed to prepare reports on them. These subjects were Carrying the Gospel to All the World, The Native Church and Its Workers, Education in Relation to the Christianization of National Life, The Missionary Message in Relation to Non-Christian Religions, The Preparation of Missionaries, The Home Base of Missions, Relation of Missions to Governments, and Cooperation and Promotion of Unity. Dr. Mott was chairman of the Commission on Carrying the Gospel to All the World. Dr. Speer was co-chairman for the report on The Missionary Message. W. Douglas Mackenzie, president of Hartford Theological Seminary, was chairman of the group reporting on The Preparation of Missionaries.

Mott was the masterful chairman of the Conference throughout its

---

18 The report of the Conference appears in nine volumes under the title, *World Missionary Conference, 1910* (New York: Fleming H. Revell Co., [n.d.]). An interesting interpretation of the Conference is W. H. T. Gairdner, *Echoes from Edinburgh, 1910* (New York: Fleming H. Revell Co., 1910).

19 Quoted by W. Richey Hogg, *Ecumenical Foundations* (New York: Harper & Brothers, 1952), p. 105. This is an invaluable account of the International Missionary Council and its historical background.

20 ARTHUR J. BROWN (1856–1963), Presbyterian minister, pastor in Ripon, Wis., Oak Park, Ill., and Portland, Ore., 1883–1895; secretary of Presbyterian (U.S.A.) Board of Foreign Missions, 1895–1929; joint president, Universal Christian Conference on Life and Work, Stockholm, 1925.

ten days of sessions, June 14–23. His skill as a presiding officer has become almost legendary, especially his successful insistence on limiting each participant in the discussion, even if he were an archbishop, to seven minutes. Quietly planning everything behind the scenes as the secretary of the Conference was the young Scottish layman, Joseph H. Oldham, who was to do some of the most basic ecumenical thinking during the decades ahead.

A feature of Edinburgh, 1910, which had a decisive influence on subsequent ecumenical history was the participation of Anglo-Catholic leaders as well as Evangelicals. Their support had been secured on the assurance, carefully adhered to throughout the Conference, that there would be no resolutions or recommendations involving "questions of doctrine or church polity with regard to which the Churches or societies taking part . . . differ among themselves." In the geographical distribution of delegates the Conference was less adequately representative than in the denominational. Nearly all came from Europe and North America. Out of twelve hundred delegates only seventeen were nationals from Asia and Africa, and they came as appointees of Western organizations.

In deference to some of the Anglican leaders, who were concerned to guard against anything that might seem unfriendly toward the Roman Catholic Church, Latin America was the one part of the globe to which no attention was given. A considerable group of American delegates were not happy over this exclusion. Led by Robert E. Speer, they held an unofficial session to discuss Latin American needs. This had an important outcome in the decision to arrange a subsequent conference to deal specifically with that area. This took place in New York in March, 1913, and led to the creation of the permanent Committee on Cooperation in Latin America, representing the North American boards and agencies with responsibilities in that part of the world. Three years later a Congress on Christian Work in Latin America was held in Panama. At that time there was not a single union institution of any kind in Latin America. Five years later there were twenty-two.[21]

The only formal decision that was made at the Edinburgh Conference was that a Continuation Committee should be appointed, "international and representative in character," to carry forward the processes that the Conference had begun and to work toward the formation of a permanent international missionary committee. This was in line with a proposal which the Foreign Missions Conference of North America had put forward earlier in the same year.[22] Due to the coming of world war,

---

[21] The Committee on the War and the Religious Outlook, *The Missionary Outlook in the Light of the War* (New York: Association Press, 1921), p. 304.

[22] *Seventeenth Annual Report* (1910), p. 18. A similar proposal had been made by the German Standing Committee for Foreign Missions.

more than a decade was to elapse before the goal was reached in the founding of the International Missionary Council.

The impact of Edinburgh, 1910, upon cooperation among the American boards was quickly felt. Up to this time they had not moved much beyond annual gatherings for consultation, with a Committee of Reference and Counsel to study a few matters in the interim. Under the inspiration of Edinburgh, the boards now organized the Foreign Missions Conference of North America on a constitutional basis and began to look to its Committee of Reference and Counsel for continuous service in its behalf.

The constitution of the Foreign Missions Conference, framed in 1911, carefully limited its role and functions. Its purpose was "the consideration of questions relating to the administration of foreign missions" and "the investigation and consideration of matters of practical interest to the participating boards and societies." Following the Edinburgh pattern, it explicitly declared that "no resolution shall be considered which deals with theological or ecclesiastical questions that represent denominational differences."

In the same year in which the Foreign Missions Conference received its constitutional form a Board of Missionary Studies (a little later renamed Board of Missionary Preparation) was established, following a note strongly emphasized at Edinburgh, and in 1914 it acquired a full-time director. Also in 1914 the Missionary Research Library was founded, financially aided by John D. Rockefeller, Jr., and gradually became the most important center of its kind in the world.[23] The years immediately after Edinburgh also saw a series of important conferences on certain fields and special interests, including those on Japan (1912), China (1912), the Moslem world (1913), and the relation of missions with governments (1913).

The Edinburgh Conference has often been referred to as "the beginning of an era." This description is appropriate, if the era is clearly understood to be that of the ecumenical movement in its world-wide dimension. It was not, however, the beginning of the era of official cooperation among the churches or church agencies. In America the Federal Council and the Home Missions Councils, as well as the annual conferences of foreign missions boards, were all a part of the official life of the churches prior to 1910.

If the Edinburgh Conference was the beginning of an era, it was also the end of one. It marked the passing of the time when foreign missions could be thought of in terms of extending "the blessings of Christian civilization" from the West to other parts of the world. The decline of

---

[23] As the Library expanded and its budget increased the problem of financial support led to its transfer in 1929 to the Union Theological Seminary where it was conducted as a joint project until 1967, when the Seminary took it over.

the political power and prestige of the West set in soon after the war. In missions the center of gravity began to shift from boards and societies in the West to the emerging churches which the missionaries had helped to bring into being in Asia and Africa and Latin America.

The Beginnings of Faith and Order

An indirect consequence of the World Missionary Conference of 1910 was the action of the Protestant Episcopal General Convention, held in Cincinnati in October of the same year, proposing a World Conference on Faith and Order. While at Edinburgh as the missionary bishop of the Philippine Islands, Charles H. Brent had become convinced that cooperation in common tasks, however important as a next step, was not enough.[24] He had caught a vision of a united church, embracing the heritage of the whole Christian movement. "I was converted," he wrote. "I learned that . . . the Spirit of God was preparing a new era in the history of Christianity." He felt that the churches must make a concerted effort to understand each other at the level of their doctrinal and ecclesiastical differences—matters which the Edinburgh agenda had carefully excluded as too controversial—in the faith that the denominational system could eventually be superseded by an undivided Church of Christ.

What happened in the life of Bishop Brent during the weeks between the Edinburgh Conference and the Episcopal Convention is interestingly described by his biographer:

> His mind had been dwelling on how the disaster of disunity might be overcome. He had grown increasingly sure that one essential was to bring the points of difference out into the open and examine them frankly. By such a course they might be robbed of much of their power; many of them might be seen to be complementary rather than mutually exclusive, especially if the disagreements were viewed in the light of what the churches held in common. He records in his diary that at the early Eucharist on the opening day of the convention there came upon him vividly a conviction that a world conference should be convened to consider matters of faith and order.[25]

On the day before the opening of the Convention, Bishop Brent addressed a mass meeting in which he spoke of the impression that the Edinburgh missionary conference had made upon him and indicated his hope for a future world gathering that would consider issues of

---

[24] CHARLES H. BRENT (1862–1929), Episcopal priest, rector of St. Stephen's, Boston, 1891–1901; missionary bishop of the Philippines, 1901–1917; senior chaplain at A.E.F. headquarters, 1918; bishop of Western New York, 1919–1929; chairman, Lausanne Conference on Faith and Order, 1927.

[25] Alexander C. Zabriskie, *Bishop Brent: Crusader for Unity* (Philadelphia: Westminster Press, 1948), p. 147.

faith and order. On October 19, William T. Manning,[26] then rector of New York's Trinity Church, introduced a resolution which was unanimously adopted, proposing

> that a Joint Commission be appointed to bring about a conference for the consideration of questions touching Faith and Order, and that all Christian Communions throughout the world which confess Our Lord Jesus Christ as God and Saviour be asked to unite with us in arranging for and conducting such a conference.

When the Joint Commission was created to further the purpose of this resolution, Robert H. Gardiner became its secretary and during the rest of his life carried the main burden of the preparations for the Conference.[27] Although the project necessarily called for the collaboration of theological experts, Gardiner was a layman. It was he who contributed the organizing skill that provided the setting for their work. As Bishop Brent's biographer summarizes:

> To Brent was given the vision of the prophet and the gift of expressing in biting and vigorous language the challenge. Behind him, usually in the shadow, was Gardiner, always ready to bring to a knotty problem his keen, legally trained mind, and eager to work out the details of such organization as was necessary to realize the vision of his colleague.[28]

Supporting the movement were other Episcopal laymen, notably George Zabriskie, who became its treasurer, and J. Pierpont Morgan, who contributed $100,000 to launch it on its course.

Although it was the Episcopal Church which took the bold initiative, there were other contemporary forces moving in a similar direction. On the day before the resolution was introduced at its General Convention, Peter Ainslie was giving an address as president of the International Convention of the Disciples of Christ. In large part, it was an appeal for greater activity in behalf of Christian union. He followed up his appeal by founding a journal devoted to the cause, *Christian Union Quarterly,* and by organizing the Commission on Christian Union, soon renamed the Association for the Promotion of Christian Unity. In the same week the National Council of Congregational Churches, independently of what was happening among either the Episcopalians or the Disciples, appointed a commission to participate in any "fraternal discussion of church unity" that might prove feasible.

The first action of the Joint Commission of the Episcopal Church

---

26 WILLIAM T. MANNING (1866–1949), Episcopal priest, professor of theology at University of the South, 1893–1895; rector in Lansdowne, Pa., and Nashville, Tenn., 1896–1903; vicar of St. Agnes Chapel, New York, 1903–1908; rector of Trinity Church, 1908–1921; elected bishop of New York, 1921.

27 ROBERT H. GARDINER (1855–1924), Boston lawyer, leader in the Brotherhood of St. Andrew, devoted the last fourteen years of his life to serving the Faith and Order movement, entirely without remuneration.

28 Zabriskie, *op. cit.,* p. 149.

was to invite other churches to appoint commissions which would co-operate with it in planning for a world conference. The first responses, naturally, came from American churches. By the next summer eighteen Protestant denominations had already acted affirmatively on the invitation. From the outset the Faith and Order movement was planned to include other churches than those arising from the Reformation. Within the first year informal contacts were made with a few Eastern Orthodox leaders in the United States and with Cardinal Gibbons, the Roman Catholic archbishop of Baltimore.

In the summer of 1912 the Joint Commission sent a deputation to consult with the heads of the Anglican churches of the British Isles.[29] In the spring of 1913 came the first meeting of the American commissions that had thus far been appointed in response to the Episcopal invitation. Fifteen of them were represented. It was at this point that the movement ceased to be entirely under Episcopal control and began to be effectively interdenominational.

The most important step at this time was a decision of the interdenominational group to send a deputation to confer with the Free Churches of Great Britain and the Presbyterian Church of Scotland.[30] The deputation carried out its mission early in 1914, securing assurances of interest and the appointment of cooperating commissions.

While these deputations were developing personal contacts in Great Britain, an extensive correspondence was being carried on with other churches around the world. The responses were uniformly sympathetic, but Cardinal Gasparri, Secretary of State at the Vatican, concluded his friendly reply with an outspoken reminder that the Roman Pontiff, "as the one to whom all men have been given over to be fed, is the source and cause of the unity of the Church."[31]

Then came the First World War, rudely interrupting the hopeful prospect for a world conference. The Joint Commission of the Episcopal Church had planned to send a deputation to the churches of the European continent, including the Orthodox and the Roman Catholic, in 1914 but had to postpone it till after the war. In the meantime, during the period while the United States was still a neutral, some preliminary spadework for the agenda of the conference could be done by the Americans. In 1916 a North American Preparatory Conference was held in Garden City, Long Island, at which a tentative draft of

---

[29] The deputation was headed by Charles P. Anderson, Bishop of Chicago, who was chairman of the Joint Commission.

[30] This deputation consisted of Peter Ainslie (Disciples), Newman Smyth (Congregational), and William H. Roberts (Presbyterian).

[31] The full text of this letter is printed in Ruth Rouse and Stephen Charles Neill, *A History of the Ecumenical Movement, 1517–1948* (Philadelphia: The Westminster Press, 1954), p. 413.

subjects was outlined. At this point the Faith and Order movement was essentially an American project. Not until 1920 was it to become effectively international.

The Faith and Order movement and the movement of cooperation among church agencies soon tended to become polarized. Each represented an important interest which was a rival of the other for the support of those concerned for something beyond denominational self-sufficiency. Those who were trying to build up interboard agencies— like the Foreign Missions Conference, the Home Missions Council, and the Council of Church Boards of Education—were intent on getting as much unity as was immediately practicable in their own fields. Many of them thought the idea of an organic union of the churches was utopian. Those, on the other hand, who were planning for a World Conference on Faith and Order had their gaze focused on the ultimate goal. Some of them feared that successful cooperation in current tasks might make Christians satisfied with a reformed denominationalism.[32]

The Federal Council of the Churches of Christ in America occupied a middle position between these two other approaches. It went beyond the agencies of functional cooperation in being concerned not only with more effective service in specific fields but also with the basic relation of the churches, as churches, with one another. It did not, however, go as far as the Faith and Order movement, which involved an effort to resolve the doctrinal and ecclesiastical differences that stood in the way of a united church. The Federal Council concentrated its interest on a federated relationship rather than union, though leaving it an open question whether fellowship in Christian life and work might prepare the way for a fuller form of unity in the future.

---

[32] Both Brent and Gardiner, however, were active in the Federal Council as well as being officers in Faith and Order.

5

Wartime Testing of Church Cooperation

(1914–1918)

Less than six months before the assassination of an Austrian arch-duke in an obscure Serbian town precipitated a world war, Andrew Carnegie made a gift of $2 million to assist the churches in working together in behalf of peace. The gift was in the form of an endowment to be administered by a new foundation known as the Church Peace Union. Its trustees included prominent clergymen and laymen, predominantly but not exclusively Protestant. One of its most influential leaders, and its president for many years, was William P. Merrill, Mrs. Carnegie's pastor.[1] Its first secretary was Frederick Lynch, a Congregational minister and editor of *Christian Work,* who had encouraged Mr. Carnegie in the project.[2]

Although war clouds were gathering over Europe when Mr. Carnegie made this benefaction, his optimism, in keeping with the general mood of Americans at the time, was boundless—even naïve. In making the gift he inserted in the legal instrument a proviso that "if in the judgment of the trustees, the time shall come when peace is fully established and no more need be done in that cause, the income of the grant may be spent for the alleviation of poverty or other good causes."[3]

The first major undertaking of the Church Peace Union was to arrange for a conference, international and interdenominational in scope, to be held in Constance, Germany, in the early days of August, 1914. This was to be the occasion for launching an organization which would work for peace through the churches of the world. In Europe some preliminary groundwork for such a structure had already been laid by British and German churchmen who had created two "Associated Coun-

---

[1] WILLIAM P. MERRILL (1867–1954), Presbyterian clergyman, pastor in Philadelphia and Chicago, 1890–1911, and of Brick Presbyterian Church, New York, 1911–1936; president of Church Peace Union, 1918–1947; author of the hymn, "Rise Up, O Men of God."

[2] See Charles S. Macfarland, *Christian Unity in the Making* (New York: The Macmillan Company, 1948), p. 93. For an interpretation of Dr. Lynch's international idealism, see his *The Peace Problem* (New York: The American Peace Society, 1911).

[3] Quoted in *Christian Century Pulpit* (November, 1931), p. 2.

cils for Fostering Friendly Relations." Dr. Macfarland had made personal contacts with both of these, in behalf of the American churches, during a visit to Europe three years earlier.[4]

War Clouds Over Plans for Peace

By one of the most ironical coincidences in Christian history, this first international conference of churchmen in the interest of peace met on the very day, August 2, on which Germany declared war on Russia. In spite of the hazards of international travel in such a crisis, ninety delegates reached Constance, approximately half of those who had accepted invitations to attend. Notified by German authorities that the last train leaving Germany before the closing of the border would be on the following morning, the conference had to adjourn a few hours after it had convened. Before breaking up, however, it had approved the creation of a permanent body to serve as an instrument of cooperation among national groups of churchmen working for peace, and had appointed an international committee to carry on from this point. On the following day, August 3, the delegates made a hasty exit from Germany. It was the day on which Germany declared war on France.[5] Forty-eight hours later, those delegates who were able to get together in London met for a brief session to make organizational arrangements for the future. It was the day after England had declared war on Germany.

The name which was at first chosen for the new body was "The World Alliance *of Churches* for Promoting International Friendship." The name reflected the hope that the organization might represent the churches in their corporate capacities. But the abnormal circumstances of the time prevented much consultation across national boundaries, and the degree of official recognition that would warrant the ambitious title was not forthcoming. In the following year the name was modified to describe the character of the movement more accurately. It became the World Alliance for Promoting International Friendship *through the Churches.* The organization represented individual churchmen, devoted to the cause of peace and influential in the religious life of their various countries, but it was not destined to fulfill their dream of becoming an alliance of churches.

Several national branches of the Alliance were soon formed in spite of the cannonading. When its international committee held its first annual meeting in Switzerland in 1915, there were already ten such groups. Not long after the end of the war, the number of national councils had grown to twenty-six. During the two decades between the First

---

[4] The story is told in detail by Nils Karlstrom in Chapter XI of Rouse and Neill, *op. cit.*

[5] A first-hand report of the Constance meeting and its aftermath is given by Frederick Lynch in *Through Europe on the Eve of War* (New York: Church Peace Union, 1914).

and Second World War the Alliance, with its bases in these units, fostered international contacts which later proved to be of high value in preparing the way for the official World Council of Churches.

During the period of the First World War the American branch of the Alliance and the Federal Council's Commission on Peace and Arbitration were so closely associated in an educational program that they functioned almost as a single body, Dr. Lynch being the chief link between the two. As they both became more firmly established, the tie between them was looser, the Alliance acting as a free association of concerned individuals—including some Roman Catholic laymen and Jewish leaders—and the Council's Commission maintaining an official relation with the denominations in its constituency.

Until the entry of the United States into the war in 1917, the Federal Council strongly supported a policy of American neutrality. Early in 1915 its officers joined with representatives of the Church Peace Union in a letter to the churches expressing regret that "partisanship is adding fuel to fires of passion" and voicing the hope that the church would not abdicate "its sacred function as the maker of peace and concord."[6] Informal personal approaches were made to church leaders in both Great Britain and Germany to ascertain whether there was any possibility of American mediation for a settlement of the conflict. At Christmas time in 1915 Dr. Macfarland went to Germany, England, and France—as well as to the neutral countries of Holland and Switzerland —to confer with religious leaders in the interest of maintaining some measure of international contact between the churches in wartime and looking forward together to postwar reconstruction.[7]

As the war dragged on, however, the interest of the American churches in neutrality and reconciliation shifted to open sympathy with the Allies and active support of their cause. This was especially the case after the sinking of the *Lusitania* in the spring of 1915 and the unrestricted attacks of German submarines on American shipping.

Facing the Crisis Together

Two weeks after the United States entered the war, the Federal Council called a special meeting to consider the role of the churches in the crisis. It met in Washington, May 8–9, 1917, and proved to be more widely representative than any official Protestant gathering up to that time. The detailed report gives abundant evidence that it moved on a high spiritual plane. This is especially clear in the Message issued for the guidance of Christian people in the struggle that lay ahead. In the records of the meeting there is no indication of its authorship, but

---

[6] *The New York Times,* March 1, 1915.

[7] A vivid account of this mission is given in Charles S. Macfarland, *Across the Years,* Chapter VII.

it was no secret that it was primarily the work of William Adams Brown.[8] It is remarkably free from intemperate nationalism and the bitter passions which were soon to engulf the country. It conceived the war aims of America in very idealistic terms—more idealistic than the subsequent course of events sustained. It spoke of vindicating "the inviolability of faith as between nation and nation," of safeguarding "the right of all the people, great and small, alike, to live their lives in freedom and peace," and of overcoming "the forces that would prevent the union of the nations in a commonwealth of free peoples."

The outline of the duties to which all members of the churches were summoned revealed an unusual degree of Christian insight. They included:

> To purge our own hearts of arrogance and selfishness . . .
>
> To hold our own nation true to its professed aims of justice, liberty and brotherhood;
>
> To testify to our fellow-Christians in every land, most of all to those from whom for the time we are estranged, our consciousness of unbroken unity in Christ;
>
> To unite in the fellowship of service multitudes who love their enemies and are ready to join with them in rebuilding the waste places as soon as peace shall come;
>
> To be diligent in works of mercy and relief;
>
> To care for the welfare of our young men in the army and navy, that they may be fortified in character and made strong to resist temptation;
>
> To be vigilant against every attempt to arouse the spirit of vengeance and unjust suspicion toward those of foreign birth or sympathies;
>
> To protect the rights of conscience against every attempt to invade them.[9]

These high goals, specifically Christian in purpose and spirit, were enunciated plainly at a time when the nation was swept by war fever. They were, however, much easier to announce than to attain. As the strain of the conflict intensified, the whole national effort became more and more concentrated on the one goal of victory. Winning the war came to be regarded as in itself a moral and spiritual achievement. It is even possible that the lofty idealism which the Message voiced had an unintended effect of making people less shocked by the butchery of war. As all organs of public opinion came increasingly under the dominance of governmental propaganda, pulpits more and more joined

---

[8] WILLIAM ADAMS BROWN (1865–1943), Presbyterian theologian, Roosevelt professor of systematic theology at Union Theological Seminary, New York, 1898–1930, and research professor, 1930–1936; chairman of the General Wartime Commission of the Churches, 1917–1919, and of the Federal Council's Department of Research and Education, 1920–1936; co-president of the Oxford, 1937, Conference on Church, Community, and State. See his autobiography, *A Teacher and His Times* (New York: Charles Scribner's Sons, 1940).

[9] The full text of the Message is printed in *Report of the Special Meeting*, Federal Council of the Churches of Christ in America (New York, 1917), pp. 22–26.

uncritically in the rationalization of the conflict as a glorious crusade or even a "holy war." This lent considerable justification to the title of a postwar book, *Preachers Present Arms*, a sweeping indictment of the stance of religious leaders during the war.[10]

Preachers Present Arms, however, should not be accepted as a fair picture of the attitude and activity of the churches as a whole during the war. The facts which it cites are true enough, but it leaves too much unsaid that also belongs in the record. It quotes a host of preachers and evangelists and editors of the religious press who denounced the Germans as Huns and whipped up undiscriminating enthusiasm for everything that looked toward victory, but it ignores the beneficent work and influence of both local churches and national agencies during the struggle.

Among the practical duties which the Message of the Federal Council set before the churches, and which they undertook in a responsible way, were the maintenance of a close relationship with chaplains and Y.M.C.A. workers among the armed forces, support of the American Red Cross, working for wartime prohibition of the liquor traffic, conserving the food supply of the nation, protecting standards of social welfare, and safeguarding democratic processes in wartime.[11] These tasks clearly pointed to the need for greater cooperation of the churches in each community. Fortunately a national Congress on Purpose and Methods of Interchurch Federation was already in a preliminary planning stage before the United States was involved in the war. It was held in Pittsburgh, Pa., October 1–4, 1917. Out of it came *The Manual of Interchurch Work*, which served as a standard handbook of local cooperation both during the war and after.[12]

As the war continued, the propaganda of the government became so powerful that the churches tended increasingly to accept it too uncritically. In the main, however, the Federal Council avoided nationalistic excesses. It justified its patriotic support of the war on the ground that the war was a just one and that the winning of it was essential to the establishment of an international order of peace and justice. Its leaders felt duty-bound as citizens to share fully in the national struggle but they did not entirely forget that the Christian community transcended the nation. There is no record, in any of the Council's many wartime utterances, of any appeal to hate the Germans or condemn German

---

[10] Ray H. Abrams (New York: Round Table Press, 1937).

[11] An objective and thoroughly documented study of the Federal Council's wartime service is "The Social Policy of the Federal Council of the Churches of Christ in America during World War I," an unpublished doctoral thesis at Duke University, 1964, by John F. Piper, Jr. It is also available in microfilm at Union Theological Seminary, New York.

[12] Edited by Roy B. Guild (New York: Federal Council of the Churches of Christ in America, 1917).

Christians. Its primary attention was focused on providing a religious ministry to the millions of men drafted into the armed forces.

Emergency Wartime Tasks

Even before the American entrance into the war, the Federal Council of Churches had taken the initiative in getting the chaplaincy in army and navy established on a more satisfactory basis. Up to this time the process of selecting chaplains had been slipshod, often depending on the recommendation of a member of Congress. Sometimes an appointment to the chaplaincy became an easy resort for a minister who was in trouble with his parish or denominational officials. Among even the best of the chaplains morale was low, due in part to their isolation from the churches, in part to lack of support for their religious function by their commanding officers. As General John J. Pershing observed in his reminiscences, they had often been relegated to "the status of handy men who were detailed to write up boards of survey or operate libraries."[13]

Moreover, the chaplains were few in number. As early as 1913, the Federal Council had petitioned Congress to provide for at least one chaplain on every major ship and at every navy yard and army post.[14] In 1914 the Council established an office in Washington, one of whose functions was to give support to better provision for the chaplaincy.[15] In the same year an increase in the number of chaplains in the navy was authorized by the government.

As the result of a joint approach to the War Department by representatives of the Federal Council and the National Catholic War Council, an arrangement was made in 1916 by which all chaplains would henceforth be screened and nominated by the churches.[16] For coordinating the activities of the Protestant denominations in discharging this responsibility, a General Committee on Army and Navy Chaplains was formed at the beginning of 1917.

When, later in 1917, a reorganization of the army raised the size of a regiment from 1,200 to 3,600 men, the quota of chaplains continued to be only one per regiment, which reduced the ratio of chaplains to men by two-thirds. To secure legislation that would assure more chaplains required a long struggle. In spite of persistent efforts by the Federal Council and the National Catholic War Council, no governmental action

---

[13] John J. Pershing, *My Experiences in the World War* (New York: Frederick A. Stokes Co., 1931), Vol. I, p. 283.

[14] *Annual Report, 1913,* p. 6.

[15] *Annual Report, 1914,* pp. 71–73.

[16] The National Catholic War Council was formed in 1917 to deal with the wartime emergency. It became a permanent agency of the Roman Catholic Bishops after the war, changing its name to National Catholic Welfare Conference.

was forthcoming for almost a year. Meanwhile, the situation overseas was deplorable, as described in a message from Bishop Charles H. Brent, then Senior Chaplain on General Pershing's staff, on April 18, 1918:

> We are dreadfully short-handed here. As far as statistics can advise, we have not one chaplain to 5,000 men. . . . It is cruel beyond words to send our young men across the sea to live in conditions of unwonted hardship and temptation, to encourage them to be ready to die for their country, and then neglect to furnish them with those spiritual ministrations which are at the door of every citizen in home life.[17]

The bill for the increased number of chaplains was finally passed by Congress in May, 1918. At the outbreak of the war there had been only 113 chaplains—Protestant and Roman Catholic—in the army and navy. By the end of the war, 7,931 applications for appointment as Protestant chaplains had been received and investigated. Of these 2,731 were approved, and 1,439 were duly commissioned by the government.[18]

The Council also gave attention to other needs of the chaplaincy than greater numbers. It pressed successfully for the establishment of a Chaplains Training School by the government for clergymen entering the service. It secured provision for a modest amount of necessary equipment for each chaplain. Before the war was over the chaplaincy was on a new and more satisfactory basis.

A few weeks after the outbreak of the war it became evident that the tasks requiring cooperative attention were multiplying so rapidly that a special interdenominational agency was needed. The Federal Council accordingly created the General Wartime Commission of the Churches on September 20, 1917. In its relation to the Council the Wartime Commission was given a greater freedom than earlier commissions. Instead of being under the direction of the Council's executive committee, it operated as an autonomous unit, although always working closely with the Council and being domiciled in the same quarters. The main reason for the freer relationship was that there were important denominations, like the Southern Baptist Convention and most of the Lutheran bodies, which were not members of the Council but which, in the wartime emergency, were ready to cooperate with a temporary agency. Another reason was that there were important organizations for wartime service, like the Y.M.C.A., which did not fit into the established pattern of the Federal Council.

The General Wartime Commission consisted of one hundred persons representing the many Protestant agencies dealing directly with tasks and problems connected with the war. It had as its chairman Robert E.

---

[17] Piper, *op. cit.*, pp. 325–326. Dr. Piper gives a detailed account of the efforts to secure more chaplains, based on an examination of materials in both governmental and Federal Council archives.

[18] *Wartime Agencies of the Churches,* ed. Margaret Renton (New York: General Wartime Commission of the Churches, 1919), pp. 187ff.

Speer, already widely known for his missionary leadership, and as its secretary William Adams Brown, who was granted a leave of absence from his professorial chair at Union Theological Seminary to permit him to assume executive responsibility for the Commission. This was the beginning of Dr. Brown's active dedication to the movement of interchurch cooperation, which was to continue for the next twenty-five years.

During its limited life of about eighteen months, the General Wartime Commission succeeded in commanding a greater measure of official cooperation than had been seen in any interdenominational organization up to this time. This was doubtless due, in the main, to the external pressure of wartime circumstances. The crisis which the nation faced greatly reinforced the impulses to work together. The careful definitions of policy and procedure in the Commission were an additional source of confidence among the cooperating agencies. Its executive committee met regularly twice a month, which was time-consuming but rewarding. It assured to each agency a full knowledge of what the others were planning, thus avoiding serious duplication and commanding strong support for those projects which were selected for joint action.[19]

Ministering to the Armed Forces

In the early stages of mobilization of the armed forces the chaplains in the training camps were so few that several denominations felt impelled to send clergymen to minister as "camp pastors." These civilians were sometimes so numerous in a camp that they created problems for the commanding officer. Their desire to serve was commendable but their functions and relationships were vague and undefined. When several pastors of different denominations found themselves in the same camp, all uncertain as to their role and all unfamiliar with military conditions, there was a real danger that the commandant might find the situation too confused to be tolerable. Into this scene the General Wartime Commission brought sufficient order to make it acceptable to the military authorities. Interdenominational conferences were held in several geographical areas for the guidance of camp pastors and local churches near the camps. The denominational agencies that were appointing camp pastors were kept in continuous consultation with one another. The magnitude of the problem is indicated by the fact that in 1917–1918 there were more than 1,500 camp pastors. A single denomination, Southern Baptist, appointed 200 for varying periods of

---

[19] It was at this juncture that my own connection with the Federal Council began. At the invitation of Dr. Brown I became an assistant secretary of the Wartime Commission, expecting to resume my graduate study after a year, but I spent the next forty years in interdenominational and ecumenical service. In 1920, I became associate secretary of the Federal Council. From 1921 to 1930 I was junior general secretary; from 1931 to 1950, general secretary. When the National Council of Churches was formed, I served as its first general secretary, from January, 1951, to February 1, 1954.

service. The National Lutheran Commission for Soldiers' and Sailors' Welfare had 150, the Presbyterian Church in the U.S.A. 100, the Episcopal Church 95, and others in proportion.[20]

Another problem which involved tension was the respective roles of the churches and the Y.M.C.A. in their service to men in the armed forces. The work of the "Y," supported by a civic campaign that raised the United War Fund, was by far the most extensive of all the organizations that were officially recognized as "welfare agencies." It operated in 333 camps, army posts, and naval stations in the United States, and in 1,680 centers in France. The total number of men recruited for its staff was over 12,000, of whom about 3,000 were ordained ministers.[21] From the standpoint of the War and Navy Departments of the government, the status of all "Y" secretaries, including the clergy, was that of laymen. This was true even of those who were secretaries for specifically "religious work." The chaplains, on the other hand, were officially commissioned by the churches for a pastoral ministry, including the conduct of worship and the administration of the sacraments.

In the main, the relation between Y.M.C.A. workers and chaplains was reasonably satisfactory. The "Y" huts were placed at the disposal of chaplains as needed; and the attitudes on both sides—with a few exceptions—were fraternal. But there was never any adequate definition of relationships between the churches and the Y.M.C.A., and the lack of it contributed to misunderstandings and rivalries. The vast program of the Y.M.C.A., although it leaned heavily on the churches for personnel and support, was launched without any clear agreement with them. Its War Work Council was set up without consultation with either denominational or interdenominational leaders. A little later, when a Cooperating Committee of the Churches was initiated by the Y.M.C.A., its members were chosen by the "Y" itself, not by the churches.

The one established point of contact between the Y.M.C.A. and the churches was in the General Wartime Commission. Thanks to the representation of the "Y" in the Commission, and even more to relations of personal friendships and trust between the leaders on both sides, the over-all picture showed more unity than might have been expected in the absence of common planning in advance.[22]

An important behind-the-scenes function of the General Wartime Commission was to provide a nexus between Protestantism on the one hand and the National Catholic War Council and the Jewish Welfare

[20] Renton, *op. cit.*, pp. 20, 55, 94, 100.

[21] *Ibid.*, pp. 231–232. Not so well known is the extensive humanitarian ministry of the Y.M.C.A. to prisoners of war of all nations while the United States was still a neutral.

[22] For a frank appraisal of the relations between the Y.M.C.A. and the churches in the war, see the Committee on the War and the Religious Outlook, *Christian Unity: Its Principles and Possibilities* (New York: Association Press, 1921), pp. 34–36.

Board on the other. Although there was no joint action in terms of program, there was consultation from time to time. This was effected through an informal "Commitee of Six," made up of representatives of the three faiths, under the chairmanship of Father John J. Burke. The Protestant members were Robert E. Speer, William Adams Brown, Bishop William Lawrence, and John R. Mott. On a few occasions the Committee of Six made a united approach to the War Department and the Navy Department in the interest of all the chaplains, and to the governmental Commission on Training Camp Activities in behalf of the moral welfare of the troops.

The lack of any serious tension between the three faiths in their wartime roles is illustrated by a felicitous incident affecting the chaplaincy. When the first Jewish chaplains were commissioned, they complained against the regulation which prescribed the wearing of the cross as the official insignia of the chaplaincy. In response to their protest the Secretary of War issued a new regulation against the use of any religious insignia by chaplains—a regulation which applied to Christian as well as Jewish chaplains. When the chairman of the Jewish Welfare Board heard of this, he promptly requested a rescinding of the order so far as Christian chaplains were concerned. The problem was solved by another directive authorizing Christian chaplains to wear the cross and Jewish chaplains to wear the star of David.[23]

A phase of the General Wartime Commission's work which began at a rather late date but was to have postwar consequence was the activity of a Committee on the Welfare of Negro Troops. Negroes were, of course, drafted—like other citizens—to fight a "war for democracy," but the conditions under which they fought were far from democratic. When complaints of serious racial discrimination arose, the Commission employed two field secretaries to make investigations both in army camps and in adjacent communities. Discriminatory practices were reported to the War Department both in a series of detailed studies and in a conference in which white and Negro representatives shared. The presentation to the War Department was made by a Southern white churchman, M. Ashby Jones, minister of the First Baptist Church of Atlanta, with seven concrete recommendations for improving conditions. In some instances corrective measures followed. The significance of the program, however, was less in any concrete reforms that resulted than in forcefully registering the critical judgment of the churches against policies of racial discrimination.[24]

At a few camps, situated in the open country or near small towns with wholly inadequate church facilities, cooperative Protestant head-

[23] William Adams Brown, *op. cit.,* pp. 235–236.

[24] Piper, *op. cit.,* pp. 251–267. Dr. Piper's account is based on a detailed study of the documentary evidence.

quarters were erected. Especially noteworthy was the chapel, with adjoining offices and living rooms, at Camp Upton, Long Island. The responsibility for financing and erecting it was shared by five denominations—Baptist, Congregational, Episcopal, Methodist, Presbyterian—
but it was placed at the service of all religious workers in the camp.
Less ambitious building projects were a parish house at Camp Dix, N.J.,
and central offices or social centers for religious workers at Camp
Devens, Mass., Camp Meade, Md., Camp May, N.J., Camp Cody, N.M.,
and Camp Kearney, Cal.[25]

Other Wartime Ministries

In the mushrooming centers for the production of wartime munitions
and ships a different method of assuring a religious ministry was followed. A quick survey of 115 such communities revealed situations in
which there was no church or religious center whatever. When the findings were laid before the national boards of home missions and other
interested agencies, an agreement was reached that in each place where
an edifice was needed, one denomination would assume the responsibility for developing a community church for all Protestant people and
for providing a pastor. Under this unprecedented agreement "Liberty
Churches"—as they came to be called—were established at seven
ordnance reservations. Each was staffed and financed by a denominational agency—Episcopal, Lutheran, Methodist Episcopal, Methodist
Episcopal South, Presbyterian U.S., Presbyterian U.S.A.—all under the
general supervision of a joint committee of the Home Missions Council
and the Federal Council of Churches.[26] The war ended before the program of Liberty Churches had been carried far, but four of the seven
became permanent institutions. In certain more stable areas, like
Newport News, Va., and the Calumet area of Chicago, in which ship-
building and other emergency industries expanded on a large scale
almost overnight, the joint committee reinforced the ministry of the
local churches by appointing community workers to serve a group of
cooperating parishes.

For the considerable groups of interned aliens in the United States,
citizens of countries with which our nation was at war, some spiritual
ministry had to be provided. Since many of them were of German
background, with which the Lutheran churches had the closest tie, the
National Lutheran Commission for Soldiers' and Sailors' Welfare, as a
cooperating unit in the General Wartime Commission, agreed to represent all the Protestant agencies in discharging this responsibility.

The most popular of the religious activities of the period was a cam-

---

25 Renton, *op. cit.*, pp. 16, 162.
26 *Ibid.*, pp. 193–199.

paign on "The Churches and the Moral Aims of the War," in 1918. Its primary sponsors were the Church Peace Union and a civic organization called the "League to Enforce Peace," headed by former president William Howard Taft. More marginally related to the campaign were the Federal Council of Churches and the American Council of the World Alliance for International Friendship Through the Churches. The project sought to arouse widespread support for President Wilson's avowed aims of winning the war against autocracy, making the world safe for democracy, securing justice for all nations, and creating a League of Nations. Within a period of three months 300 great rallies were held, addressed by prestigious speakers including a score of American clergymen and three British—George Adam Smith, the eminent Biblical scholar, Charles Gore, Bishop of Oxford, and Arthur Guttery, the president of the Free Church Council of England and Wales.[27] The three visitors made no fewer than 360 addresses in three months. The meetings helped to build an impressive support among the churches for a League of Nations. A less fortunate result was too great a glamorizing of the war as essentially a holy crusade.

One point at which the Federal Council of Churches hardly measured up to the full responsibility that could rightly have been expected of it was in connection with the conscientious objectors to war. At its special meeting in Washington at the beginning of the conflict, the Council had recognized that the churches were "under particular obligation to see that the conscientious objector is allowed such non-combatant service as does not violate his conscience."[28] But as the war came increasingly to be regarded as a wholly black-and-white encounter between the forces of evil and the forces of righteousness, there was less sensitivity to the problem of the conscientious objector. An honored pacifist leader, Norman Thomas, even said that the Federal Council's early commitment to protecting the rights of conscience turned out to be only "a scrap of paper" and that the Council gave no "aggressive or effective help during the days when a small body of liberals was struggling for a more human treatment of conscientious objectors and other political prisoners."[29] The statement was partly justified but too unqualified. Even Mr. Thomas's "small body of liberals" in the National Civil Liberties Bureau had felt, until late in the war, that it was a more effective strategy to maintain unpublicized contacts with a friendly War Department than to carry on a widespread agitation. When, in the fall of 1918, it became clear that in certain places the treatment of conscientious objectors was

---

[27] Renton, *op. cit.*, pp. 121ff.

[28] *Report of the Special Meeting, May 7–9, 1917*, p. 18.

[29] In *The Conscientious Objector in America* (New York: B. W. Huebsch, Inc., 1923), p. 265.

harsh, the General Wartime Commission presented such evidence as it could secure to the War Department. Assurance was given that the reported cases of mistreatment would be investigated. A departmental order subsequently curbed extreme disciplinary measures, but by this time the war was over.

Forerunners of Ecumenical Action

An undertaking of long-range significance, although begun as only an emergency program, was the effort of the American churches to provide relief for overseas churches suffering from the devastation of war. It began in a small way as early as 1915 in response to pleas to the Federal Council from Protestant bodies in France and Belgium. In 1917 two representatives of French Protestantism came to America in quest of greater help and received an encouraging response. Early in 1918 a Committee on Christian Relief in France and Belgium was officially organized. Its primary purpose was to enlist financial aid for evangelical institutions struggling to survive in those countries. In the four years of war about $400,000 was raised for their assistance. After the war a much more extensive program of aid, including the rebuilding of more than a score of French churches destroyed by the war, was carried out. These efforts had important consequences other than financial. By furthering an appreciative understanding of a little known sector of European Protestantism they contributed to the coming ecumenical movement.

Although at this time the contacts of the American churches with the churches of Europe were limited to the Allied nations, the vision of a truly ecumenical fellowship, embracing Christians on opposite sides of the battle lines, was not wholly absent. At the beginning of 1918, for example, a declaration of the American Council of the World Alliance for International Friendship said:

> The Church in all its branches should humbly and devoutly pray for recovery of its lost consciousness of its essential unity and universality in Christ, establishing in its membership the feeling of a fellowship that transcends the barriers of nation and race. . . . [It] should build in all its branches throughout Christendom a worldwide fellowship of goodwill and reconciliation. It should practice self-sacrifice and service in the relief of suffering, earnestly cultivate love of enemies, and stand ready to share in the pressing tasks of reconstruction and rehabilitation when this war is ended.[30]

Toward the end of 1918, only a month after the armistice, a strong plea was made by the Federal Council for the formation of a League of Nations "by which common standards of right and privilege for all

---

[30] *Federal Council Bulletin* (February, 1918).

people and nations shall be guaranteed by the united power of all."
Provision was made for a day of prayer for such a League.[31] The
idealism which was reflected in the enthusiasm for the League at this
time was boundless. It was even referred to in a Federal Council publication as "a political expression of the Kingdom of God."

More significant for the future of the ecumenical movement was a
proposal authorizing "a few leaders of the churches to meet at this time
in Europe . . . to consult with our European brethren, especially with
British churches, as to the advisability and feasibility of a World Conference on a large scale."[32] This was one of the early steps moving in
the direction of the Universal Christian Conference on Life and Work
of seven years later.

Where the War Left the Churches

Although the cooperative efforts of the churches during 1917 and
1918 were mainly focused on the emergencies of the war and the international situation, there were considerable gains in ongoing programs.
The fresh energies evoked by the wartime crisis were felt in several aspects of the Federal Council's life. One of these was in the Commission
on Social Service. It had had no full-time executive after Dr. Macfarland
assumed responsibilities in general administration in 1912. Now it
called Worth M. Tippy to the task. With a background of unusual pastoral experience in relating the church to the whole life of a community,
he was to give creative national leadership in this field for the next two
decades.[33]

In evangelism also a fresh advance was made. For the first time the
Federal Council provided a full-time executive in this field in the person
of Charles L. Goodell.[34] The Commission on Evangelism now began to
find its way to giving guidance in pastoral evangelism as an alternative
to mass revivalism. One of its major emphases was on simultaneous
efforts in evangelistic outreach by all the pastors of a community, including cooperation in a house-to-house canvass to locate the unchurched.

The wartime experience had been a great training school for the
American churches in working together. Robert E. Speer summed it up

---

[31] Charles S. Macfarland, *Christian Unity in the Making*, p. 147.

[32] *Ibid.*, p. 148.

[33] WORTH M. TIPPY (1866–1961), Methodist minister, was a pastor of Indiana churches,
1893–1904, and of Epworth Memorial Church, Cleveland, Ohio, 1905–1915, where he was
one of the organizers of the Cleveland Church Federation. From 1915–1917 he was pastor
of New York's Madison Avenue Methodist Church, and from 1917 to 1937 the executive of
the Federal Council's work in social service.

[34] CHARLES L. GOODELL (1854–1937), Methodist pastor in Providence, R. I., 1880–1888,
Boston, 1888-1896, Calvary Church, Brooklyn, and St. Paul's, New York, 1897-1918; executive secretary, Federal Council's Commission on Evangelism, 1918–1935, and radio preacher,
1931–1937.

in an address at the end of the war in these words:

> We have been taught clearly this last year the absolute indispensability
> of an adequate, unselfish instrumentality for cooperation in the name of
> the Church and with the consciousness of the Church in its richest his-
> torical and spiritual significance. . . . It can never be an open question
> again as to whether the Federal Council, or something that fills that
> ground, is an absolute necessity.[35]

While the war was still at its peak the General Wartime Commission
of the Churches took the initiative in constituting a Committee on the
War and the Religious Outlook. It grew out of the conviction that the
war had laid on the churches the duty of the most thorough self-examination. Its distinctive feature was the fact that its members were
appointed to do nothing except study and think together. Its first chairman was President Henry Churchill King of Oberlin College. When prolonged responsibilities in Europe in behalf of the Y.M.C.A. led him to
resign, he was succeeded by William Adams Brown, who brought to
his task not only his practical experience as the chief official of the
General Wartime Commission but also his ripe theological scholarship
and an active concern with the role of the church in society.[36]

In its several studies the Committee enlisted the service of about
a hundred active participants in addition to its own members. As preliminary publications, aiming to foster discussion, it issued a series
of nine brief monographs on "The Religious Outlook" in the early months
after the war. They were "tracts for the times," bearing such titles as
"The Local Church after the War," "Christian Principles Essential to a
New World Order," "Christian Principles and Industrial Reconstruction,"
"Christian Aspects of Economic Reconstruction." They reflected the social idealism which the wartime mood had encouraged but most of
them were too sharply oriented to the immediate situation to have
much long-range significance.

The major contribution of the Committee on the War and the
Religious Outlook was a series of five reports, each a substantial volume.
The first was *Religion Among American Men: As Revealed by a Study of
Conditions in the Army*.[37] It was based on an extensive body of observa-
tions and experiences of chaplains and other workers in the armed
forces. Viewing the men in uniform as a revealing cross section of
Americans of the younger generation, the report diagnosed "religious
illiteracy" as very widespread. This was the precursor to a report on
"The Teaching Work of the Church," which sought to stimulate a
greater sense of responsibility for the Christian education of both chil-

---

[35] Quoted in Charles S. Macfarland, *Christian Unity in the Making*, p. 151.

[36] It was my privilege to serve as secretary of the Committee, with Angus Dun, later Episcopal bishop of Washington, D.C., as associate secretary during the earlier period of its work.

[37] (New York: Association Press, 1920).

dren and adults.[38] One of its main accents was on a greater recognition of the role of religion in all education.

Another report was concerned with *The Missionary Outlook in the Light of the War*.[39] This magnified the opportunity for missionary advance by reason of the increasing recognition of the world as a single community, and reviewed emerging situations in different parts of the world. A fourth report focused on *Christian Unity: Its Principles and Possibilities*, a survey of interchurch cooperation and union in America and of lessons learned from the wartime experience.[40] The fifth report was *The Church and Industrial Reconstruction*, a study of Christian social responsibility in relation to economic and industrial problems.[41]

The circulation of these volumes did not reach large proportions. By the time they came from the press, a disillusionment over the war and an impatience for a "return to normalcy" had set in, which did not provide a favorable climate for intensive reflection on the mission of the church in the remaking of society. The report on *The Church and Industrial Reconstruction* was the one which provoked the most discussion. The British economist, R. H. Tawney, called it "the most useful contribution" yet made to the subject.[42] On the other hand, it was criticized, especially in a later era, as lacking social realism and assuming that Christian ideals of love and brotherhood are directly applicable to the economic and social realm.[43] Probably the most important influence of the Committee on the War and the Religious Outlook was the indirect one of offering a concrete example of the kind of cooperative study that was later to become characteristic of the ecumenical movement.

---

38 (New York: Association Press, 1923).

39 (New York: Association Press, 1920).

40 (New York: Association Press, 1921).

41 (New York: Association Press, 1921).

42 Quoted in William Adams Brown, *A Teacher and His Times*, p. 257.

43 See, for example, Donald B. Meyer, *The Protestant Search for Political Realism* (Berkeley, Calif.: University of California Press, 1960), pp. 19–25, 32–34.

6

Testing by Postwar Disillusionment

(1919–1924)

After the war there was a brief period when the crusading spirit of the earlier years of the twentieth century still lived on. "The air was full of banners," as a discerning observer said, "and the trumpets called from every camp."[1] This mood, however, was soon followed by a psychological reaction, tersely expressed in the title of a ruminative book of the time, *Disenchantment*.[2]

The disillusionment took many forms. Enthusiasm for the League of Nations gave way to resurgent nationalisms. Ardor for social reform yielded to a nostalgia for "normalcy." National prohibition, adopted in a wave of crusading zeal, was defiantly flouted. The community of national feeling evoked by the common perils of war was succeeded by the anti-Negro, anti-Catholic, anti-Jewish nativism of the Ku Klux Klan. The cooperation of the churches during the wartime emergency was followed by the divisiveness of the fundamentalist controversy. The vision of a bold united advance in an Interchurch World Movement ended in failure.

Collapse of Postwar Crusades

In the churches there was a spirited rallying to Woodrow Wilson's plea for the League of Nations. It appeared to most religious leaders as a noble political expression of the oneness of mankind. It was especially extolled by the Federal Council of Churches, which gave unqualified endorsement and at a critical juncture called for a Day of Prayer for the League. Robert E. Speer, who had been chairman of the General Wartime Commission of the Churches, voiced the general view of Protestant leadership when he described the League of Nations as "an in-

---

[1] Gaius Glenn Atkins, *Religion in Our Times* (New York: Round Table Press, 1932), p. 156.

[2] By C. E. Montague (New York: Brentano, 1922).

dispensable and unavoidable implication of all our Christian faith."[3] While the Peace Conference was in session in Paris, the Federal Council sent a delegation to present resolutions in enthusiastic support of the League. Even after American membership became a sharply controversial issue in politics the churches continued to urge American duty to join. The appeal fell on increasingly deaf ears. The American people were moving toward the political isolationism that sent Warren G. Harding to the White House.

The churches, however, continued an active interest in international affairs, directing their main attention to the armaments race. In February, 1921, the Federal Council petitioned the Congress and the President to initiate measures "looking toward general disarmament by all the nations." After the International Conference on the Limitation of Armament, which met in the following November, had drafted a treaty, the Council launched a campaign for approval by the Senate. The Committee on General Information of the Conference reported that out of 13,878,671 letters received on the subject more than 12,500,000 indicated that their action was related to the interest of the churches.[4]

The concern for cooperation in behalf of peace was further expressed in the Federal Council's activity in support of American membership in the Permanent Court of International Justice. Throughout the years 1922 to 1924 this was repeatedly urged, climaxed by an appeal to the Senate Committee on Foreign Relations in May, 1924, by a delegation headed by Bishop Brent.[5] The dominant temper of the nation, however, was too isolationist to respond to such a plea.

Another crusading movement which evoked an exuberant response from the churches called for the prohibition of the manufacture and sale of alcoholic beverages. This was, of course, no new interest. The American Society for the Promotion of Temperance, the National Temperance Society and Publication House, and the Women's Christian Temperance Union—all organized in the nineteenth century—had drawn most of their support from the churches. What was new was the method of attacking the problem. Instead of concentrating on an educational program, the Anti-Saloon League, growing in strength since its creation in 1895, decisively shifted the emphasis to legal and political strategies. It openly entered the arena of election campaigns, endorsing candidates who were committed to the "dry" position and mobilizing to defeat candidates who were regarded as "wet."

Although not an official organization of the churches, the League

---

[3] In an address at the special postwar meeting of the Council held in Cleveland, Ohio, May 6–8, 1919. *Federal Council Bulletin* (June, 1919).

[4] *Federal Council Bulletin* (December, 1921).

[5] *Ibid.* (June, 1924).

commanded strong support from most of them, notably from the Methodist and the Baptist. It often described itself as "the church in action against the saloon." It was markedly effective in carrying its program into tens of thousands of local churches, probably more successful in this respect than any other nondenominational agency before or since. During the war the patriotic appeal for food conservation had helped to popularize the campaign for prohibition, which after the war was pressed with greater vigor. Within a year after the end of the war, the eighteenth amendment to the Constitution of the United States had been adopted and national prohibition went into effect in 1920. A widespread reaction against its enforcement then set in and grew in intensity until the repeal of the amendment in 1933.[6]

The Federal Council of Churches had been on record since its first meeting in warm support of the principle of prohibition, although not participating in the political maneuvers of the Anti-Saloon League. When the flagrant violations of the Volstead Act became more and more scandalous, the research department of the Council, early in 1925, undertook an inquiry into the situation. The report frankly admitted that the evils which had led to the adoption of the eighteenth amendment were far from being solved. To the stalwarts of the Anti-Saloon League, whose policy was to make no concessions whatever, the nationwide publicity attending the report was a nettling irritation. Some of the denominational representatives in the Council who were also active in the League (notably Bishop James Cannon, Jr.) sought to reprove the research department and challenged its authority to release its findings without their having been endorsed by the Council as a whole. The result was sharp debate and no little strain within the Council for several months. The fortunate outcome was a strong affirmation of the importance of "impartial and unbiased research," including the dictum that "the bewildering complexity of modern life makes this function all the more imperative, and also makes it imperative that it be discharged with all possible freedom and scientific thoroughness."[7]

The success of the drive for prohibition was a dramatic example of the power of the churches when mobilized for what was regarded as a clear moral issue. It also demonstrated that there are methods of dealing with an evil which are of dubious appropriateness for the churches. In this case a majority within the churches was trying by legal measures to impose on the whole nation a way of life to which large numbers of their own members were not really committed.

---

[6] For a sympathetic account by an "insider," see Ernest H. Cherrington, *The Evolution of Prohibition* (Westerville, Ohio: American Issue Publ. Co., 1920). For a critical analysis, see Peter Odegard, *Pressure Politics: The Story of the Anti-Saloon League* (New York: Columbia University Press, 1928).

[7] *Federal Council Bulletin* (December, 1925).

Theological Conflict

In the years immediately following the war the theological divergencies within Protestantism were greatly accentuated. Two decades of open conflict lay ahead. This was precipitated by the attempt of the fundamentalists to protect orthodoxy from the encroachments of science and to eliminate from leadership in the church all who could not subscribe to their rigid positions. They insisted on a literal adherence to the inerrancy of Scripture, the Virgin Birth of Jesus, His substitutionary atonement, His physical resurrection, and His imminent second coming. The central issue was over the interpretation of Scripture and the historical method of studying the Bible. The World Conference on Christian Fundamentals, held in Philadelphia in the spring of 1919, marked the onset of the struggle. Soon most of the major denominations were involved in calamitous controversies, especially the Presbyterians, the Northern Baptists, and the Disciples.[8]

The divisive effect of the Fundamentalist movement was much more obvious within the denominations than between them. In the Presbyterian Church in the U.S.A. a glare of publicity followed the effort to oust Harry Emerson Fosdick, a Baptist, from the pulpit of New York's First Presbyterian Church, an issue brought to focus by his sermon in 1922, "Shall the Fundamentalists Win?" This was followed by attacks on the orthodoxy of Princeton Theological Seminary and the Presbyterian (U.S.A.) Board of Foreign Missions, culminating in the founding of a splinter denomination, the Orthodox Presbyterian Church. In the Northern Baptist Convention a long-continued dissension resulted in the withdrawal of a group of congregations in 1933 to form the General Association of Regular Baptists, and in 1947 another withdrawal produced the Conservative Baptist Convention of America.

In almost every major denomination there was controversy between fundamentalist conviction and pietistic ethics on one side and evangelical liberalism on the other. The fundamentalists rightly emphasized the need for a theology which preserves historical continuity with the past. Their opponents rightly insisted that theology could not ignore the best thought of every changing age. The struggle between them became so bitter as to have a hurtful impact on every movement that tried to magnify cooperation on the basis of a common loyalty to Jesus Christ. The acrimony and distrust which were stirred up ran directly counter to the ecumenical spirit.

At first little attention was paid to the interdenominational agencies by the fundamentalists. Their strategy was directed to capturing the

---

[8] See Stewart G. Cole, *The History of Fundamentalism* (New York: Harper & Brothers, 1931) and Norman F. Furniss, *The Fundamentalist Controversy, 1918–1931* (New Haven: Yale University Press, 1954).

great denominations. The Federal Council, however, did not long escape the consequences of the strife. When Dr. Fosdick became the preacher for the National Radio Pulpit, sponsored by the Council, it came directly into the line of fire. The feeling that the Council was "liberal," in spite of its having the active participation of moderate conservatives, was a main factor in the official withdrawal of the Southern Presbyterian Church in 1931.

Failure of Interchurch World Movement

Of all the postwar crusades the most ambitious was the Interchurch World Movement. Buoyed up by the unprecedented outpouring of money for all good causes during the national crisis of wartime, Protestant leaders embarked on a more extensive program of common effort than had ever been undertaken before. It appeared on the horizon as suddenly as a meteor—and disappeared almost as quickly.

On December 17, 1918, less than a month after the end of the war, a conference of executives of denominational boards—missionary, educational, and benevolent—launched the Movement. It boldly proposed to bring together in an associated enterprise not merely denominational agencies engaged in the same line of work but all the boards operating in all areas of service. It was conceived as a great combination of promotional interests, designed to reinforce and supplement the postwar "forward movements" which many of the denominations were organizing.[9] Its role was defined as the making of comprehensive surveys of needs in the most important fields of Christian concern and the securing of greatly multiplied resources for meeting these needs.

Projected hastily, under the impulse of enthusiasms generated by the war, the Movement lacked clear delineation of its relationships either to the denominations or to the existing interdenominational agencies. Whether it was to be temporary or permanent, whether it was to be promotional only or might assume certain administrative responsibilities, were unanswered questions. It was organized by operational boards without waiting to secure the approval of the denominations as corporate bodies. When, some months later, the importance of such approval became more evident, it was forthcoming in varying degrees, and assurance was given that at least two-thirds of the Movement's general committee would be persons approved by denominational authority.[10]

---

[9] These included the New Era Movement of the Presbyterian Church in the U.S.A., the New World Movement of the Northern Baptist Convention, the Men and Millions campaign of the Disciples of Christ, the Progress Campaign of the Reformed Church in America, and a score of others.

[10] For information about the Movement as conceived by its leaders see *Handbook of the Interchurch World Movement* (New York, 1919). For a summary of its survey material, see the two-volume *World Survey by the Interchurch World Movement* (New York, 1920).

The interdenominational agencies already existing were regarded by the Interchurch World Movement as too slow-paced for dealing with the new postwar situation. Ignored at the outset, they related themselves to the Movement in different ways after it had gathered momentum. The Missionary Education Movement became completely integrated with it. Other interboard agencies were more or less cooperative, including the Foreign Missions Conference, the Home Missions Council, and the Council of Church Boards of Education. The Federal Council of Churches, however, pursued an independent course, sympathetic with the aim of the Movement but establishing no connection with it.[11]

The culmination of the Movement was a simultaneous campaign for funds, totaling no less than $336 million, in the spring of 1920. The participating agencies were to carry on their solicitations within their own constituencies, each benefiting by a common publicity. There was, however, no provision for the expenses of the Movement itself to be defrayed out of the denominational funds thus collected. Its needs would be cared for—so it was sanguinely assumed—by a community appeal to "friendly citizens." This proved to be a fateful miscalculation. The Movement asked for $40 million for itself but received less than one-tenth of that amount. Having built up an extensive staff and conducted expensive surveys, mainly on borrowed money, it was left with a staggering debt of more than $6 million. Most of this had to be met by denominational boards that had contemplated no such contingency. Their appeals to their own local churches for their own denominational needs were generally successful, but the appeal to "friendly citizens" for support of the cooperative phases of the program broke down. Following this deflation of exaggerated hopes, an attempt was made to salvage the tottering Movement by a drastic reduction of budget but it was too late. By the end of June, 1920, after a life-span of eighteen months, the Movement had collapsed. The crusading era was over.

The magnitude of the task which the Interchurch World Movement set for itself required a greater development of cooperation than could be achieved by a burst of promotional energy. The immobility and lethargy in the rank-and-file of the denominations with reference to any great advance in unity was vaster than had been realized. Moreover, the Movement suffered seriously from a lack of clarity as to its own character. It had been put together so speedily that even among those responsible for its affairs there were confusing interpretations of its role. To some it was a way of strengthening the denominations in their work; to others, a way of transcending the denominations. It also suffered

---

11 See *Federal Council Bulletin* (January, 1920), for the statement in which the Council and the Interchurch World Movement expressed their friendly attitude toward each other while preserving their separate structures.

from an unfortunate public image of itself as enamored of size and publicity and financial standards of success.[12]

The weakest point in the armor of the Movement was the inadequate measure of authentic representation in its relation to the churches. It was launched by a group of responsible officers of denominational agencies but without the official commitment of the agencies. When formal approval was subsequently given by the agencies, it was without full consideration of assuming a weighty responsibility. Not until a late stage was authorization sought from the denominations themselves in their corporate capacity. The unhappy outcome indicates that unless an interdenominational project is grounded in the denominational consciousness, it is on an unstable foundation. One of the unexpected results of the collapse of the Movement was to strengthen the Federal Council of Churches in the eyes of its member denominations. The values of its constitutional structure now stood out in clearer light.

Steel Strike Investigation

The one feature of the ill-starred Interchurch World Movement which is remembered today is its investigation of the steel strike of 1919. The chief issues involved were the long hours of labor—especially the twelve-hour day—working conditions, and recognition of the union. The report, made by a committee headed by Bishop Francis J. McConnell, gave strong support to the contentions of the workers, who had given up their strike before the report was issued.[13] It was publicly attacked on two grounds: first, that a church agency had no business to inject itself into a secular field; second, that the report was unreliable in its factual data. In retrospect, neither complaint appears justified. The conflict was so grave in its human consequences that in the absence of other attempts to shed light on the issues the churches would have been derelict in their social responsibility if they had done nothing. The subsequent reforms in the industry were evidence of the substantial correctness of the conditions depicted in the report.

Three years later, the issue of the twelve-hour day in the steel in-

---

[12] A discriminating analysis of elements of both strength and weakness in the Movement, written only a few months after its collapse, is given by Robert E. Speer in the Committee on the War and the Religious Outlook, *Christian Unity: Its Principles and Possibilities*, pp. 140–150. A less critical appraisal is found in the article, "The Truth About the Interchurch," by a member of the General Committee, in *Christian Work*, December 11, and December 18, 1920. The most complete record of the Movement is an unpublished manuscript, "History of the Interchurch World Movement," in the libraries of Union Theological Seminary, New York, and the University of Chicago. It was apparently prepared by the Committee that was charged with the task of liquidating the Movement.

[13] FRANCIS J. MCCONNELL (1871–1953), Methodist minister, educator, and bishop; pastor in West Chelmsford, Newton Upper Falls, Ipswich, and Cambridge, Mass., 1894–1903, and New York Avenue, Brooklyn, 1903–1909; president of DePauw University, 1909–1912; elected a bishop in 1912; president of Federal Council of Churches, 1928–1932.

dustry was reopened by the Federal Council of Churches, with the collaboration of the National Catholic Welfare Conference and the Central Conference of American Rabbis. Their joint statement bluntly characterized the twelve-hour day as "morally indefensible." The Iron and Steel Institute had reported a few months earlier that nothing could be done about it because the furnaces had to be kept going twenty-four hours a day and more than two shifts of workers would be too costly. To this the introduction to the joint statement replied: "If industry objects that we churchmen are invading a technical realm when we discuss engineering problems, we must reply that when industry employs men twelve hours a day it is committing a moral trespass and challenges the churches in their own field." The statement had a pronounced public impact, due partly to the unprecedented common front of the religious bodies, partly to the force of a moral judgment well buttressed by facts. The statement appeared in June, and before the end of the year the twelve-hour shift was abolished.[14]

Whether the attacks on the Interchurch World Movement for its investigation of the steel strike were responsible for the Movement's failure was a question which was much debated at the time, and which it is impossible to answer with confidence. It seems fairly clear, however, that even if there had been no such investigation, the Movement had too much internal weakness to be a viable enterprise. But some positive values emerged from it. It challenged both the denominational and the interdenominational agencies to find more dynamic ways of moving ahead on the cooperative road. It led indirectly to the inauguration of certain new programs of cooperation, such as that which brought the United Stewardship Council into being as a clearing house of methods for promoting Christian responsibility in the use of money. The Movement also gave needed impetus to the development of scientific research and survey as instruments in the service of the churches.

When the Movement was liquidated, much of the survey material which it had gathered and not yet published was distributed among the several interdenominational agencies. The main task of continuing surveys and intensive studies fell to a new organization, privately initiated, the Institute of Social and Religious Research. Organized at the beginning of 1921 as an independent agency, it was financed chiefly by grants from John D. Rockefeller, Jr. During the next thirteen years, it carried on forty-eight research projects, published in seventy-eight volumes, in such fields as the rural church, the urban church, home missions, foreign missions, Christian education, theological education, and racial

---

[14] For a summary of the joint statement, see *Information Service*, Federal Council of Churches, June 16, 1923. For the full text of the Interchurch World Movement's findings, see *The Report on the Steel Strike of 1919*, by the Commission of Inquiry (New York: Harcourt, Brace & Co., 1920).

aspects of organized religion. In all of these the development of cooperation among religious forces and the importance of objective study of
socio-religious conditions were constant interests.[15]

Abortive Plan for Organic Union

Simultaneous with the quick rise and fall of the Interchurch World
Movement were the similar fortunes of the American Council on Organic
Union, an adventure in unity of a very different kind. In 1918, while
the war was still going on, the General Assembly of the Presbyterian
Church in the U.S.A. invited other evangelical churches to a Conference
on Organic Union. Representatives of the nineteen denominations that
accepted the invitation convened in Philadelphia in the month after the
end of the war. At a second meeting in February, 1920, "the Philadelphia
Plan" was formulated for "a visible body" to be known as "The United
Churches of Christ in America," and an "American Council on Organic
Union" was set up to sponsor the proposal.

In spite of the title of the sponsoring organization, it really proposed
a federal rather than an organic union. There was, however, an explicit
statement of hope that this would be the first stage on the road to "complete unity."

The Plan contemplated a Council of the "United Churches" whose
role would be chiefly advisory but which would have power, if the member denominations so desired, "to direct such consolidation of the missionary activities in over-churched areas as is consonant with the law of
the land, or of the particular denomination affected." There was, however, nothing in the Plan which made the proposed consolidations man-
datory. They were to be "progressively achieved" and "accelerated, de-
layed, or dispensed with as the interests of the kingdom of God may
require." There was a moral commitment to consolidation but a very
flexible process of moving toward it. The Plan further conferred a limited measure of judicial authority upon the proposed Council by providing that two or more constituent churches "might submit to the Council
for its arbitrament any matter of mutual concern."

The Plan was to become operative when officially adopted by six denominations. It soon became evident that there was no prospect of such
an outcome. The main objection that was raised was that it did not go
sufficiently beyond the existing Federal Council of Churches to warrant
creating the confusion that would arise from having two Councils. This
viewpoint was voiced by the General Assembly of the United Presby-

---

[15] The best-known, though hardly the most important, of the studies was *Middletown,*
by Robert and Helen Lynd (1929), an inquiry into the religious and social attitudes of a
Midwest industrial city. It was through the Institute that H. Paul Douglass conducted most
of his valuable studies. When it was discontinued in 1934, he joined the staff of the Federal Council of Churches.

terian Church of North America when it said that the projected Council "proposes at the present time a little further advance toward real organic union, but has as yet not accomplished anything practical in the field of Christian activities," while the Federal Council "has made less progress toward organic union, but has already accomplished much practically for Christian activities."[16]

Others were apparently against the proposal not because it did not go far enough but because it went too far. In its declared purpose it looked beyond cooperation and made a long-range commitment to union, in at least a preliminary form. Although each of the constituent denominations was to retain "its creedal statements, its form of government in the conduct of its own affairs, and its particular mode of worship," the Plan contemplated the transfer of at least a few functions to the new Council by the denominations, particularly "the consolidation of their missionary activities."[17] The existing Federal Council stood for interdenominational cooperation; the proposed Council stood for cooperation plus some limited authority officially delegated to a central body. The difference between the two was the difference between *federation* and *federal union.*

After two years of desultory discussion, the Philadelphia Plan was no longer given serious attention. Even in the Presbyterian Church in the U.S.A., which had initiated it, it did not secure the final assent of the number of presbyteries that was requisite for adoption. The time was not ripe for any form of union beyond partially federated efforts of wholly autonomous denominations.

Some Hopeful Trends

Although the postwar years are rightly described as a period of reaction, it would be a great mistake to suppose that this tells the whole story. In the field of cooperation there were several hopeful and constructive developments. As a concrete example, consider Near East Relief. Although not an official agency of denominations, it was formally endorsed by many of them and drew both its moral and its financial support primarily from the churches. It raised $91 million, plus food and supplies valued at about $25 million, for Greek and Armenian refugees and other sufferers from war's aftermath. It rescued and fed and gave a measure of education to 132,000 orphaned children, and initiated experiments in agriculture that led to a permanent Near East Foundation.[18] Leaders in the movement, like James L. Barton and Charles V. Vickrey, regarded the task as an expansion of their missionary concern.

---

16 *Christian Unity: Its Principles and Possibilities,* p. 159.

17 *Ibid.,* p. 356. The full text of the Plan is printed as an appendix of the volume.

18 James L. Barton, *Story of Near East Relief (1915–1930): An Interpretation* (New York: The Macmillan Co., 1930).

A secular historian like Samuel Eliot Morison can point to the work of Near East Relief as an outstanding humanitarian achievement.[19]

In the field of religious education the postwar period witnessed an important advance in national leadership. These were the years in which the International Council of Religious Education was being created by the merger of the Sunday School Council of Evangelical Denominations and the older International Sunday School Association. The genius of the plan of union was a combination of the "territorial principle," which had been embodied in the statewide Sunday School Associations, and the "denominational principle" embodied in the national boards of the Sunday School Council. In the governing body of the unified structure the state associations and the denominational boards were given equal representation. One of the chief architects of the merger, consummated in 1922, was Robert M. Hopkins, who served as the chairman of the Council for the next decade.[20]

For the Federal Council of Churches the years from 1920 to 1924 were among the most creative. A Committee on Goodwill between Christians and Jews was organized to oppose anti-Semitism and work for better understanding. A Committee on Religious Work in the Panama Canal Zone was formed, which developed a pattern for a united ministry to American personnel living abroad. Of special significance for future developments was the establishment of the Commission on Race Relations in 1921. This was to prove a steadily increasing factor in bringing the Negro and the white denominations (both of which had been in the Council from its beginning) into cooperation in special efforts for interracial understanding and justice. The first chairman was a distinguished Southern layman, John J. Eagan of Atlanta. The first executive, who was to provide notable leadership for the next twenty-four years, was George E. Haynes, a Negro with wide experience as educator and sociologist.[21]

A program of interchurch aid was also set in motion at this time which prepared the way for what is known today as Church World Service. Even before the war was over the Federal Council had undertaken a special effort to help the hard-pressed Protestant bodies in France and Belgium. In the summer of 1922, as a result of a confer-

---

[19] In *The Oxford History of the American People* (New York: Oxford University Press, 1965), pp. 922–923.

[20] Robert M. Hopkins (1878–1954), minister of the Disciples of Christ and its leader in religious education; secretary of the American Christian Missionary Society, 1910–1920, and general secretary of the United Christian Missionary Society, 1920–1928; general secretary of the World's Sunday School Association, 1928–1939; president of the United Christian Missionary Society, 1939–1946.

[21] George E. Haynes (1880–1961), Congregational layman, a secretary of the International Committee of the Y.M.C.A., 1905–1908; professor at Fiske University, 1910–1920; staff member in U.S. Department of Labor, 1918–1921; executive secretary of Federal Council's Department of Race Relations, 1922–1946; co-founder of the National Urban League.

ence in Copenhagen initiated by the Federal Council and sponsored by the Swiss Church Federation, the Central Bureau for the Relief of the Evangelical Churches of Europe was created. Under the direction of the Swiss Adolf Keller, with headquarters in Geneva, it found its chief support in America and continued an increasing ministry of interchurch aid until the World Council of Churches took over the responsibility in 1948.[22] The financial resources of the Bureau were not large, as compared with the amounts raised after the Second World War, but the contribution to ecumenical understanding and fellowship was pronounced.

Other creative influences were combining to lend impetus to the ecumenical movement in three nascent organizational forms. Almost as soon as the armistice was signed, steps were being taken which developed international contacts in "Faith and Order," in "Life and Work," and in the International Missionary Council.[23]

Advance in Faith and Order

The four years of war, cutting off normal channels of communication with churches overseas, interrupted the preparations for the World Conference on Faith and Order just as they were getting under way. Within America, however, where the proposal for the World Conference had originated, the Protestant Episcopal Commission had kept up a measure of activity in its behalf. Less than four months after the end of the war, an Episcopal deputation sailed for Europe and the Near East to confer with heads of churches and solicit their participation. They visited Athens, Smyrna, Istanbul, Sofia, Bucharest, Belgrade, Alexandria, Cairo, Jerusalem, Damascus, Paris, Oslo, Uppsala, and Rome. Everywhere except in Rome they met with affirmative responses.[24]

The interview with Pope Benedict XV was a keen disappointment. The deputation had to report that although he received them graciously, he gave an unqualified declination to their invitation. His written reply said that "the teaching and practice of the Roman Catholic Church regarding the unity of the visible Church of Christ was well known to everybody and therefore it would not be possible for the Catholic Church to take part in such a Congress as the one proposed." His statement ended

---

[22] See Charles S. Macfarland, *Steps Toward the World Council* (New York: Fleming H. Revell Co., 1938).

[23] In his valuable book, *The Great Tradition in the American Churches* (New York: Harper & Row, 1953), pp. 222–225, Winthrop S. Hudson seems to me to give an exaggerated picture of "decline in cooperative activities" in the first decades of the twentieth century. More significant developments were taking place in the 1920's and 1930's than his statement implies. Moreover, the cooperation in the nineteenth century, which he extols, did not enlist the churches as churches; it was a cooperation of Christians made possible by going outside the churches.

[24] The story is told in Faith and Order Pamphlet No. 32. See also Tissington Tatlow, "The World Conference on Faith and Order," Chapter IX in Rouse and Neill, *op. cit.*

with the prayer that the participants in the Congress might "become reunited to the visible Head of the Church."[25]

After the extensive visitations in Europe and the Near East, and letters to churches not reached by personal contacts, the Episcopal Commission invited all the cooperating bodies to a preliminary meeting "to decide what subjects should be prepared for the World Conference." This took place in Geneva, Switzerland, August 12–20, 1920, and was attended by spokesmen of seventy churches. With the exception of the Church of Rome, all the major families of Christendom that confess "Our Lord Jesus Christ as God and Saviour" were represented. An historic aspect of the occasion was the presence of representatives, eighteen in number, of the Eastern Orthodox Churches. It was the first time they had participated on any such scale in an interdenominational gathering.

The most important action at Geneva was the creation of a Continuation Committee to carry forward all preparations for the World Conference. It was at this point in 1920 that the responsibility for the Faith and Order movement ceased to be carried by American churchmen and became international. The chairman and the secretary of the Continuation Committee, however, were both American Episcopalians, Bishop Brent and Robert H. Gardiner. The Committee functioned chiefly through two subcommittees, one on Subjects, the other on Business. The latter was composed almost entirely of Americans. A secretariat was established in Boston under the direction of Gardiner, who, after his lamented death in 1924, was succeeded by another American Episcopal layman, Robert W. Brown.[26]

Not only in its origin and early leadership but also in its antecedents the Faith and Order movement was predominantly American. The "Quadrilateral" which defined the general Anglican approach to union was formulated by the Episcopal Church in 1886, and affirmed, with slight changes, by the Lambeth Conference of Bishops two years later.[27] The American initiative in Faith and Order, the nurturing of the infant movement for a decade, and the continuous American support run counter to the popular impression that American churches have little concern for theology or the nature of the church.

Beginnings of Life and Work

During the war Archbishop Nathan Söderblom of Uppsala, primate of the Church of Sweden, had persistently tried to bring about an international conference of leaders in the churches of both the belligerent

---

25 *Ibid.*, p. 416.

26 H. N. Bate, *Faith and Order: Lausanne, 1927* (London: S. C. M. Press, 1927), p. 41.

27 See p. 28.

and the neutral nations. The aim of such a meeting, as he conceived it, was to testify to the supra-national character of the church of Christ and to exert a reconciling influence even in the midst of the conflict. He failed to secure support from the churches in any of the warring nations, including the American, the general view being that the project must be deferred until the war was over. Söderblom had a keen sense of the strategic importance of international cooperation among the churches not only in their social witness but also in their missionary outreach. As a young man he had visited the United States for a student conference at Northfield, Mass., and had come strongly under the influence of Dwight L. Moody and John R. Mott.

The first meeting of Christian leaders on an international scale after the war was that of the World Alliance for International Friendship through the Churches, convened at Oud Wassenar, near the Hague, on September 30, 1919.[28] Intense feeling over "war guilt" between the French and Belgian delegates on the one hand and the German delegates on the other made it difficult to do any constructive planning. Archbishop Söderblom, however, pleaded that an "Ecumenical Council of the Churches" be held to further international cooperation in meeting their social responsibilities. He was interested also in the prospect of a World Conference on Faith and Order, but held that the churches must not wait for formulated agreements in doctrine before coming together to face their duty in relation to the social and international problems of the immediate hour. The archbishop's proposal found its strongest support among the American delegates. In fact, they were already committed to an international conference as a result of earlier discussions in the Federal Council, especially at its quadrennial meeting in St. Louis in 1916.

Before the World Alliance adjourned at Oud Wassenar, it provided for a small international committee with full powers to proceed in preliminary planning for a conference along the lines urged by Archbishop Söderblom. The members of the Committee were only three—the Swedish archbishop, the general secretary of the American Federal Council, and the president of the Conference of Swiss Churches. They decided that a preparatory conference should be held in Geneva the next summer, and responsibility for arranging it was entrusted to the Federal Council.[29] It was held August 9 to 12, 1920, with ninety representatives of the churches of fifteen countries. The American delegation was the largest and included among others Arthur J. Brown, Fred-

---

[28] A detailed account of this meeting and of the succeeding steps that led up to the Universal Christian Conference on Life and Work is given by Nils Karlstrom in Chapter XI of Rouse and Neill, *A History of the Ecumenical Movement.*

[29] *Ibid.,* p. 534–535.

erick Lynch, Charles S. Macfarland, William P. Merrill, and Bishop Brent.[30]

Again Archbishop Söderblom was the outstanding interpreter of what the proposed "Ecumenical Council" (as he called it) should be. His conception of it involved an invitation not only to all the Protestant churches but also the Eastern Orthodox and the Roman Catholic. Some of the delegates held that the official doctrine of Rome made cooperation with it impossible. The archbishop firmly maintained the position that if any church were to be excluded it must be by its own act. The decision was that "all Christian Churches" should be invited.[31]

The steps taken at Geneva led to the active participation of the Orthodox Churches in the movement. The way had been opened for this through a remarkable letter addressed in January, 1920, by the Ecumenical Patriarch of Constantinople "to all the Churches of Christ, wheresoever they be" proposing a "League of Churches" for common tasks.[32]

At Geneva it was apparently assumed that the conference might be held within two years or so. Arrangements for it were entrusted to a committee of which Archbishop Söderblom was chairman, with two Americans, Charles S. Macfarland and Frederick Lynch, as secretaries.[33] The committee soon decided to establish three geographical sections for the preparatory work—American, British, and European. It adopted, as the official designation of the proposed assembly, "Universal Conference of the Church of Christ on Life and Work," later reworded as "Universal Christian Conference on Life and Work." After 1920 "Life and Work" was the term which designated an organized phase of the emerging ecumenical movement.

Behind "Life and Work" in its institutional structure lay two noteworthy developments. One was the rising social conscience which had for some time been gathering strength, especially in America and England. The other was the more recent concern to find the way of giving embodied expression to the supra-national character of the Christian church. This had been sharpened by the tragedy of a world war which the churches had been powerless to prevent, and which had engaged Christians of different nations in internecine conflict with one another. From his vantage point in a neutral country Archbishop

---

[30] Bishop Brent, although chairman of the Faith and Order group that met in Geneva the following week, actively supported the parallel plan for an international conference on Life and Work.

[31] Faith and Order, on the other hand, invited only those Churches that "confess our Lord Jesus Christ as God and Saviour."

[32] For the full text, see G. K. A. Bell, *Documents on Christian Unity* (London: Oxford University Press, 1924), Vol. I, pp. 44–48.

[33] This committee was later succeeded by a larger group of representatives of the churches.

Söderblom saw this with prophetic clarity. The marriage of Anglo-American concern for the social meaning of the Gospel and Scandinavian concern for international reconciliation gave birth to the Life and Work movement.

Formation of International Missionary Council

While "Faith and Order" and "Life and Work" were thus acquiring organizational form, the movement of missionary cooperation symbolized by Edinburgh 1910 was assuming a more representative character. This took place through the gradual transformation of its Continuation Committee into the International Missionary Council. In this development the leadership of two men was crucial. One was J. H. Oldham, the Scot who had became secretary of the Continuation Committee.[34] The other was its chairman, the American John R. Mott.

Mott's combination of organizing genius with world-wide vision was the chief factor in bringing agencies of cooperation to birth in the lands of the churches that were the result of the missionary movement. In the fall of 1912 and the spring of 1913 he had undertaken an extensive tour of Asia, partly in the interest of Christian evangelism among students, partly in the interest of missionary cooperation. Over a five-month period he was the central figure in twenty-one interdenominational conferences of missionaries and national Christian leaders in Ceylon, India, Burma, Malaya, China, Manchuria, Korea, and Japan. In each case the conference was not an end in itself but the beginning of an enduring cooperative structure. At first these structures were only "Continuation Committees" but they were the nuclei of what were to evolve within a few years into National Christian Councils. In retrospect, Dr. Mott considered his role in the formation of National Christian Councils to have been his greatest contribution to the missionary movement.[35]

The world war sounded the death knell of the Edinburgh Continuation Committee which had been set up in 1910. Although it still had a nominal existence, it was no longer able to function internationally. The fact that Mott had accepted an appointment by President Woodrow Wilson to serve on a diplomatic mission to Russia in 1917 was the final factor in producing a loss of confidence on the part of German missionary leaders. An Emergency Committee of Cooperating Missions accordingly functioned in place of the immobilized Continuation Com-

---

[34] In *Ecumenical Foundations*, pp. 141 and 399, William R. Hogg refers to the Continuation Committee as having "the first full-time paid secretariat in interdenominational work." This is an incidental error in a book remarkable for its historical accuracy. After 1908 the newly organized Federal Council of Churches had a full-time "corresponding secretary" in the person of Elias B. Sanford.

[35] Hogg, *op. cit.*, p. 156.

mittee of Edinburgh, operating chiefly through the Foreign Missions Conference of North America and the British Conference of Missionary Societies. In the postwar process of reconciliation Arthur J. Brown, of the Board of Foreign Missions of the Presbyterian Church in the U.S.A., played a key role by a visit to Germany in the summer of 1919. Largely as a result of his influence, the four Germans who had been members of the Edinburgh Continuation Committee shared in an unofficial conference at Crans, Switzerland, a year later. There it was decided that the time had come for creating a representative International Missionary Committee, to take the place of the moribund Continuation Committee.

At Lake Mohonk, New York, in 1921, eleven years after the Edinburgh Conference, the International Missionary Council was organized. Its structural units were not denominational boards but the interdenominational conferences of missionary boards in the several geographical areas of the older churches and the embryonic National Christian Councils in the lands of the younger churches.[36] The largest of the component units was the Foreign Missions Conference of North America. At Lake Mohonk the German Missions Committee was not represented —the strains of wartime were not yet sufficiently relaxed—but it was enrolled as a charter member of the Council. The Council, according to its modestly defined role, was to "enlist thinking and investigation on missionary questions . . . help coordinate the efforts of the national missionary organizations . . . bring about united action where necessary," and "call a world missionary conference" when deemed desirable.[37] It was clearly understood on all sides that the Council would not deal with "any matter involving an ecclesiastical or doctrinal question on which the members of the Council or bodies constituting the Council may differ among themselves." Of the new Council John R. Mott was the chairman and another American, A. Livingstone Warnshuis, who had rendered distinguished service in China, became a co-secretary. For the first few years the office was in London but the American boards were so important in the missionary enterprise as a whole that in 1925 Warnshuis was transferred to a New York office, closely associated with the Foreign Missions Conference of North America.

An immediate responsibility assumed by the International Missionary Council had to do with the German missions which had been forced by the war to cease their work or which could not be supported by the German churches during the disastrous postwar inflation. The

---

[36] The term "younger churches" is no longer satisfactory, but it is a convenient shorthand for such a cumbrous term as "the churches of Asia, Africa, Latin America and the Pacific Islands."

[37] The story of the formation of the Council is told in careful detail by Hogg, *op. cit.,* Chapter V.

Council, after persistent appeals, secured permission for German missionaries to return to their fields and regain their properties in areas subject to governments with which Germany had been at war. It also coordinated the efforts that gave financial support to German and other European missions during the years (1921–1925) when they could hardly have survived without help.

The greatest long-range contribution of the International Missionary Council was in an intangible realm, the development of increasing fellowship among leaders in the younger churches and in the older churches of Europe and America. The significance of this for the ecumenical movement of a generation later can hardly be overemphasized. It laid foundations which enabled the World Council of Churches to be not merely Western but world-wide.

7

Widening Ecumenical Horizons

(1925–1929)

ALTHOUGH a keen European observer of the American scene could conclude in 1927 that "Protestantism is the only national religion," the description was rapidly becoming outdated.[1] As a result of the massive immigration from Southern and Eastern Europe in the decades immediately preceding the war, the religious pluralism of American society was greatly accentuated, with profound effects upon church relationships of the future.

The numerical strength of Roman Catholicism, of Eastern Orthodoxy, and of Judaism was vastly increased. Henceforth Protestantism would not have as great a predominance in the statistical picture nor would it operate from its earlier position of unique identification with American culture. The Roman Catholic, the Eastern Orthodox, and the Jewish enclaves were moving out of quasi-ghetto situations into a much more integral relation with American life. Before long, the period after the world war would often be referred to as the "post-Protestant era."

The Changing Status of American Catholics

The most significant aspect of the changing religious scene was the evolving status of Roman Catholicism. Until after the world war it had been chiefly a church of recent immigrants. Now it was on the way to becoming a truly indigenous American church. The cutting off of large-scale immigration gave it an opportunity to consolidate its structure and to find itself in relation to American culture. Before this time, American Catholicism had been seriously segmented by ethnic and linguistic differences. There were Irish Catholics, Italian Catholics,

---

[1] André Siegfried, *op. cit.*, p. 33.

Polish Catholics, German Catholics, and Catholics of still other backgrounds, in rather obvious blocs. Now they could develop into an increasingly homogeneous and cohesive American Catholic Church, a process which was virtually complete within a generation after the world war.

The war itself had a unifying influence on Catholicism in America. The formation of the National Catholic War Council to meet the emergency had given the church a national coordinating body for the first time. Prior to this each diocesan bishop had gone his own way, subject only to the oversight of a distant Rome. The values of the wartime organization in shaping policies at more than a diocesan level were so evident that in 1922 it was transformed into a permanent National Catholic Welfare Conference, with the blessing of the Vatican. The conference consisted of all the American bishops, with an administrative board of ten and a staff equipped to give guidance in specialized fields of responsibility, such as education, social action, and missions. Other agencies of a non-hierarchical character for developing special national programs were also created, such as the National Catholic Rural Life Conference in 1922 and the Catholic Interracial Council in 1934.

While manifesting these signs of vigorous vitality the Catholic Church still held itself generally aloof from other religious bodies. The encyclical of Pope Pius XI in 1928 on "Fostering True Religious Unity" (*Mortalium Animos*) effectively cut off any participation in the ecumenical movement for a generation. The time for open dialogue with non-Catholics had to wait until the Vatican Council of Pope John XXIII.

Most Protestants hardly realized their own changed situation in the nation until mid-century. There were, however, perceptive leaders who were aware of what was taking place and of the new kind of responsibility that the change entailed. An important illustration of this was the creation of the National Conference of Christians and Jews in 1928. It was in large measure the outgrowth of an earlier move that the Federal Council of Churches had made in an effort to offset a rising anti-Semitism. In 1924 the Council had formed a Committee on Goodwill between Christians and Jews, under the chairmanship of Alfred Williams Anthony.[2] After four years of quiet educational work and friendly contacts with an increasing number of Jewish leaders, it became clear that there was an urgent need for a body in which Jews and Christians could meet on an equal basis. This was hardly possible in a committee

---

[2] ALFRED WILLIAMS ANTHONY (1860–1939), pastor of Free Baptist Church in Bangor, Maine, 1885–1888; professor in Cobb Divinity School, 1890–1908; professor in Bates College, 1908–1911; corresponding secretary, general conference of Free Baptists, 1911–1915; one of the organizers of the Interdenominational Commission of Maine; executive secretary of the Home Missions Council, 1918–1923.

of the Federal Council because of its constitutional limitation to evangelical Christians. It was accordingly decided to establish a new organization, independent and non-ecclesiastical, made up of influential Protestants, Catholics, and Jews, committed to working together for better relationships.

The direction of the National Conference was in the hands of Everett R. Clinchy, at that time the secretary of the Federal Council's Committee on Goodwill between Christians and Jews, who resigned to become president of the new organization and devoted the next thirty years to its development. S. Parkes Cadman, who was president of the Federal Council from 1924 to 1928, became a co-chairman of the new organization.[3] Associated with him as co-chairmen were Roger W. Straus, a Jewish layman, and Professor Carlton J. H. Hayes of Columbia University, a Roman Catholic layman. In large measure the National Conference was a lay organization, more civic than religious in character. It had no close relation with either church or synagogue but it exercised an indirect and informal influence on both. The participation of Jews was more extensive than that of Protestants, and of Protestants much more extensive than that of Catholics, but together they did pioneer work in furthering mutual respect and understanding.

Eastern Orthodox Enter the Scene

A new ecumenical factor in the postwar years in America was the development of relations between Protestant and Eastern Orthodox churches. Up to this time, although Greek and Russian and other immigrants from Orthodox areas had been coming in substantial numbers, they were virtually unknown to Protestants. This was not surprising since there were still few of the Orthodox priests who used the English tongue readily. Overseas, however, a measure of contact between Protestant and Orthodox had begun earlier through the channels of the World's Student Christian Federation. In 1911 its conference had been held in Constantinople. It was held in that historic base of the Ecumenical Patriarch because the Federation, under Dr. Mott's guidance, desired to give convincing evidence that in extending its work into that area there would be full collaboration with Orthodoxy. In the years immediately following, before Europe was engulfed in war, student Christian movements were organized in several Balkan and Near Eastern countries, with Orthodox priests as the spiritual guides.[4] Another im-

---

[3] S. Parkes Cadman (1864–1936), Congregational minister; pastor of Metropolitan Methodist Church, New York, 1895–1901; Central Congregational Church, Brooklyn, 1901–1936; president of Federal Council of Churches, 1924–1928, and radio minister, 1928–1936.

[4] Rouse and Neill, *op. cit.,* pp. 602–606.

portant contribution to widening ecumenical relations was made after the war by the Russian Student Christian Movement in Exile, with its headquarters in Paris, where an important bridge of understanding was built between Orthodoxy and Protestantism, largely through the co-operation of the American Y.M.C.A.[5]

A bond of friendship that originated in America was forged by the extensive humanitarian work of Near East Relief during the years immediately after the war. This fostered a sympathetic knowledge of Eastern Christianity and cultivated the American soil for subsequent cooperation between Protestant and Orthodox churches.

The meetings in Geneva in the summer of 1920 in preparation for the first World Conference on Faith and Order and the first Universal Christian Conference on Life and Work marked the inauguration of contacts between Protestant and Orthodox on the official ecclesiastical level. Eighteen representatives of seven Eastern Churches were in attendance at the Faith and Order meeting, and some of them also shared in the Life and Work meeting. This was an assurance that Orthodox bodies would come into the main streams of the ecumenical movement. This had an indirect consequence for American Christianity. Henceforth Protestant leaders would have a growing interest in the Eastern Orthodox in America.

In 1923 the Federal Council of Churches moved definitely along this line by creating a Committee on Relations with Eastern Churches "to promote fellowship and conference and to take such steps as may be of mutual service." Bishop Charles H. Brent of the Episcopal Church became the chairman of the group, even though that Church was not yet an official member of the Council. The focus of interest at this stage was more on the Orthodox in their homelands than in the United States. The chief function of the Committee was to give American expression to fraternal regard for the Orthodox by providing a point of contact with their representatives when they visited this country and by seeing to it that American Protestant leaders, when they visited Europe, did not overlook the Orthodox. The Committee also undertook to secure some scholarships for Orthodox students in American theological seminaries.

Beginning in 1926, William W. Peet, a Protestant layman who had had a long and honored career as a missionary of the American Board in the Near East and whose primary conception of missionary strategy in the area was that of strengthening the ancient churches, served for

---

[5] Two American Protestants, Paul B. Anderson and Donald Lowrie, both of whom had served the Y.M.C.A. in Russia before the Revolution, became especially influential interpreters of American Protestantism and Eastern Orthodoxy to each other.

two years in Athens as a representative of the Federal Council of Churches. He had no defined duties other than to be of friendly personal helpfulness to leaders in the Eastern Churches, but this had no little effect. "It seems to be taken for granted by the prelates of the Eastern Churches," he reported in 1928, "that my mission here marks the end of that feature of American mission work which has been in the past characterized by an effort to gather groups of people out of the old churches into separate communions."[6]

In 1927 the Federal Council's Committee was authorized to study the possibilities of establishing "closer relationships" with the Eastern Churches in America "on the basis of a cooperative program of practical work." Another decade passed, however, before the "closer relationships" resulted in any of the Eastern Churches in America becoming a constituent member of the Council.

The Influence of World Conferences

Within the years from 1925 to 1928 there were three world conferences, each of which marked a further stage in the commitment of American churches to the rising ecumenical movement and each of which afforded fresh evidence that churches of widely divergent backgrounds, cultural and confessional, were sharing a common life. The first moved in the realm of Christian social concern. The second was theological in nature. The third was oriented to world-wide evangelism.

As a result of these three conferences the number of American churchmen who had first-hand contacts with the ecumenical movement in its world-wide dimension was multiplied many fold. More important than the increase in numbers was the cross fertilization that took place between American and European viewpoints. In each of the conferences there was a dialectical tension between them, often disconcerting at the time but creative in the outcome.

In general, the American approach to issues was more pragmatic, the Continental European more theoretical. In thinking of unity, most Americans accented the urgency of practical tasks, while Europeans stressed the need for agreement in theological foundations. European Christians tended to regard American Christians as activist (an adjective with pejorative overtones) and Americans criticized Europeans for carrying on theological discussions in academic detachment from contemporary life and the social context of the times.

This ecumenical encounter affected American Christianity in interesting ways. For one thing, American churchmen discovered that their religious enthusiasms needed more theological depth. Their pragmatic

---

[6] Quoted in Charles S. Macfarland, *Christian Unity in the Making*, p. 310.

temper underwent modification as a result of exposure to Christians more deeply concerned with basic thinking about the nature of God and man. For another thing, the Americans came to have a fuller appreciation of the church as a corporate community. Although they had been concerned with the significance of the Gospel for society, they had not given much attention to the social significance of the church itself. Now, as a result of their international contacts, they began to see the church more clearly as a community transcending national cultures.

The influence of this ecumenical experience was paralleled by what was happening in theological circles. In 1928 Karl Barth's *The Word of God and the Word of Man* was translated into English by Douglas Horton, the first of the Basel theologian's works to appear in America.[7] Although at first it seemed strangely un-American in its orientation, its influence was soon to be widely felt.

Impact of Stockholm, 1925

On August 19, 1925, six hundred delegates from thirty-seven countries met in Stockholm as the Universal Christian Conference on Life and Work, aiming to "unite the different churches in common practical work, to furnish the Christian conscience with an organ of expression, and to insist that the principles of the Gospel be applied to the solution of contemporary social and international problems."[8] It was hoped —in the words of Arthur J. Brown, the chairman of the American Committee on Arrangements—that the Conference would thereby help to "emancipate the churches in all lands from the spirit of sectionalism and provincialism, and to take wide views of the Kingdom of God."

The Conference surveyed the social-ethical meaning of Christianity under the following heads:

The Obligation of the Church in the Light of God's Plan for the World

The Church and Economic and Industrial Problems

The Church and Moral and Social Problems

The Church and Education

Ways and Means for Promoting Cooperation Between the Churches

Archbishop Söderblom of Sweden was the central figure in every way, but the American participation was extensive. Dr. Brown was a co-president. Henry A. Atkinson, executive of the Church Peace Union,

---

[7] (Boston: Pilgrim Press, 1928).

[8] G. K. A. Bell, ed., *The Stockholm Conference, 1925* (London: Oxford University Press, 1926), p. 1. See also Charles S. Macfarland, *Steps Toward the World Council.*

was the general secretary of the Conference. Among other Americans who were close to the heart of the project were Peter Ainslie, William Adams Brown, S. Parkes Cadman, Frederick Lynch, and Charles S. Macfarland.[9]

The Stockholm gathering was not as widely representative as subsequent ecumenical conferences. Only thirteen American denominations sent delegates, although these included most of the larger bodies. There was only one American Negro, and only a handful of spokesmen for the churches of Asia and Africa. Some of the delegates had only a semi-official status. These limitations, however, paled into insignificance in the light of the fact that for the first time there was an international conference to which representatives of widely separated churches had come together by corporate ecclesiastical authority.

In terms of its reports and findings the Conference did not break new ground—at least not so far as American experience was concerned. The content of its message was "tame, timid and thin."[10] But it takes on greater significance when it is borne in mind that it represented the collective judgment of Christians from widely different historical and cultural backgrounds. The international consensus gave strong reinforcement to those in each country who were most concerned for Christian witness and Christian action in the public sector of life. Henceforth national spokesmen would be supported by the moral authority of a world conference which had affirmed the obligation of the churches to apply the Gospel "in all realms of human life." Henceforth there would also be a deeper understanding of the church as a supranational community and a penitent realization of the extent to which churches which ought to have Christianized the nations had themselves been nationalized.

The conference had disavowed in advance any intention of dealing with theological issues. These, it was explained, would be left to a subsequent World Conference on Faith and Order. It was assumed that immediately urgent problems could be handled without becoming involved in doctrinal differences. But in the very first session at Stockholm a theological issue of crucial import intruded. The opening sermon by the Anglican Bishop of Winchester had spoken of "setting up the Kingdom of God on earth." Soon afterward the Lutheran Bishop of Saxony said that "nothing could be more mistaken or more disastrous than to suppose that we mortal men have to build up God's kingdom in the

---

[9] Söderblom wrote to a friend that the Conference "could never have been brought about but for the Federal Council." Quoted in *Christian Union Quarterly,* Vol. XVI, No. 1 (July, 1926), p. 11.

[10] The description is that of Bishop Brent, an active participant in the Conference. See his *Understanding: Being an Interpretation of the Universal Christian Conference on Life and Work* (New York: Longmans, Green, 1926), p. 11.

world." The divergent viewpoints revealed in these two statements were still unreconciled when the Conference came to an end, but each was affected by exposure to the other. Partly as a result of the ecumenical give-and-take, partly as a consequence of the economic depression that soon followed, the American interpretation of the "Social Gospel" gradually became more realistic in its appraisal of the possibilities of human nature and human society.

For the next five years after the Conference, the Life and Work Movement, as it was now called, had a rather ineffective organization. There was a continuation committee, appointed at Stockholm, "to carry on the work of the Conference and to consider how far and in what ways its practical suggestions may be made operative." The four "sections," which had been organized in preparation for Stockholm—American, British, European, Eastern Orthodox—were continued. A fifth section which was authorized to represent the Younger Churches failed to materialize, due to difficulties of distance and lack of financial resources. In 1930 the continuation committee was reorganized as a permanent body known as the Universal Christian Council for Life and Work, with the American, Henry A. Atkinson, as general secretary and the Swiss, Adolf Keller, as associate general secretary. The appointment of Dr. Keller was due to European, especially German, feeling that American activism ought to be balanced by more historical and theological factors. In the United States the American section of Life and Work and the Federal Council's Department of Relations with Churches Abroad were combined into a single body under the administrative direction of Henry S. Leiper.[11] From this time onward the Federal Council was officially interlocked with the Life and Work Movement.

Impact of Lausanne, 1927

In the summer of 1927, seventeen years after the General Convention of the Episcopal Church had proposed it, a World Conference on Faith and Order was convened in Lausanne. Of the 108 churches officially participating, 22 were American. The British, Continental European, and Eastern Churches were also well represented, but out of the 400 delegates only 5 were Asian or African.[12] The presiding officer was

---

[11] HENRY SMITH LEIPER (1891–   ), Congregational minister, missionary in China, 1918–1922; editorial secretary, Congregational Commission on Missions, 1923–1929; executive secretary, American Section of Universal Christian Council for Life and Work and Federal Council's Department of Relations with Churches Abroad, 1930–1938; associate general secretary, World Council of Churches, 1938–1952; executive secretary, Missions Council of the Congregational Christian Churches, 1952–1959.

[12] The official record of the Conference is *Faith and Order, Lausanne, August 3–21, 1927,* ed. H. N. Bate (London: S.C.M. Press, 1927). An important interpretation from an American angle is Edmund D. Soper, *Lausanne: The Will to Understand* (New York: Doubleday, Doran, 1928).

Bishop Brent, whose imagination had first caught the vision of such a gathering.

The major themes to which the Conference addressed itself were:

> The Church's Message to the World: The Gospel
> The Nature of the Church
> The Church's Common Confession of Faith
> The Church's Ministry
> The Sacraments
> The Unity of Christendom and the Relation Thereto of Existing Churches

The reports drafted by the several sections were not formally adopted by the Conference as a whole but "received for transmission to the churches" for study. There was no attempt to lend the authority of the Conference to any position by a majority vote or to cover up unresolved difficulties by compromise formulas.

From the standpoint of reconciling doctrinal and ecclesiastical differences or indicating a path to union, Lausanne was disappointing. Instead of solving problems it set them in a sharper light. The Conference should be judged, however, not as an isolated occurrence but as the beginning of a long process. Its significance lay in the fact that the main bodies of Christendom (with the exception of the Roman Catholic) had become engaged in a serious effort to understand each other at the level of their deepest differences. The differences were not merely those which are characteristic of Protestantism but also those which mark the more basic separation between the Catholic tradition—as represented at Lausanne by Eastern Orthodox, Old Catholics, and Anglo-Catholics—and the Protestant Reformation. These differences had especially to do with the nature of the church, its ministry, and its sacraments.

The Eastern Orthodox felt so little at home with some of the presuppositions which others brought to the conference that they refrained from voting except in the case of the Message. They further felt it necessary to make a formal statement explaining that they regarded Eastern Orthodoxy as in itself a complete embodiment of the unity of the church.[13] There was also a corporate statement from the Lutheran delegation which emphasized the view that unity consists in agreement concerning the doctrine of the Gospel and the administration of the sacraments and urged that formulations of the Conference should be

---

[13] Bate, *op. cit.*, pp. 382–386.

put forward only as "material for further consideration."[14] A representative of the Society of Friends, while welcoming the statements of the
Conference for purposes of discussion, felt it necessary to make it clear
that for Friends "the unity of Christians never did, nor ever will or can,
stand in uniformity of thought or opinion but in Christian love."[15]

Bishop Brent once wrote about an anonymous churchman that "the
only kind of unity he can grasp is where every one agrees with him."[16]
The situation of Lausanne left no doubt that there were such churchmen in all denominations and that the first task of Faith and Order
was to bring about a fuller knowledge of the diverse historic traditions
within the Christian community. The most important thing about the
Conference was its evidence of a widening will to understand. The delegates were not inclined to blur their differences for the sake of general
amiability. The disposition to deal with one another in complete hon-
esty sometimes accentuated the polarity of theological viewpoints, but
the divergences were voiced without acrimony.

The main difference in ecclesiastical practice was sharply illustrated
when William Adams Brown proposed that the report on the sacraments
include a suggestion that future Faith and Order conferences provide
for a communion service in which all might participate as a means of
expressing their spiritual unity. He also voiced hope for a recommendation that in certain circumstances, especially among the younger
churches in lands where Christians are small minorities, there might
be provision for some form of intercommunion. This precipitated so
much objection that Dr. Brown withdrew his suggestions.[17] A later plea
by Peter Ainslie, as a representative of the Disciples of Christ, that the
Lausanne Conference conclude with a communion service as a manifestation of "the equality of all Christians before God" met with even
less favor.

In addition to Lausanne's insoluble problem of intercommunion, there
was another issue which proved divisive enough to prevent the Conference from transmitting the report of one of its sections to the churches.
This had to do with "the unity of Christendom and the relation thereto
of existing churches." The report as drafted recommended cooperation
in Life and Work as a way of advance in unity. Some of the delegates
of Anglo-Catholic convictions, including the American Episcopal layman Frederick C. Morehouse, were not in sympathy with this. They
feared that such cooperation or federation might come to be accepted
as an adequate goal. There was also a serious questioning of another

---

14 *Ibid.*, pp. 373–375.
15 Bate, *op. cit.*, pp. 410–411.
16 Rouse and Neill, *op. cit.*, p. 427.
17 Bate, *op. cit.*, pp. 393–395.

part of the report which set forth the "essentials" for a united church. If there had been an opportunity for less hurried discussion, a more satisfactory procedure might have been found, but to avoid a rift during the closing hours of the Conference it was decided to refer the statement to the Continuation Committee instead of sending it to the churches. After making minor revisions the Committee printed it as an appendix to the official report, not as an integral part of it.

The fact that there was so much tension over the nature of the church's unity and the method of manifesting it indicates how difficult was the course which the Faith and Order movement had set for itself. The only statement on which the Conference as a whole could agree with sufficient unanimity to adopt it as its own was "The Message of the Church to the World—The Gospel." Here solid ground was found on which the churches could formally stand together. However much they might differ in interpretations and applications, they could unhesitatingly agree that at least there was a common unifying tradition which underlay all the different traditions developed in the course of Christian history.

In spite of its inconclusive character, the Lausanne Conference was an enlarging and liberalizing education for the participating churches. It drew them out of theological isolation into dialogue. If it made them more conscious of the seriousness of their differences, it demonstrated that these could be faced frankly in a quest for deeper understanding and in hope for fuller light upon the way. It signalized the substitution of dialogue in an ecumenical spirit for sectarian self-sufficiency or controversy.

The face-to-face exposure of the different ecclesiastical positions to one another had two important consequences of contrasted kinds. One result was to make each confessional group more aware of its own historical heritage. In the process of encounter with others it was necessary for each to define more clearly what it stood for that was of enduring value for the Church universal. This meant a considerable revival of denominational consciousness. The other result was to induce a realization within each denomination that while it had something vital to contribute to others it also had something to receive. It became more clear, as Bishop Brent said, that "most of us are devotees of the cult of the incomplete" and that no single historical group represents the wholeness of the truth that is in Christ.[18]

If the Conference hardly came up to the high expectations which some had entertained, it was definitely a starting point on a new road. It established a pattern of common study and consultation which gath-

---

[18] Bate, *op. cit.*, p. 8.

ered momentum during subsequent years. On the American churches it exerted a continuing influence which resulted, a generation later, in the incorporation of Faith and Order studies into the permanent program of the National Council of Churches.

For carrying on the process of ecumenical dialogue after Lausanne a Continuation Committee of ninety-five persons was appointed. Its chief officers were three Americans—Bishop Brent as chairman, Ralph W. Brown as general secretary, and George Zabriskie as treasurer.[19] When Bishop Brent, who was in precarious health while at Lausanne, died two years later, he was succeeded in the chairmanship by Archbishop William Temple, with J. Ross Stevenson as head of the American group.[20]

Some of the American delegates at Lausanne were so impatient with the slow pace of Faith and Order discussions that they felt other methods must also be followed. Conspicuous among them was Peter Ainslie, who took the initiative in creating The Christian Unity League. This was an association not of churches but of individuals who were prepared to ignore denominational restrictions which seemed to them contrary to brotherhood in Christ and "the equality of all Christians before God." In a Pact of Reconciliation they agreed that "no Christian shall be denied membership in any of our churches, nor the privilege of participation in the observance of the Lord's Supper, and that no Christian minister shall be denied the freedom of our pulpits by reason of differences in ordination."[21] This short-cut approach to problems of unity appealed to many whose viewpoint was pragmatic and untheological, but it gained little organizational strength. After Dr. Ainslie's death in 1934, the League ceased to be active.

Impact of Jerusalem, 1928

In the three weeks concluding with Easter Sunday in 1928 an enlarged meeting of the International Missionary Council met on the Mount of Olives overlooking the Holy City. The conference was primarily devoted to an intensive examination of urgent issues confronting the missionary enterprise. One of its most important aspects was its evidence that the younger churches were coming of age. Up to this time

---

[19] For a full record of Bishop Brent's life and work, see Alexander C. Zabriskie, *Bishop Brent, Crusader for Christian Unity* (Philadelphia: The Westminster Press, 1948).

[20] J. ROSS STEVENSON (1866–1939), Presbyterian minister, pastor in Sedalia, Mo., 1890–1894; professor in McCormick Theological Seminary, 1894–1902; pastor of Fifth Avenue Presbyterian Church, New York, 1902–1909, and of Brown Memorial Church, Baltimore, 1909–1914; president of Princeton Theological Seminary, 1914–1936; moderator of Presbyterian General Assembly, 1915.

[21] See *Christian Union Quarterly*, Baltimore, Md., Vols. XVIII–XXIII.

the missionary movement had been dominated by Western missionaries. Edinburgh, 1910, in spite of all its ecumenical significance, had
been virtually a conferring of American and European Christians with
a few invited guests from Asia and Africa. Jerusalem, 1928, was representative of world-wide Christianity, about a quarter of its membership
being leaders of the younger churches.

The American influence at Jerusalem was strong, not only through
the primary role of John R. Mott as chairman but also through invited
participants from outside the inner circle of the missionary boards,
including Professor William E. Hocking of Harvard, Dean Luther A.
Weigle of Yale, President Kenyon L. Butterfield of Michigan State College, and Professor Rufus M. Jones of Haverford College. Moreover, the
preparatory papers for the meeting owed much to American thinking,
especially to the trenchant analysis of modern secular civilization by
Dr. Jones. He set forth the view—little recognized in previous missionary gatherings—that the greatest rival of Christianity is not Buddhism,
Islam, or Hinduism, but the secularism that finds no room for God in
either thought or life. This focus on secularism led to the conclusion
that the missionary task could no longer be conceived in simple geographical terms. Instead, the Western world, from which the missionary enterprise was projected, was itself seen as a great missionary field.
As Dr. Jones put it: "We go to Jerusalem not as members of a Christian
nation to convert other nations which are not Christian, but as Christians within a nation far too largely non-Christian, who face within
their own borders the competition of a rival movement as powerful,
as dangerous, as insidious as any of the great historic religions."[22]

Many of the Continental Europeans feared that this emphasis opened
the door to a dangerous syncretistic approach to non-Christian religions.
It seemed to imply too much of a common front between all religious
faiths over against a common foe and to invite a cooperation between
Christians and non-Christians which would obscure the uniqueness of
Christianity. Even before the conference began, the misgivings of some
of the most influential European delegates—including Julius Richter
and Karl Heim of Germany and Hendrik Kraemer of the Netherlands—
were so pronounced that Dr. Mott invited them to meet him and a few
others in a pre-Jerusalem session in Cairo to canvass the situation together. After Cairo they still continued to warn against the dangers of
over-appreciating the values in non-Christian religions but they shared
constructively in the discussions in Jerusalem.

The feature of the Jerusalem meeting which did most to draw it
together in a sense of unity was the Message, drafted by a group with

---

[22] *Jerusalem Meeting of the International Missionary Council, March 24–April 8, 1928*
(New York: 1928), Vol. I, p. 273.

William Temple, then Bishop of Manchester, and Robert E. Speer as co-chairmen. It was Christocentric from beginning to end. "Our Message," it held, "is Jesus Christ. We must give nothing less and we can give nothing more." This left many questions of missionary philosophy and strategy still unanswered but at least it indicated the unifying center of the missionary movement. It also provided a partial synthesis of the viewpoints of those (chiefly American and British) who stressed the Christian responsibility for society and those (chiefly European) who feared that this would lessen the concentration of missions on personal conversion to the Christian faith. "The message of Christ," Jerusalem affirmed, "has meaning not only for the individual soul but for the world of social organization and economic relations in which individuals live."[23]

The years immediately following the Jerusalem meeting were exceedingly problematical ones in all sectors of the ecumenical movement both in our own country and throughout the world. The economic depression, beginning in 1929, brought crises of financial support. There were increasing international tensions as totalitarian movements gained strength. Sharp differences in theology, signalized by the rise of neo-orthodoxy on the one hand and a drift toward humanism on the other, put heavy strains on cooperative enterprises that had been developed during the two previous decades.

---

[23] *Ibid.,* pp. 401ff.

8

Recession and Rethinking

(1930–1935)

AFTER buoyant optimism in the early decades of the twentieth century came the Great Depression. The crisis in the economy after the collapse of the stock market in 1929 was paralleled by a recession in organized religion. For the churches the most obvious aspect of the gloomy situation was the shrinkage in financial resources. As denominational receipts declined, interdenominational income plummeted. Cooperative activities, being new and experimental, suffered more than the firmly established programs of denominations. In the Federal Council of Churches, for example, an income which exceeded $400,000 in 1929 had fallen to less than half that amount by 1934.

More significant than the financial losses of the churches were the evidences of declining spiritual vigor. These had been noticeable for some time prior to the economic slump. A discerning editorial several months before the Depression spoke of "unusual conditions that are causing more or less anxiety" and referred particularly to waning support of home missions as one of the signs. "More money is being given in the total," it was reported, "but less and less to our missionary boards."[1] The whole decade from 1925 to 1935 has been characterized by a careful historian as a period of "American religious depression."[2]

An unhappy aspect of the era, and one which was bound to slacken any advance in unity, was increasing theological strain. The central evangelical tradition, which had provided a common base for the cooperative agencies, was involved in difficulties on both the right and the left. At one extreme was a militant fundamentalism which demanded that its own brand of rigid orthodoxy be the accepted standard. Rejecting the methods of historical study of the Bible, it proclaimed belief in Scriptural inerrancy to be essential to Christian faith. At the

---

[1] *Federal Council Bulletin* (April, 1929).

[2] Robert T. Handy, *Church History,* Vol. XXIX (1960), pp. 3–16.

opposite pole was a radical humanism, espoused by a few far-out liberals for whom scientific method was a substitute for revelation in any form. The "Humanist Manifesto" of 1933, of which John Dewey was the most influential signer, marked the extreme point of this leftward swing.[3] Although the Manifesto won only a handful of adherents in the churches, it contributed to a mood of uncertainty and doubt which was far from conducive to either evangelical vigor or cooperative action.

The fundamentalists were interested in cooperation only on the basis of their own inflexible terms, and they tended to oppose social as well as theological change. The humanists were too absorbed in their *avant-garde* position to be interested in cooperation with those whom they regarded as bound to blind tradition. The main body of Protestants, who were either conservative without being fundamentalists or liberal without being humanists, were confused and perplexed.

Rethinking Foreign Missions

The questionings and confusions of the period were especially evident in the controversy that arose in the early thirties over the Laymen's Foreign Missions Inquiry. Projected by a group of influential laymen who were committed to the world-wide mission but felt the need for an objective review of program and policies, it resulted in putting the whole missionary enterprise under heavy tension.

The inquiry was an independent undertaking, financed mainly by John D. Rockefeller, Jr., not officially connected with any missionary agency but involving the cooperation of seven denominational boards. It was conducted in two stages. The first was a Fact-Finders' Survey in China, Japan, India, and Burma, directed by the Institute of Social and Religious Research. This produced a massive body of valuable information. The second stage was an appraisal of missionary strategy, *Rethinking Missions*, made by a group of laymen under the chairmanship of Professor William E. Hocking of Harvard University.[4]

On the side of missionary strategy, the laymen's appraisal was very critical of separate denominational approaches to the tasks and urged that a single administrative unit be given direction of all missionary work in each area. On the side of missionary philosophy, the viewpoint was equally radical. It brought into the arena of open discussion a crucial difference among missionary leaders in their attitude toward non-

---

[3] For the contents of the Manifesto, see H. Shelton Smith, Robert T. Handy, and Lefferts A. Loetscher, *American Christianity* (New York: Charles Scribner's Sons, 1963), Vol. II, pp. 248–253.

[4] The Survey material is found in seven volumes, edited by Orville A. Petty, under the title *Laymen's Foreign Missions Inquiry, Fact-Finders' Report* (New York: Harper & Brothers, 1933). The report of the Committee on Appraisal was published as *Rethinking Missions. A Laymen's Inquiry After One Hundred Years* (New York: Harper & Brothers, 1932).

Christian religions. Departing from the traditional position, the laymen wanted to see Christianity standing in an appreciative relation with other religions as allies—at least to some extent—over against world-wide irreligion and secularism. They proposed that missions look forward "not to the destruction of these religions but to their continued coexistence with Christianity, each stimulating the other in growth toward the ultimate goal, unity in the completest religious truth."[5] Their report conceived the missionary as "a co-worker with the forces within each religious system which are making for righteousness." It accordingly stressed Christian service and Christian influence through educational, medical, and social work more than direct evangelization and conversion.

The lines were now more sharply drawn between those who adhered to established patterns and those who advocated a more flexible and adaptable course. In reply to the laymen's appraisal and in clear contrast with its underlying philosophy was Hendrik Kraemer's *The Christian Message in a Non-Christian World.*[6] It rejected the view of missions as a search for truth rather than a proclamation of God's unique self-revelation in Christ and insisted that other religions offer no real point of contact with Christian faith. Kraemer's influence was strong at the Madras meeting of the International Missionary Council in 1938. In general the reaction to the laymen's appraisal strengthened the evangelical commitment of many missionary boards.

The cumulative results of the tensions within missionary circles during the next dozen years were to produce new interdenominational agencies. American boards and societies that regarded the Foreign Missions Conference of North America as "liberal" came together in the Evangelical Foreign Missions Association in 1945. Still another national organization for missionary cooperation emerged, the Interdenominational Foreign Missions Association, representing a group of "faith" missions, not related to ecclesiastical bodies, such as the Sudan Interior Mission, the African Inland Mission, the Wycliff Bible Translators. By mid-century the constituent boards and societies of the conservative associations had as many missionaries on the field as the boards which were members of the Foreign Missions Conference.

Rethinking Home Missions

In home missions a period of rethinking at this time was due more to sociological than to theological factors. During the nineteenth century the missionary task in America had meant the planting of churches in the expanding West or aiding churches that were not self-supporting.

---

[5] *Rethinking Missions*, p. 44.
[6] (New York: Harper & Brothers, 1938).

In the latter part of the nineteenth century and the early part of the twentieth, it came to mean also ministries to immigrants and to underprivileged minorities, such as Indians, Negroes, Orientals, and Spanish-speaking peoples. By the thirties the establishing of more churches was a less urgent need.[7] The day was past when the distinctive role of home missions could be described as church extension. It was increasingly to be thought of as the Christianizing of the life of the nation.

As the agencies of home missions addressed themselves to this broad task, they found themselves more and more involved in problems of the social order. It was not enough to organize schools for Negro children without giving thought to the pattern of community and economic life in which they would live. It was not enough to minister to migrant workers without being concerned with legislation for protecting their human rights. In engagement with such issues the Home Missions Council and the Federal Council of Churches worked in close collaboration.

In church extension one serious problem remained. This was the almost complete lack of what is technically called comity, the process of interdenominational planning in locating and assisting local churches so as to avoid "the twin evils of over-lapping and over-looking." In 1928 a National Church Comity Conference, the first of its kind, was held in Cleveland, which adopted a "five year program of survey and adjustment." It was directed to four main objectives: (1) eliminating missionary aid to churches that were competing with other churches in over-churched areas; (2) working progressively for the elimination of competition among self-supporting churches; (3) allocating responsibility among missionary boards for new work on a non-competitive basis; (4) providing joint support of certain common projects. To undergird this program and to build up support for a missionary advance, an interdenominational Home Missions Congress was scheduled to be held in Washington in 1930. Before the Congress met, the Depression had made "advance" seem a very unrealistic word. Instead, the immediate problem was to hold the lines and rally the forces to prevent a retreat.

The importance of comity was magnified by the financial stringency of the times. If there were limits to the resources available to the missionary boards, it was all the more urgent that no resources be wasted in maintaining churches where they were not really needed. The intensified accent on comity resulted in 1935 in a national agreement by six denominations (Northern Baptist, Congregational, Disciples, Evan-

---

[7] A book published in 1931, *The Challenge of Change: What Is Happening in Home Missions,* by John M. Moore (New York: Missionary Education Movement, 1931), marks the transition that was taking place. The changing orientation had been discerned earlier by H. Paul Douglass in *The New Home Missions* (Philadelphia: American Baptist Publication Society, 1914). See also Hermann N. Morse, *Home Missions Today and Tomorrow: A Review and Forecast* (New York: Home Missions Council, 1934).

gelical and Reformed, Methodist Episcopal, and Presbyterian U.S.A.), pledging to withdraw aid in local situations in which an aided church was competitive with other churches.[8] In the following four years, aid was accordingly withdrawn from 346 points in thirty-four states.

This, however, remedied only slightly the problem of overchurching. Congregations that were not dependent on missionary assistance could continue in parochial loyalties even when it was obvious that the community would be better served by fewer and stronger churches. A few of the old-line denominations, especially the Southern Baptists, rejected the principle of comity agreements as limiting their freedom in missionary activity. They even began to invade the territory of Northern Baptists. New sectarian groups were arising which appealed strongly to disadvantaged people unreached by any middle-class church. The Church of the Nazarene, for example, which in 1926 had only 60,000 members, reported more than 200,000 two decades later. Pentecostal groups had a phenomenal growth and bizarre cults like Father Divine's Peace Mission sprang up almost over night. All these were entirely uncommitted to policies of cooperation or comity. In justification of their go-it-alone attitude they could say that they were ministering to religious needs of people whom the main-line churches had neglected.

Rethinking Religious Education

During the first quarter of the twentieth century enthusiasm for religious education was a conspicuous feature of American church life. The founding of the Religious Education Association in 1903, the inauguration of weekday schools of religious education in 1913, and the formation of the International Council of Religious Education in 1922 were organizational expressions of a movement which had almost a crusading character. But by the mid-thirties religious education presented a confused and uncertain picture. Its condition was described by one of its outstanding representatives in these depressing terms:

> Obviously it is in distress. The machinery has broken down. All the denominational boards of education have suffered great losses. The International Council of Religious Education is struggling on with a greatly reduced staff and budget. The Religious Education Association is in abeyance, trying to maintain itself with a handful of volunteers who are holding it together in spite of a staggering debt. . . . The professional leadership is discouraged; directors of religious education are transferring to social work or public education or joining the ranks of the unemployed.[9]

---

[8] Home Missions Council: *Annual Report, 1935,* p. 12.

[9] Adelaide T. Case, in *The Church Through Half a Century,* ed. Samuel McCrea Cavert and Henry P. Van Dusen (New York: Charles S. Scribner's Sons, 1936), pp. 243–244.

Side by side with the financial problem was a deepening tension within the leadership over basic theory and theological assumptions. This was vividly illustrated by two books, which appeared a little later, championing contrasted philosophies of Christian education current at this time. One was Harrison S. Elliott's *Can Religious Education Be Christian?*[10] The other was H. Shelton Smith's *Faith and Nurture.*[11] Elliott opposed any "transmissive" concept of religious education and interpreted it as a process of growth through purposeful social activity, centered not in the Bible or Christian doctrine but in the experience of the child. Smith represented a sharp reaction against this position, although it was one which he himself had earlier held. He came to feel that it was making Christian education merely a part of general education, with no particular truth of its own, and that it virtually equated the experience of God with the experience of human community. He concluded "that the thought patterns of modern liberal religious nurture have largely exhausted their vitality, and that failure to reconstruct them in terms of a more adequate faith will ultimately result in the collapse, or at least the slow death, of the twentieth-century movement of religious education."[12]

The conflict in educational theory presented grave problems to those who were struggling to establish a firm base for interdenominational cooperation. Up to this time the enthusiasts for Sunday School work had not concerned themselves with defining a theological position. They had been content with working for common action in practical matters in which basic differences of conviction did not arise. Now, however, the International Council of Religious Education became a focal point in the struggle between the two views, at a time when it was engaged in formulating a new graded curriculum after the long reliance on uniform lessons. Under the leadership of William C. Bower, professor of religious education in the University of Chicago, the view of the progressive educators was dominant in the *International Curriculum Guide* of 1932. This conceived Christian Education as "a guided experience in Christian living in which the growing person is assisted in interpreting, judging, and bringing through to Christian outcomes the actual life-situations which he faces in every area of his experience, with the aid of the resources of the past religious experience of the race."

As the result of the work of a Committee on Basic Philosophy and Policy, beginning in 1937 under the chairmanship of Luther A. Weigle, more explicit stress was laid on the role of the Christian faith and the

---

[10] (New York: The Macmillan Company, 1940).

[11] (New York: Charles Scribner's Sons, 1941).

[12] *Ibid.,* p. vii.

Christian church.[13] In the final report of the Committee the central emphasis was on "the induction of growing persons into the Christian community," while continuing to affirm the necessity of reinterpreting the faith "in terms of the living experience of our own day" and to "discover its wider and deeper implications."[14] This mediating viewpoint helped to draw the forces of religious education together after a very controversial period.

Rethinking the Social Gospel

In the year 1932 two events took place which were clear symptoms of changes in Christian social thought. One was the revision of the "Social Ideals of the Churches." The other was the publication of Reinhold Niebuhr's *Moral Man and Immoral Society*. The first indicated the influence which the movement commonly known as the "Social Gospel" had acquired. The second revealed the need for rethinking some of the assumptions on which it had rested.

The decision to restate the Social Ideals was prompted by the fact that during the twenty-four years since the original formulation new areas of social concern had forced themselves on the Christian conscience. The statement of 1908 had been focused almost entirely on justice for industrial workers. Now other issues had come to the fore. The war and its aftermath had made international relations an inescapable topic. The long relegation of the Negro to second-class citizenship was becoming a challenge to professed democratic standards. The increasing plight of the farmer, as cities gained the balance of political power, demanded attention. Most obvious of all, the continuing economic depression, with unprecedented unemployment and worsening poverty, raised the question whether the churches had any corporate witness to bear in the economic realm.

The sobering impact of the Depression was mirrored in statements by major denominations. Conspicuous illustrations were the report of the Social Service Commission of the Northern Baptist Convention and the report on the State of the Church at the General Conference of the Methodist Episcopal Church, both in the spring of 1932 and both sharply critical of undue dominance of the profit motive. In December of the same year came the Federal Council's revision of the Social Ideals, retaining the substance of the original statement but becoming more specific at some points and adding others.

---

[13] LUTHER A. WEIGLE (1880–   ), professor at Carleton College, 1905–1915; professor of religious education, Yale Divinity School, 1916–1949, and dean, 1928–1949; president of Federal Council of Churches, 1940–1942; chairman of the committee which prepared the Revised Standard Version of the Bible; chairman of World Council of Christian Education, 1928–1958.

[14] See William C. Bower and Percy R. Hayward, *Protestantism Faces Its Educational Task Together* (Appleton, Wis.: C. C. Nelson Publ. Co., 1949), pp. 61–64.

Among the new articles in the Social Ideals were proposals urging social security for all, economic justice for the farmer, the repudiation of war and a drastic reduction of armaments, and equal rights for all races.[15] The most controversial points were two articles directly reflecting the economic crisis through which the nation was then passing. Making a definite break with *laissez-faire* economics, they declared that the churches should stand for:

> Practical application of the Christian principles of social well-being to the acquisition and use of wealth; subordination of speculation and the profit motive to the creative and cooperative spirit;
> Social planning and control of the credit and monetary systems and the economic processes for the common good.

The interpretation which accompanied the revision was a synthesis of personal evangelical faith and social concern. This was even more explicit in a statement issued the following year over the signatures of thirty-one denominational heads, "The Present Crisis as a Summons to Advance." They said:

> We are agreed in holding the personal experience of fellowship with God in Christ to be the supreme value in life and the foundation of any Christian program adequate for a fear-stricken and bewildered world. Unless the Gospel is first lodged in the heart of the individual as a renewing and transforming power, it can have no healing for society as a whole. . . . We are agreed that a renewed spiritual life for each of us as individuals must lead straight out into the great social issues of our day. . . . We cannot be interested in the salvation of individual personalities without being at once concerned about the slums that damn them or the unemployment that works havoc to the spirit of man no less than to his body.[16]

The revised Social Ideals represented a realistic confrontation with social and economic problems of the time. They anticipated some of the measures of President Roosevelt's New Deal. During his political campaigning, on at least one occasion, Roosevelt replied to charges of radicalism by saying that he was "as radical as the Federal Council of Churches."

The new statement did not, however, reveal any serious rethinking of the theological assumptions of the Social Gospel. It did not expound the Biblical and doctrinal foundations from which the Social Ideals presumably derived their moral and spiritual authority. As F. Ernest Johnson, one of the ablest spokesmen for the Federal Council, said several years later in recalling what had been earlier said and done:

---

15 The full text of the revised Social Ideals, with an extensive commentary on it, is found in the *Quadrennial Report of the Federal Council of the Churches of Christ in America, 1932,* pp. 57–74.

16 *Annual Report, Federal Council of the Churches of Christ in America, 1933,* p. 28.

It is a valid criticism of this liberal social gospel Christianity that its phi-losophy, its ideals, and its programs as commonly stated have little dis-tinctive character in terms of Christian postulates. Many of the social pronouncements of church bodies in this country might have been made by any high-minded group of educators or social workers claiming noth-ing more than a secular sanction. . . . The task of deriving ethical man-dates directly and irresistibly from Christian assumptions about man's relation to God, about sin and redemption, about love and sacrifice, about the Church, and implementing these mandates in the corporate life of the Christian community—this task we have not done in any effective way.[17]

A theological reorientation of the Social Gospel was, however, soon to set in. The most convenient date for marking it is the same year (1932) in which the Social Ideals were revised, for in this year Reinhold Niebuhr's *Moral Man and Immoral Society* appeared. Niebuhr had re-cently begun his distinguished career at Union Theological Seminary after a pastorate in Detroit where he had gained an unusual understand-ing of modern industry. He had had close associations with the Federal Council for a decade as a representative of the Evangelical Synod of North America and had recently served as the chairman of its Commis-sion on the Church and Social Service.

Niebuhr's critique of society in his epoch-making book was a major factor in bringing about a deeper realization of "the power of self-interest and collective egoism in all intergroup relations."[18] Earlier spokesmen of the Social Gospel had taken it for granted that Christian motivation could be transferred from the realm of individual action to the realm of social action, if only there were sufficient understanding of the social significance of Christianity. Niebuhr undercut this assumption by his analysis of the strength of human pride and sin in their group manifes-tations. He made it clear that to expect society to be transformed into a community of harmony and justice through the individual responses of those in positions of power to Christian ideals was illusory. At the same time he constantly insisted on Christian social responsibility.

Stimulated by Niebuhr and disciplined by the disillusionment which the Depression brought, those who were concerned for the Christian witness in society became more realistic in their estimate of human nature and more aware of the inevitable tension between the Kingdom of God and every economic or political order. They became, accordingly, less utopian in their expectations. While maintaining the command-

---

[17] F. Ernest Johnson, *The Social Gospel Re-examined* (New York: Harper & Brothers, 1940), pp. 4, 9. Dr. Johnson (1884–   ), Methodist minister and educator, was research sec-retary for the Federal Council of Churches, 1918–1924, and executive of its Research De-partment, 1924–1950. He was also professor of education in Teacher's College, Columbia University, 1931–1950.

[18] Reinhold Niebuhr, *Moral Man and Immoral Society* (New York: Charles Scribner's Sons, 1932), p. xx.

ment of love as the Christian absolute, they put the emphasis on responsible action to achieve proximate goals.

During the thirties there was a growing insight into the tension between the Christian faith and every human society. This was dramatically evident in European countries where churches were confronting
totalitarian régimes. In America, though much less obviously, there was
a pervasive tendency of the local church to conform to its environmental
culture and to lose its character as a distinctive community with standards of its own. A reaction against this found influential voice in 1935
in a book that was significantly named *The Church Against the World*.
In it three young scholars—H. Richard Niebuhr, Francis P. Miller, and
Wilhelm Pauck—critically examined the latent syncretism of the church
with nationalism and capitalism, and pleaded for the independence of
the church from captivity to any secular culture.[19] The unconscious alliance of American Protestantism with the "American way of life" was
coming under increasing scrutiny. The participation of the American
churches in the rising ecumenical movement was to be a decisive factor
in developing a perspective in which the church is seen as a community
transcending nation, race, and class.

Rethinking Church Federation and Union

In connection with the twentieth anniversary of the Federal Council
in 1928 a Committee of One Hundred reviewed its relation to the
churches. One of the main questions raised was whether the time had
come for a restructuring of the Council in a way that would make it a
fuller expression of unity. A syllabus drafted by William Adams Brown
suggested that the denominations might carry the principle of federation further by officially "delegating certain defined functions to the
federal body."[20] The discussion in the Council made it clear that there
was no general support for such a modification of denominational patterns, but a committee on Function and Structure was appointed to give
further study to the Council's role. Irritated by this delaying tactic, *The
Christian Century* called the whole process "a complete washout" and
gloomily editorialized:

> It is vain to expect a body of delegates containing an overwhelming pre-
> ponderance of men and women employed by the denominations—bish-
> ops, board secretaries, college presidents, theological professors—to face
> such questions. They are already too deeply and humanly implicated in
> the denominational system to be either able or willing to consider the

---

19 Niebuhr, Miller, Pauck, *The Church Against the World* (Chicago: Willett, Clark & Co.,
1935).

20 *Federal Council Bulletin* (June, 1928).

transfer of any important denominational functions to an organism representing all the churches.[21]

In 1932 the Committee on Function and Structure, under the chairmanship of George W. Richards, presented a report which outlined an internal reorganization of the Council with a view to greater operational effectiveness, and this was duly approved.[22] The report also suggested a more radical proposal, which would have modified the relationship of the denominations to the Council by authorizing it "to administer for any of the constituent bodies such activities as they may commit to it and as the Council may accept." This was put forward as a deliberate step, though a small one, in moving from a loose confederation toward federal union.[23] It contemplated the possibility that the denominations might commit certain substantial powers to the Council, thereby endowing it with an authority that had not been given to it at its founding. During the twenty-four years of its life the Council had gradually assumed more and more administrative responsibilities, and this had been generally welcomed as useful, but there had been no formal transfer of any function from denominations to an interdenominational agency and no surrender of any denominational authority. Nor was there to be any now. After extended debate the only action taken on the proposed amendment was to "defer action." It was evident that until denominational tempers changed there was little prospect of even a limited form of federal union. Relationship among the denominations reflected a growing spirit of mutuality and cooperative helpfulness but this did not reach the point of willingness to give up any part of their separate denominational sovereignties. Among thoughtful leaders, however, the idea persisted that some manifestation of unity beyond working together at certain common tasks was called for.

Within more limited circles actual unions of certain denominations were taking place at this time. Three Lutheran bodies—the Synod of Buffalo, the Synod of Iowa and other states, and the Synod of Ohio and other states—came together in 1930 to form the American Lutheran Church.[24] In 1931 the Congregational Churches and the Christian

---

[21] December 20, 1928.

[22] GEORGE W. RICHARDS (1869–1955), professor of church history in the Theological Seminary of the Reformed Church in the U.S., 1899–1939, and president, 1920–1939, was the leader of the movement for uniting the Reformed Church in the U.S. and the Evangelical Synod of North America to form the Evangelical and Reformed Church, of which he was president, 1934–1938.

[23] See *Quadrennial Report, 1932*, pp. 24–56, for the full text of the proposals, and pp. 221–228 for the discussion of them.

[24] A unifying process had been under way in American Lutheranism for some time, evidenced by the coming together of three Norwegian Lutheran bodies in the United Norwegian Church in 1917, and of three general and older bodies in the United Lutheran Church in America in 1918.

Churches (General Convention) united to establish the Congregational Christian Churches. Although these two groups were similar in polity, their historical antecedents were very different. In 1934 the Reformed Church in the United States and the Evangelical Synod of North America joined in creating the Evangelical and Reformed Church. This merger was noteworthy by reason of its bridging greater differences than any other American union up to this time. Although the two denominations had a common German ancestry, they represented different theological backgrounds. One was wholly in the Reformed tradition, while the Evangelical Synod, as an American offspring of the Evangelical Church of Prussia, had an admixture of Lutheranism. The union was further remarkable for another reason: it was fully consummated in advance of the adoption of a constitution or a decision as to how the agencies of the two denominations would be combined.

In the Methodist family a vigorous movement for reunion got under way in 1931. Undiscouraged by the failure of earlier efforts to unite the Methodist Episcopal Church and the Methodist Episcopal Church South, these two bodies, with the additional participation of the Methodist Protestant Church, resumed negotiations and by 1934 had drafted a complete plan of union. The differences to be resolved were not doctrinal but practical and psychological. The toughest problem was racial. This issue was resolved by a compromise providing for a "central jurisdiction" which, unlike the other jurisdictions, did not follow geographical lines but embraced all the non-white annual conferences.[25] The Methodist Church, when officially constituted by a uniting general conference in 1939, included virtually all of American Methodists except those in Negro denominations. It represented the largest number of American Protestants who have ever been involved in an organic union.[26] Negotiations which were to eventuate in the union of the Evangelical Church and the Church of the United Brethren in Christ were begun in 1933. It would be a dozen years, however, before the consummation was reached in the formation of the Evangelical United Brethren Church.[27]

The developments in cooperation, federation, and union at the national level had partial parallels at state and local levels. In 1929, just before the Depression, a survey showed that there were 43 councils in cities of 50,000 or more.[28] They were mainly limited to the larger urban areas. With a single exception, all cities with a population of more

---

[25] This arrangement was to be increasingly challenged and was modified as time went on.

[26] See John M. Moore, *The Long Road to Methodist Union* (New York: Abingdon Press, 1943).

[27] A complete chronological list of church unions in America during the twentieth century is given in a forthcoming companion volume.

[28] H. Paul Douglass, *Cooperation in American Cities* (New York: Institute of Social and Religious Research, 1930).

than 300,000 had a council of churches. Many of the local councils at this stage were expressions of the concern of forward-looking churchmen for a united Protestantism more than they were well-supported agencies of the churches. Only three- councils were receiving as much as half of their resources directly from the member churches.

At the state level the ordinary difficulties in cooperation had been accentuated by the fact that new councils of churches and older councils of religious education (or Sunday School councils) often existed side by side and were competing for sufficient support for an adequate program. One of the unanticipated consequences of the financial crisis after 1929 was that dwindling resources had an almost coercive effect in inducing the two types of councils to unite. In the thirties the process of union between them began. The first statewide merger took place in Connecticut in 1932 under the leadership of J. Quinter Miller.[29] By 1940 there had been twenty such mergers.

Rethinking Local Unity

Impatient with the slow progress of national agencies in dealing with overchurching, Christians in local communities sometimes took matters into their own hands. Their experiments, especially numerous in the twenties, resulted in a unique American phenomenon, the "community church movement."

Being the product of diverse local initiatives, the community churches were a heterogeneous group, both organizationally and theologically. Their one distinguishing feature was their community-centered orientation. Some were radically independent, wholly autonomous, and unrelated to any denomination. A few, like New York's Riverside Church, established in 1930, maintained a very loose affiliation with a denomination for narrowly limited purposes.[30] Others involved no serious break with the established order, adopting a federated structure under which two or more congregations of different denominations functioned locally as a single unit while maintaining "overhead" relations with the parent bodies. Sometimes in rural areas the federated groups might be scattered over several towns, in which case they constituted a "larger parish."[31] There were also congregations which assumed the designation of

[29] J. QUINTER MILLER (1899–   ), minister of the Church of the Brethren; director of religious education, Cleveland Church Federation, 1923–1927; general secretary of the Connecticut Council of Churches, 1930–1940; associate general secretary of Federal Council of Churches, 1940–1950; executive of National Council of Churches, 1950–1966.

[30] The affiliation of the Riverside Church was with the Northern Baptist Convention. Later it established a similar affiliation with a second denomination, the United Church of Christ.

[31] See Edmund deS. Brunner, *The Larger Parish* (New York: Institute of Social and Religious Research, 1934).

"community church" and served more than denominational constituencies while remaining completely within the denominational system.

In 1928 an enthusiastic interpreter of the community churches located more than 1,200, but many of these were units within a denomination.[32] A survey at about the same time by the Institute of Social and Religious Research, limited to towns and villages of less than 5,000 population, found 312 federated, 137 independent, and 37 affiliated churches.[33] In 1926 the Federal Census of Religious Bodies for the first time included both federated and independent churches in its report, listing 361 of the former and 257 of the latter, and the census of a decade later indicated a substantial increase in both types. Since 1936 there has been no similar census but there is abundant evidence that after the thirties there was a marked decline of enthusiasm for the short-cut approach to unity that the independent community church represented.

In its federated form the community church had its greatest development in rural areas with a declining population, where the problem of maintaining unneeded churches was most acute. The pressure of economic circumstances was usually a more decisive factor than a spiritual impulse to unity. The independent type of church gained special favor in new suburban areas, where there was more than the average concern for "togetherness" and a feeling that a single Protestant Church would contribute to the unity of the community.[34]

In a few exceptional situations a community church of a strictly interdenominational character has come into existence through a joint approach by national bodies. A striking illustration is found at Hoover Dam, Nevada. Seven denominations—Northern Baptist, Disciple, Congregational, Methodist Episcopal, Presbyterian U.S.A., United Brethren, and United Presbyterian—agreed in 1930 to establish a united center for religious and social life in the new community that was growing up around a great governmental project. After a period of missionary aid, the church became self-supporting.

Theologically, the community churches have ranged over the entire doctrinal spectrum. Some of the earliest were so conservative that they finally joined fundamentalist or holiness denominations. A few went to the opposite extreme, like the First Community Church of New York, formerly Unitarian, which in 1919 opened its membership to all on the basis of ethical idealism and humanitarian concern. Most community churches, however, have tended to reflect a "common-core Protestant-

---

[32] David R. Piper, *Community Churches: The Community Church Movement* (Chicago: Willett, Clark & Co., 1928).

[33] Elizabeth H. Hooker, *United Churches* (New York: George H. Doran Co., 1926).

[34] For a discriminating analysis of the different types of community church at the beginning of the 1960's, see Robert Lee, *The Social Sources of Church Unity* (New York: Abingdon Press, 1960), Chapter VI.

ism," with an inclination toward a liberal viewpoint. Members of denominations that stress the sacramental and the liturgical have less often been found in community churches.

The strength of the community church has been its witness to a Christian unity that transcends denominations. Its weakness has been its lack of a fellowship wider than its own parish and an uncertain sense of missionary responsibility. As a means of providing for some of the services which a denominational headquarters ordinarily renders, the Community Church Workers of the U.S.A. was formed in 1923. Beginning in 1929, it had an established relationship for a time with the Home Missions Council, which maintained for a few years a field secretary with special responsibility for helping overchurched communities to deal with their problem. In the late forties, the Community Church Workers developed into a Council of Community Churches.[35]

The community church, contrary to some early expectations, has not resulted in any basic modification of Protestant structures. Clearly useful in certain circumstances, it has not shown the way to a comprehensive solution of the problems of denominationalism. The decline of ardor for the community church is probably due, paradoxically, to the growth of the ecumenical movement. During the twenties and thirties when the denominations seemed to be progressing at only a snail's pace in overcoming their separateness, independent churches kept springing up as a reaction against the established order. After the ecumenical spirit became more pervasive, local groups that might otherwise have broken away from the denominational system began to have greater hopes for a change within it. If there was ground for believing that unitive influences were at work in the "going order," the old reasons for cutting loose from it had less weight.

A distinctive reason for a special type of united church was found in communities of Americans living overseas. The development of the seven union congregations in the Panama Canal Zone is an impressive example. Begun informally while the Canal was still in process of building, in 1920 they came under the sponsorship of the Federal Council of Churches and were indebted to seven cooperating denominations for generous assistance in erecting their places of worship. As American personnel have gone in rapidly increasing numbers to all the continents, union churches have been formed to minister to them in more than a hundred foreign cities. Each congregation is an independent body, but affiliated with the National Council of Churches for purposes of contact with American church life.

---

[35] In 1950 an organization of Negro community churches merged with it. The present Council of Community Churches maintains a consultative tie with the National Council of the Churches of Christ in the U.S.A.

Strains and Stresses

The internal strains and stresses which were characteristic of the Federal Council from the beginning were especially severe in the confused period of the Depression. A conspicuous illustration of them was the controversy in 1931 over the statement on "Moral Aspects of Birth Control," a subject on which, at that time, none of the constituent denominations of the Council had spoken. The members of the Committee on Marriage and the Home, which drafted the statement, were not themselves in complete agreement on all points. Twenty-two of them held that "the careful and restrained use of contraceptives by married people is valid and moral," and three dissented. All were convinced, however, that education on the subject was urgently needed and published the results of their study as a contribution to that end.

In the light of all the contemporary interest in planned parenthood and the widespread ethical and religious support for it in all Protestant circles today, it is difficult to realize why the Federal Council's pioneering study of it in the early 1930's should have created a great furor. But it did. There was a stormy debate over it in most of the denominations.

In the Southern Presbyterian General Assembly it precipitated a formal withdrawal from the Council.[36] In the Presbyterian Church U.S.A., its Committee on Marriage, Divorce and Remarriage, which had voted to give approval to birth control, deleted the item from its report to the General Assembly because of the controversy. In the Northern Baptist Convention a resolution from the floor was adopted which disclaimed support of it. The General Synod of the Reformed Church in America received overtures to withdraw from the Council but turned them down. In the United Lutheran Church the Synod of New York, after a heated argument over breaking its consultative relation with the Council, finally let the matter die without taking action.

In the religious press there was spirited and extended editorial discussion, pro and con. The most condemnatory judgment came from *Commonweal,* a lay Catholic magazine ordinarily regarded as on the liberal side, which went to the extreme of seeing in the report the "voluntary bankruptcy of the Reformation," the "dissolution of Christian morality," and the "liquidation of historic Protestantism by its own trustees."[37]

The criticisms of the statement raised sharp questions about the representative character of the Council. Should it "represent" only what its denominational constituencies were officially committed to? What significance would there be in statements which merely registered views

---

[36] It returned to membership in 1940.

[37] New York, April 1, 1931.

already well established? Was it not an asset to have an interdenominational body which would not confine itself to a cautious consensus but try to provide a sense of direction in relation to the newer and more puzzling issues? These questions had often risen before and would continue to rise again and again. While they have had no definitive answer, there has been an increasing tendency to recognize the value of two different types of statement. One speaks *for* the churches in order to inform the general public where they stand and why. The other speaks *to* the churches in order to afford them as much guidance as careful study by a delegated group can give.

In addition to such tensions within the Federal Council there were tensions between it and external forces. Its forthright stance on social and racial and international issues precipitated many attacks. In 1929, to take a typical year, an article in the *U.S. Naval Institute Proceedings*, protesting against the Council's activity in behalf of reduction of armaments, alleged that alien influences and resources were behind its program. Later in the same year the American Legion in its annual convention demanded an investigation of ten organizations, including the Council. In the following year a congressman, Hon. George H. Tinkham, publicly denounced the Council for "meddling in secular affairs." In 1931 the volume *Tainted Contacts*, by E. N. Sanctuary, launched a diatribe against what he described as the "socialism, communism, internationalism and pacifism" of the Council. The most frenetic point was reached in 1934 in Elizabeth Dilling's widely circulated *Red Network*, which "exposed" both "dangerous" individuals, including Mrs. Franklin D. Roosevelt and Chief Justice Charles E. Hughes, and organizations deemed "subversive," including the Federal Council of Churches.[38]

---

[38] See Charles S. Macfarland, *Across the Years,* Chapter XIII, for an account of some of the cases in which he was involved. For extensive documentation of these attacks, and others of a later period, see Ralph Lord Roy, *Apostles of Discord* (Boston: Beacon Press, 1953).

9

Recovery and Advance

(1936–1940)

RALLYING from the Depression, the American churches after the mid-thirties manifested a renewal of spiritual vigor.[1] This was especially evident in a revived emphasis on evangelism, in an entrance into several new fields of cooperative effort, in a serious exploration of a fuller form of Christian unity, and in a burgeoning of ecumenical activity that culminated in the plan for a World Council of Churches.

Missions of Evangelism

The first conspicuous evidence of fresh vigor was a cooperative advance in evangelism, known as the National Preaching Mission. This was a united undertaking, organized by the Federal Council of Churches, to stimulate a stronger Christian witness in American communities. It was concrete evidence that Christian social concern had not displaced a concern for personal evangelism, and that the two belonged together.

Under the direction of Jesse M. Bader, the National Preaching Mission was launched in the fall of 1936 after two years of preparation.[2] It was conceived as a deliberate project for stirring a spiritual awakening. A note frequently sounded in the preparatory work was that great social causes require a moral and spiritual dynamic that the causes do not in themselves supply. As an editorial appraisal said, comparing the situation in 1936 with that which had been faced in 1912 by the Men and Religion Forward Movement:

---

[1] An objective student of the period, Professor Herbert W. Schneider of Columbia University, even characterized the improved condition of the religious forces as an "offensive." See his *Religion in Twentieth Century America* (Cambridge: Harvard University Press, 1952).

[2] JESSE M. BADER (1886–1963), was a minister of the Disciples of Christ, who, after pastoral service in Atchison, Kans., and Kansas City, Mo., became an executive of the United Christian Missionary Society. He was the leading figure in the Federal Council's Department of Evangelism, 1933–1950, and directed the program of evangelism in the National Council of Churches, 1950–1953. For the next decade he was general secretary of the World Convention of Churches of Christ.

Then there was a wealth of personal religious concern but too meagre channels for its expression in practical service. Today there is a wealth of channels for effective service but insufficient spiritual energy flowing through them to produce great results.[3]

For its impact the Mission depended not on any dramatized personality but on the close fellowship of a group of Christian spokesmen recruited for a nationwide program. Eighty different persons shared in the leadership, giving their service for periods varying from a few days to several weeks. One served continuously for the entire period, E. Stanley Jones, a missionary to India, whose gift for interpreting the relevance of the Gospel to contemporary life contributed greatly to the Mission's appeal. Several Christians from other lands helped in the program, among whom were John S. Whale and Muriel Lester of England, T. Z. Koo of China, and Adolf Keller of Switzerland. American participants included ministers of the caliber of George A. Buttrick, Albert W. Beaven, Henry W. Hobson, Douglas Horton, Ivan Lee Holt, John A. Mackay, and Paul E. Scherer. There were also a few lay spokesmen, such as Francis B. Sayre and Mrs. Harper Sibley.

The original schedule covered twenty-five of the largest cities between mid-September and Christmas in 1936. A typical mission lasted four days and had the service of about fifteen missioners. A typical daily program provided for a morning conference for pastors on their evangelistic influence, a noonday meeting in a downtown theater on a distinctly spiritual theme, messages at luncheon clubs, afternoon seminars on social and community problems, and a mass meeting in the evening in the largest auditorium. The response was gratifying. Nearly 25,000 ministers attended the conferences arranged for them. The evening audiences ranged from 3,000 to 18,000. In many of the cities an extension program was organized by the local council of churches, which spread the movement to hundreds of smaller communities. It so obviously met a timely need that a second schedule of missions was arranged for the spring of 1937, and during the years following several scores of other missions were held. Directly or indirectly they touched most of the major centers of population. Instead of the designation "National Preaching Mission," the term "National Christian Mission" was used after 1937, emphasizing a more than pulpit-centered approach.

There was no evidence that the Mission reached large numbers of unchurched people and there was criticism of it on this score. There was, however, no doubt that it revived the evangelistic spirit of many local churches, especially of their pastors, and did something to offset the defeatist mood current during the depression. To some extent at least, the mission helped to redeem evangelism from identification with

---

[3] *Federal Council Bulletin* (March, 1936).

stereotyped methods and high-pressure appeal. It contributed to breaking down the false division between the personal and the social aspects of the Gospel. It reinforced the influences making for greater unity by its visible testimony that the churches stood together in a common witness to a common faith.

The general plan of the National Preaching Mission proved so effective that it was followed in 1938 by the University Christian Mission, concentrated on centers of higher education. It aimed to confront students with the claims of Christ upon their lives and to interpret the meaning of Christianity and the church in a way that would win response in a community of learning. A group of about a dozen leaders, among whom were D. T. Niles of Ceylon and T. Z. Koo of China, would spend five days together on each campus, carrying on a program in which classroom visits and conversations in dormitories and fraternity houses during the day supplemented general meetings in the evening. There was also a luncheon conference with faculty members to discuss the place of religion in education. The institutions visited included state universities as well as private colleges and universities. Even in the tax-supported institutions the united approach and the lack of any sectarian note made the program welcome to the administrative authorities. The project continued until 1950, by which time missions had been held on 182 campuses in 44 states.

How to Minister to the Armed Forces

A different kind of spiritual concern was discernible in the unrest in many churches over the role of the chaplains in the armed forces. As pastors to men in a difficult environment the chaplains were conscious of their religious vocation, but as commissioned officers in army and navy they were more sympathetic than most civilian pastors to the military establishment. Chaplains criticized pastors for a tendency toward pacifism, and not a few pastors criticized chaplains as identified with the "war system." This resulted in a sharp controversy in the thirties. It had begun in a mild degree as early as 1924, when the plenary meeting of the Federal Council was asked to explore the possibility of placing the ministry to men in army and navy on a "non-military basis," but nothing had come of it. In 1936 the criticism of the chaplaincy reached a point at which two denominational bodies, the Evangelical and Reformed Church and the Disciples of Christ, went on record against further participation in the General Committee on Army and Navy Chaplains. In the same year the General Conference of the Methodist Episcopal Church proposed "a Protestant chaplaincy to be supervised through a board or department of the Federal Council." All three of these resolutions contemplated a ministry to the men in the armed forces which should be free from military control.

At the meeting of the Federal Council later in 1936 a special commission was created to "prepare a plan embodying such a modification of the status of the Army and Navy chaplains as will make clear that they are a part of the regular ministry of the Churches rather than of the armed forces of the nation."[4]

The consultations that took place during the ensuing two years indicated that a civilian chaplaincy, however sound in theory, would be confronted with insuperable administrative problems, especially in overseas and combat situations. There appeared to be a growing feeling, too, that the spiritual independence of the chaplain could be protected within the military establishment, at least in considerably greater degree, if his church maintained a more continuous touch with him and kept him sensitive to the nature of his religious vocation.

The final decision, at the Federal Council's biennial meeting in 1938, did not recommend a separation of the chaplain from the military organization. As an alternative, it proposed: (1) that the chaplain should wear no insignia of military rank, but only the cross; (2) that the training manual for chaplains be revised to place a greater emphasis upon his relation to the church; (3) that the churches make provision for closer contact with their chaplains.

This did not satisfy the whole constituency. A minority still held that anything less than a non-military chaplaincy was inconsistent with the witness of the churches in behalf of peace. The argument abated, however, after 1939 as the war clouds became darker and heightened the prospect that hosts of American youth would be in military service overseas. However right in principle it might be to have the chaplain independent of any military authorities, it seemed even more important not to leave millions of young men without a continuous religious ministry.

New Fields of Cooperation

In these years the Federal Council began to give considerable attention to the encouragement of consumers' cooperatives as a measure of economic self-help among both rural and urban workers. The project was carried on by James Myers, the industrial secretary of the Council for more than twenty years. In 1935 he organized a national seminar of churchmen on the subject, which was followed in subsequent years by numerous regional and local seminars sponsored by state and local councils of churches. There were also tours to Nova Scotia for a first-hand study of the remarkable development of cooperatives under the leadership of a Roman Catholic university, St. Francis Xavier, among the fisher folk.

---

[4] *Biennial Report, 1936,* pp. 49–59.

A pioneering program in the field of pastoral care, with a special accent on the relation of religion to health, got under way in 1937. For a dozen years previously the Federal Council's research department and the New York Academy of Medicine had sponsored a very informal Joint Committee on Religion and Medicine, consisting of a few churchmen and a few physicians who met for an occasional evening's discussion of the significance of religious faith in maintaining bodily and mental health. For some months the group had a research worker, Dr. Helen Flanders Dunbar, who had had both theological and medical training, carrying on studies in spiritual healing and psychosomatic medicine.[5]

Out of the conversations in this group emerged a Commission on Religion and Health within the Federal Council, made up of pastors, theologians, and physicians. It conceived its role as undertaking "to develop and demonstrate the distinctive function of religion in the maintenance, restoration and improvement of health and emotional balance . . . to promote practical cooperation between physicians and clergymen," and "to improve the ministry of the churches to those in hospitals and other institutions." Beginning in 1938 the Commission had a full-time director in the person of Seward Hiltner, who later became a well-recognized authority in pastoral psychology.[6] After a few years the Commission was expanded into a department of pastoral services.

Another noteworthy development in cooperation among the churches had to do with aid to suffering peoples in other lands. The chaotic conditions in both Europe and Asia elicited a Christian response in several organizational forms. In 1934 the American Committee for Christian German Refugees (later renamed the American Christian Committee for Refugees) was formed, under the initiative of the Federal Council but organized as an independent group, at the time when Nazi oppression was driving thousands out of their homelands. In 1937 the Church Committee for China Relief was constituted by joint action of the Foreign Missions Conference and the Federal Council, an expansion of an earlier China Famine Relief. In the same year a "United Christmas Appeal" was issued through the churches in behalf of German refugees, the suffering in China, and Spanish children victimized

---

[5] For a detailed account see Helen Van Voast and Ethel P. S. Hoyt, *History of the Committee on Religion and Medicine of the Federal Council of the Churches of Christ in America and the New York Academy of Medicine: 1923–1946* (privately printed; in the archives of the National Council of Churches).

[6] SEWARD HILTNER (1909–   ), Presbyterian clergyman, began his ministry as director of a newly created Council for the Clinical Training of Theological Students. After serving the Commission on Religion and Health, 1938–1950, he became professor of pastoral psychology at the University of Chicago Divinity School, 1950–1961. In the latter year he became professor of theology and personality at Princeton Theological Seminary.

by the civil war. In March, 1939, as needs multiplied, the Federal Council and the Foreign Missions Conference set up a Joint Committee on Foreign Relief Appeals to coordinate the many approaches to the Protestant churches.

Roman Catholic and Jewish agencies were effectively organized for overseas relief earlier than the Protestant. A happy illustration of the spirit that animated the programs was an unsolicited contribution of $125,000 at Christmas-time in 1939 by the United Jewish Appeal to the Federal Council, to be used for service to Christian refugees from the Nazi régime. In making the grant, the officers of the United Jewish Appeal said that it was "an acknowledgement on our part of the sympathy and support of the leaders of the Protestant Churches for all victims of religious and racial persecution."[7]

An organizational development in this period which was to have fruitful consequences for the future was the establishment of a new national agency of cooperation among church women. They had long been in the forefront of missionary activity, both home and foreign, and more recently had come to feel a collective responsibility for Christian citizenship. As a result, they had been coming together in more and more cities for cooperation in relation to community problems. These local interdenominational groups soon felt the need for a national center of information, stimulus, and guidance, and in 1929 the National Council of Protestant Church Women was organized as such a center. As it found ways of cooperation in certain projects, like the World Day of Prayer, with the groups of women organized for missionary service, a process of integrating all the interests of church women began, which culminated in 1940 in an agreement to constitute the United Council of Church Women as an inclusive agency.[8]

A Quest for Greater Unity

Encouraged by the experience of working together more and more closely, the question was again raised whether there could not be an advance to a further stage of unity among the churches. There was a growing feeling, as Bishop Ivan Lee Holt said, that "we have far more unity than we have any agency to express."[9] This point of view found organizational support in 1936 when the Federal Council established a Commission for the Study of Christian Unity. The emphasis was on

---

[7] The text of the letter, dated December 26, 1939, is printed in *Federal Council Bulletin* (February, 1940).

[8] Described in a forthcoming companion volume.

[9] IVAN LEE HOLT (1886–1967), ordained as a minister by the Methodist Episcopal Church South, was pastor of St. John's Methodist Church in St. Louis, 1918–1938, and then elected bishop. He was president of the Federal Council of Churches, 1934–1936. He also served as chairman of the Methodist Ecumenical Council.

the word "study," since there were wide differences of judgment as to what form any fuller integration should take.

The Commission proposed to give attention to (1) conditions that create the demand for a greater unity; (2) the further development of cooperation and federation in local communities, in states, in the nation, and in the world; (3) community experiments with federated and united congregations; (4) the possible delegation of certain functions by the denominations to central agencies like the Federal Council and the Home Missions Council; (5) proposals for the reorganization of American Protestantism or for unions among groups of denominations; (6) emerging ecumenical developments. The work of the Commission never attracted much public attention, but the personal influence of its secretary, H. Paul Douglass, was considerable.[10] His unsurpassed knowledge of the American churches and his long experience in research were placed at the disposal of Protestantism as a whole at a crucial time when the ecumenical movement was in a fluid condition and the World Council of Churches was emerging. His editorship of *Christendom*, a scholarly American quarterly devoted to the interests of both Faith and Order and Life and Work, was a valuable contribution to ecumenical education.

One of the interests of the Commission was in exploring some form of unity among denominations that would pass beyond voluntary cooperation. During the National Preaching Mission Stanley Jones had begun to suggest this, and his farewell message before returning to India was entitled "The Next Great Step—Unite." The type of union which he advocated was midway between a federation, in which cooperating denominations retain full sovereignty, and a merger in which the denominations disappear. In the federal union which he urged, each denomination would become a "branch" of a united church, delegating certain functions and powers to the central body and retaining all authority not thus delegated. This would be real union, Dr. Jones argued, even if the denominations maintained their own doctrinal standards, ministries, and forms of worship. He was confident that once such a union had been definitely initiated the denominational differences would be gradually overcome.

After several years of his one-man crusade Dr. Jones felt he had sufficient popular support to warrant organizing it, and launched "The Association for a United Church."[11] For more than a decade it kept up

---

[10] H. PAUL DOUGLASS (1871–1953), Congregational leader in home missions during the earlier years of his ministry, was research director of the Institute of Social and Religious Research, 1921–1933, and during the rest of his life an influential member of the Federal Council's staff.

[11] See E. Stanley Jones, *The Next Great Step* (Boston: The Association for a United Church, n.d.).

a promotional effort but the plan never reached the point of being seriously considered by any denomination.

Out of much ferment of discussion there emerged a growing conviction that, whatever might be a more remote goal, the one forward movement that was practicable in the near future was the combining of all the existing instruments of cooperation into one inclusive inter-denominational structure. It was felt that such a reorganization would have the double value of securing a more efficient operation in all fields of common responsibility and also of presenting to the nation a more adequate picture of the essential oneness of the churches. Increasingly it came to be seen that as long as the cooperative program was parceled out among several different agencies in fractional parts it would fail to kindle the imagination and command the loyalty of the Christian community as it should. Responding to a Presbyterian overture of 1938, the Federal Council on June 7, 1939, approved "the union in a single corporate body of national agencies now functioning in interchurch work."

A tentative step in this direction had already been taken in 1934 in the simple decision to form an Inter-council Field Committee which would serve several interdenominational agencies. This was at first regarded as a working arrangement for avoiding confusion in approaching local communities. It soon came to be thought of also as a way of jointly helping to build one effective agency of cooperation in each state and in each community. The national bodies that were initially most interested were the Federal Council of Churches, the International Council of Religious Education, and the Home Missions Council, but the Foreign Missions Conference and the National Council of Protestant Church Women soon saw the advantages of sharing in the arrangement. It worked so well that by 1939 it had evolved into an Inter-Council Field Department, through which eight agencies carried on their field programs. Instead of setting up a separate staff the Department depended on the collaboration of the executives of the several agencies who were responsible for extension and interpretation throughout the country. This process of drawing the agencies of cooperation together was to come to full consummation a decade later in the establishment of the National Council of the Churches of Christ in the U.S.A. under a constitution officially ratified by the member denominations. After the formation of the Inter-Council Field Department there was a steady movement of thought and practice in that direction.

An event in 1938 which, though little noticed at the time, was to have an important bearing on future ecumenical developments in America was the entry of the first of the Eastern Orthodox Churches into membership in the Federal Council. This was the Syrian Antiochian Orthodox Church. Its archbishop, Metropolitan Antony Bashir, had come to the conclusion that Orthodoxy in America should have a closer association with Protestantism.[12] His initiative along this line was all the more remarkable in view of the fact that the Episcopal Church, with which Orthodoxy had closer ties than with other churches of the Reformation, did not become a full member of the Federal Council until two years later.

Involvement in a World Council

While these changes were taking place in the United States, a development was beginning on a world-wide scale to which the American churches made a major contribution and which, in turn, exerted a strong influence on them. This was the confluence of the three tributaries that was destined to produce the World Council of Churches. Up to this time, the Universal Christian Council for Life and Work, the Continuation Committee of the World Conference on Faith and Order, and the International Missionary Council had each concentrated on its own specific objective and paid little attention to the others. Now each was becoming aware of how much it had in common with the others and of how much the unity of the church as a whole was a concern of all.

The first visible evidence of the coming confluence of the three international streams appeared in 1933 and was American in origin. While William Adams Brown was in England, on a sabbatical leave from Union Theological Seminary, he proposed to William Temple, then Archbishop of York, that representatives of all the organizations with an ecumenical commitment should come together for an unhurried conversation about their future. Archbishop Temple thought well of the suggestion and implemented it by inviting a group of conferees to his home in Bishopthorpe.[13]

In March, 1933, ten persons, all closely related to ecumenical interests, spent parts of two days at Bishopthorpe. Two of the ten were Americans, Dr. Brown and myself. All bore responsibilities in one or more of five ecumenical movements—Life and Work, Faith and Order, the International Missionary Council, the World Alliance for International Friendship through the Churches, and the World Student Christian Federation. The consultation was wholly unofficial, no one having any authority whatever to commit any organization. When it was over, no one thought that anything of much significance had happened beyond a strengthening of personal ties and mutual trust. It was plain that the time had not come when any of the agencies, with the probable

---

[12] ANTONY BASHIR (1898–1966), born in Lebanon, came to the U. S. for missionary work in 1929 and became the head of the Syrian Orthodox Church in America in 1934. He was elected an archbishop in 1936.

[13] A detailed account of the Bishopthorpe meeting is given in William Adams Brown's *Toward a United Church* (New York: Charles Scribner's Sons, 1946), pp. 134–137.

exception of Life and Work, was prepared to surrender its independent status. There was, however, a heightened recognition of the need for the several organizations to keep in continuing touch with one another and to hold at least an unofficial consultation once a year. The hope was also voiced that the organizations might hold their future world conferences under some common plan that would facilitate cooperation.

In December, 1935, while the Archbishop of York was on a visit to America, J. Ross Stevenson, as chairman of the American Section of Faith and Order, invited American representatives of the ecumenical organizations to his home in Princeton, N.J., for a conversation with the archbishop. The chief outcome was a recommendation that the informal consultative group, which had grown out of the Bishopthorpe gathering of two years earlier, should be given official status as a means of further coordination. There was also a general consensus that the Faith and Order and the Life and Work conferences, now planned for the summer of 1937, should be held in the same country and at contiguous dates. In 1936 both Life and Work and Faith and Order endorsed a further proposal that a committee representing the several agencies be appointed to prepare recommendations concerning "the future of the ecumenical movement," to be submitted to the Life and Work Conference in Oxford and the Faith and Order Conference in Edinburgh.

Carrying out this proposal, thirty-five persons met at Westfield College, London, for three days—July 8–10, 1937—on the eve of the Oxford and Edinburgh Conferences.[14] Hardly anyone expected that anything as radical as a definitive proposal for a world-wide Council of Churches under a constitutional government would emerge. The most that was generally anticipated was that some plan for more fully coordinating the operations of the several organizations would be worked out. But after reviewing the situation it became more and more clear to all at the Westfield consultation that Life and Work and Faith and Order were complementary aspects of one quest for unity. The group unanimously concluded that there should be a complete merger of the Life and Work and Faith and Order movements in a single comprehensive body, "representative of the churches and caring for the interests of each movement."[15] The representatives of the International Missionary Council, though sympathetic with the plan, were convinced that an organization devoted solely to the missionary objective was still needed.

---

[14] Of the thirty-five, ten were Americans: James C. Baker, Albert W. Beaven, William Adams Brown, Samuel McCrea Cavert, Fred Field Goodsell, William P. Merrill, John R. Mott, Lewis S. Mudge, G. Ashton Oldham, and Edward L. Parsons.

[15] *The Churches Survey Their Task: The Report of the Conference at Oxford, July, 1937* (London: George Allen and Unwin, 1937), p. 279. The full text of the Westfield College report is printed in this volume.

The World Alliance for International Friendship through the Churches felt that it should continue to maintain its non-ecclesiastical character, with a freedom of action not assured by a church-controlled body.

Even after there was unanimous agreement to propose a merger of Life and Work and Faith and Order, there was still a feeling that it would be expedient to perpetuate the old names in some way, perhaps through calling the new body "The Joint Commission on Life and Work and Faith and Order." When the question of name was being discussed in a subcommittee, I queried—on the basis of the conciliar experience in America—"Why not World Council of Churches?" Archbishop Temple broke the ensuing silence by remarking, "That's what we really want, isn't it?" Although some misgiving was expressed whether so bold a proposal could command the support of the official bodies that would make the final decision, the Westfield College group voted unanimously to present the proposal for a World Council of Churches to the Oxford and Edinburgh Conferences. In the following weeks it was adopted by both, with only a few dissenting votes, although only after considerable questioning at Edinburgh.

So many different persons in so many different countries contributed in such diverse ways to the historical evolution of the World Council of Churches that any appraisal as to who contributed most would be precarious. A strong case, however, could be made for the judgment that in the sequence of events that led to the actual emergence of the plan for the World Council in 1937, it was William Adams Brown who played the most creative role. Active in both Life and Work and Faith and Order from their beginnings, he was deeply convinced that each was incomplete without the other, and that only when they were organically integrated would the churches have a clear embodiment of ecumenical unity. His vision and his persistent interpretation of it were a catalytic factor in bringing the World Council of Churches to birth.[16]

Americans at Oxford

After the Stockholm Conference of 1925, the Life and Work movement had gone through a few years of floundering in an effort to find its way in the tangled field of international affairs. What did the churches of the world have to say and do by way of corporate Christian witness in the face of the world-wide economic depression, the rise of totalitarian dictatorships claiming authority over every aspect of man's life, and the rising threat of war? Gradually it became clear that in all these concerns the relation of church to national community was a fundamental issue. To help the churches face it, the Council for

---

[16] This personal judgment is confirmed by a letter of J. H. Oldham. See my *On the Road to Christian Unity* (New York: Harper & Brothers, 1961), p. 23.

Life and Work decided in 1934 to convene a world conference on "Church, Community and State" at Oxford three years later.[17] J. H. Oldham, the key leader in the International Missionary Council, discerned so clearly the urgency of the situation that he resigned his post in order to give his entire time to developing the new program.

Unlike the Stockholm Conference of 1925, Oxford, 1937, was not content with broad generalizations about the social and international significance of the Gospel. It was specific and realistic in dealing with the complexities of the political and economic scene. It laid the foundations for what Reinhold Niebuhr, in retrospect, called "an impressive system of Christian pragmatism."[18] Since the Conference was confronting concrete problems of secular society, it made a special point of drawing into the discussions a considerable number of lay Christians with experience in public affairs. Among the Americans of this type were John Foster Dulles, Francis B. Sayre, and Charles P. Taft.

The preparation for Oxford was more thorough than for any other ecumenical gathering up to this time. Papers on each subject were circulated in first draft to critics in different countries. Seven volumes resulted from the preparatory studies: *The Church and Its Function in Society; The Christian Understanding of Man; The Kingdom of God and History; Christian Faith and the Common Life; Christ and Community; Church, Community and State in Relation to Education;* and *The Universal Church and the World of Nations.*[19] Americans who made important contributions to these volumes included Edwin E. Aubrey, John C. Bennett, Robert L. Calhoun, H. Paul Douglass, John Foster Dulles, Walter M. Horton, Kenneth S. Latourette, Eugene W. Lyman, Paul Monroe, Reinhold Niebuhr, and Paul Tillich.

At Oxford the most conspicuous absentees were the German delegates, who were refused passports at the eleventh hour. The Americans and the British played the major roles. The American contribution to the leadership of the Conference was noteworthy. William Adams Brown was one of the presiding officers. John R. Mott was chairman of the Business Committee. John A. Mackay was chairman of the section on "The Universal Church and the World of Nations," and Henry Sloane Coffin of the section on "The Church and Education." John C. Bennett was secretary of the section on "The Church and the Economic Order."[20]

[17] *Minutes of the meeting of the Universal Christian Council for Life & Work, Fanoe, Denmark, 1934,* pp. 47ff. The term "Community" was used as the nearest English approximation to what the Germans meant by *"Volk."*

[18] In *The Sufficiency of God, Essays on the Ecumenical Hope in Honor of W. A. Visser 't Hooft,* ed. Robert C. Mackie and Charles C. West (Philadelphia: The Westminster Press, 1963), p. 124.

[19] The seven volumes were published by Willett, Clark & Co., Chicago, 1937.

[20] The official report, *The Oxford Conference,* ed. J. H. Oldham (Chicago: Willett, Clark & Co., 1937) is out of print but there is a new edition, edited with an interpretive introduction by Harold L. Lunger, under the title, *Foundations of Ecumenical Social Thought: The Oxford Conference Report* (Philadelphia: Fortress Press, 1966).

The Oxford Conference proved to be an outstanding landmark in Christian social thinking. Its authority has been described by an American scholar as "unprecedented" and the content of the reports as ranking with "the best of secular thought."[21] During the next quarter of a century they were constantly referred to as important source materials in Protestant social ethics.

In three respects the impact of the Conference on the American churches can be plainly discerned:

(1) It marked a transition to what may fairly be called "the new social gospel." After Oxford it was clearly seen that an acceptance of the ideals of Jesus and appeals to follow the way of love were not enough, and that there must be a realistic facing of the stubborn facts of man's selfishness and its manifestations in the power structures of society.

(2) Oxford paved the way to a new American interest in the relation of social ethics to theology. At Oxford it became plain that differences in social policies are often rooted in what are essentially theological understandings of the nature of God and man. After Oxford the separation between those who were concerned with the Christian faith and those who were concerned with Christian practice was much less noticeable.

(3) Oxford stimulated a new concern in America for the church in its corporate life. In considerable part, this was a reaction to the current struggle with the totalitarian state in Europe. The confrontation with what was happening in the political world emphasized the crucial significance of the church as a community of faith and life with historical rootage and continuity, not dependent on any contemporary culture and not limited to nation or race or class, but having its own distinctive standards derived from its Gospel.

Americans at Edinburgh

In preparation for the second World Conference on Faith and Order, held in Edinburgh a week after the adjournment at Oxford, the American churches carried responsibility for a study of "The Church's Unity in Life and Worship." A commission on this theme had Dean Willard L. Sperry, of the Harvard Divinity School, as its first chairman, succeeded by Professor (later Bishop) Angus Dun, of the Episcopal Theological School, Cambridge. It produced reports on "The Meaning of Unity," "The Communion of Saints," "Non-Theological Factors in Church Union," "Next Steps Toward Unity," and "A Decade of Objective Progress in Church Unity." The last of these was a world-wide survey of the fifty-five negotiations or conversations on union that had been carried

---

[21] James Hastings Nichols, *Democracy and the Churches* (Philadelphia: The Westminster Press, 1951), p. 235.

on during the decade following the Lausanne Conference.[22] The American group reflected a feeling that not all of the Faith and Order studies should be as detached from the contemporary life of the churches as the other three studies—one on "The Grace of Our Lord Jesus Christ," one on "The Ministry and the Sacraments," and one on "The Church and the Word."

The arrangements for the American participation in the Conference were in the hands of Floyd W. Tomkins, Jr., as the associate of Canon Leonard Hodgson, of Oxford, who had become the general secretary of the Continuation Committee in 1932.[23] J. Ross Stevenson, as chairman of the American section, served as one of the vice-chairmen at Edinburgh, with the Archbishop of York as the chief presiding officer.

There was a noticeable difference in the ecclesiastical climate of the Lausanne Conference of 1927 and that of the Edinburgh Conference of 1937. At Lausanne each church was anxious to make sure that its own position was understood. At Edinburgh there was more concern to understand the position of other churches. There were also indications that at some points differences were not as serious as they once had seemed. The report on "The Grace of Our Lord Jesus Christ" held that on this subject there were no longer differences which justified division. The report on "The Church and the Word" indicated that agreement on the relation of the Bible to tradition might be possible. On the subject of "The Ministry and the Sacraments," however, there was no advance beyond Lausanne.[24]

The thing for which the Edinburgh Conference is most remembered is its "Affirmation of Unity in Allegiance to our Lord Jesus Christ." This was drafted by a committee headed by Robert A. Ashworth and unanimously approved.[25] Its primary accent was on the unity which we already have, a unity "which does not consist in the agreement of our minds" and which is "deeper than our divisions." It added:

> We are convinced that our unity of spirit and aim must be embodied in a way that will make it manifest to the world, though we do not yet clearly see what outward form it should take.

---

[22] H. Paul Douglass, *A Decade of Objective Progress in Church Unity: 1927–1936* (New York: Harper & Brothers, 1937).

[23] Floyd W. Tomkins, Jr. (1887–   ), rector of St. John's Episcopal Church, Washington, Conn., served the Faith and Order movement 1928–1963, first as assistant secretary and later as associate secretary for North America. He was also counselor to the presiding bishop of the Episcopal Church on ecclesiastical relations for many years.

[24] In 1940 the Federal Council of Churches began to promote the observance of the first Sunday in October as "World Communion Sunday." The simultaneous observance was regarded as a way of testifying to the fact that although the churches are divided in their practice with reference to the Holy Communion, there is a world-wide oneness in Christ.

[25] Robert A. Ashworth (1871–1959) was a Baptist pastor in New Jersey, Connecticut, Wisconsin, and New York, 1896–1930, becoming editor of *The Baptist* in 1930. He was editorial secretary of the National Conference of Christians and Jews, 1933–1952.

In the meantime, the statement urged a great increase in cooperation:

> We believe that every sincere attempt to cooperate in the concerns of the Kingdom of God draws the several communions together in increased mutual understanding and goodwill. We call upon our fellow-Christians of all communions to practice such cooperation . . . and constantly to pray for that unity which we believe to be our Lord's will for His Church.[26]

At Lausanne, a dozen years earlier, a proposed endorsement of federation as a step toward unity had stirred enough dissent, including dissent by some American Episcopalians, to prevent its being officially received by the Conference. At Edinburgh cooperation and federation were emphasized as an advance toward a larger unity.

Americans at Utrecht and Madras

To implement the decision to form a World Council of Churches the Oxford and Edinburgh Conferences appointed a Committee of Fourteen, with fourteen alternates, under instruction to prepare a plan and submit it to the churches for their approval. Of the twenty-eight thus appointed, seven were Americans: William Adams Brown, John R. Mott, George Craig Stewart, J. Ross Stevenson, Charles P. Taft, Abdel R. Wentz, and Samuel McCrea Cavert. The Committee quickly concluded that a wider consultation than was provided within their own group was needed, and accordingly invited the churches of the different geographical areas and different historical backgrounds to send delegates to an advisory conference, to be held in the following spring, for the purpose of drafting a constitution and charting the course ahead.

At Utrecht, during a week in May, 1938, eighty persons who had been selected by varying processes in different parts of the world came together under the chairmanship of Archbishop Temple for the unprecedented task of drafting a constitution for a World Council of Churches. The chairman of the drafting committee was J. Ross Stevenson. The two questions on which the most serious differences emerged were, first, how to describe the churches which should be regarded as eligible for membership and, second, whether the basis of representation should be by geographical areas or by denominational families.

On the first point, it was readily decided to retain the formula which had been used by Faith and Order, and to define the Council as a fellowship of churches "which accept our Lord Jesus Christ as God and Saviour." Some preferred a different phrasing, pointing out that an adequate statement of the historic faith in Christ should affirm His humanity as well as His deity. The Conference felt, however, that it had

---

[26] Leonard Hodgson, ed. *The Second World Conference on Faith and Order,* Edinburgh, 1937 (New York: The Macmillan Company, 1938), pp. 275–276.

no authority to set forth a substitute for the doctrinal basis which had been associated with Faith and Order from the beginning. As to the method of representation, it was decided that the primary basis should be geographical. Under this plan ninety seats in the Central Committee, out of a total of four hundred and fifty, were assigned to the churches of the United States and Canada. At the same time, provision was made for a supplementary form of representation in the case of the Orthodox, scattered in many different countries, and minorities within world-wide confessional families who might not be adequately represented under the geographical assignments.

As an interim organization, while the Council would be in process of formation, the Utrecht Conference created a Provisional Committee, consisting of the twenty-eight persons who had been named at Oxford and Edinburgh, together with a half dozen others who had important responsibility in Faith and Order and in Life and Work. W. A. Visser 't Hooft, the young Dutchman who had given brilliant leadership to the World Student Christian Federation, was elected general secretary, and headquarters were established in Geneva. Henry Smith Leiper was elected as his associate in New York.

The International Missionary Council, although not yet prepared to give up its separate organization, heartily supported the Utrecht decision. At its meeting in Madras later in 1938, it gave much attention to interpreting the World Council to the Younger Churches and enlisting their interest. The Madras meeting was the first ecumenical gathering at which a majority of the delegates were from the Younger Churches and at which they provided a substantial part of the leadership. The American participation was extensive. Dr. Mott was at his best as chairman, at this last ecumenical gathering at which he was to preside. Americans who served as chairmen of commissions included James C. Baker, Ralph E. Diffendorfer, Fred Field Goodsell, Douglas Horton, Edward H. Hume, and Henry P. Van Dusen.[27]

The World Alliance for International Friendship through the Churches decided to continue as "a free organization," serving the churches in their work for peace, but not under their direction.[28] One of the factors in this decision was the dependence of the Alliance for its financial support on the Church Peace Union, some of whose trustees were Roman Catholic or Jewish and entirely unrelated to the World Council of Churches. The Alliance had played a pioneering role in the early years of the Life and Work movement but after the emergence of the

---

[27] See *The World Mission of the Church. Findings and Recommendations of the International Missionary Council, Tambaram, Madras, India, December 12–29, 1938* (New York: International Missionary Council, 1939).

[28] *Minutes of the International Committee of the World Alliance for International Friendship through the Churches, Larvik, Norway, 1938*, p. 23.

World Council and the increasing readiness of the churches to work together as churches, it no longer had its former function to fulfill.[29]

On the Eve of War

In July, 1939, when the war clouds were more menacing, a small conference of selected Christian leaders from eleven countries was held in Geneva, under arrangements in which the Federal Council's Department of International Justice and Goodwill had a large part, to consider what action was "open to the churches and individual Christians with a view to checking the drift toward war." The meeting, held in an atmosphere of great tension, with German delegates present, faced frankly the task of the churches in the event of war, including their duty to do everything possible to maintain contacts with each other. In the same month the first World Conference of Christian Youth was held in Amsterdam, sponsored by an Ecumenical Youth Commission which was a joint agency of the Provisional Committee of the World Council and the World Alliance for International Friendship through the Churches. The executive director was R. H. Edwin Espy, who twenty-four years later was to become general secretary of the National Council of the Churches of Christ in the U.S.A.[30] One of the oft-quoted utterances of the Youth Conference was the observation that while "the nations and peoples of the world are drifting apart, the churches are coming together." Within a month after the Conference adjourned the Second World War began.

On October 6, the Federal Council issued a statement stressing the duty of the churches to "strengthen their world-wide bonds" and to strive to be a force for reconciliation.[31] The upholding of the rights of conscience of those who could not accept military training was also a special concern at this time. In response to an overture from the General Convention of the Episcopal Church, the Federal Council on November 9 sent a delegation to confer with the Attorney General of the United States about some form of non-combatant service for conscientious objectors.[32] Although there is no documentary evidence, it seems probable that this was a factor in the governmental decision to provide an alternative to bearing arms.

Early in 1940, a National Study Conference on the Churches and the International Situation was held in Philadelphia, at which the attitude

---

[29] The Alliance voted to dissolve on June 30, 1948. The Church Peace Union became "The Council on Religion and International Affairs."

[30] R. H. EDWIN ESPY (1908–   ), layman of the American Baptist Convention, after serving as director of the Ecumenical Youth Commission, was general secretary of the Student Volunteer Movement, 1940–1943, and executive of the National Student Council of Young Men's Christian Associations, 1943–1955. Since then he has been a member of the executive staff of the National Council of Churches and in 1963 was elected its general secretary.

[31] *Annual Report, 1939,* pp. 124–127.

[32] *Annual Report, 1939,* p. 50.

of the American churches toward the war in Europe was the central issue. The general viewpoint was that the United States, in spite of overwhelming moral opposition to the Nazi régime, should not participate in the conflict of arms. Among the main duties envisaged for the American churches were enlarged efforts for the relief of wartime suffering and working for a permanent structure for maintaining peace after the war. At the end of 1940 the Federal Council took official action to establish a Commission on a Just and Durable Peace, which, under the leadership of John Foster Dulles, was to play an influential public role in the succeeding years.

In spite of all the disruptions caused by the war, the administrative group of the World Council's Provisional Committee undertook to meet at the beginning of 1940 at Apeldorn, Holland. To this meeting the American churches sent Roswell P. Barnes as their representative.[33] Its chief significance was a reinforcement of the determination of the World Council, still in the elementary stage of its formation, to make every effort to preserve ecumenical fellowship. The interim organization which had been created at Utrecht not only held together but made modest gains during the war years. In the United States a Joint Executive Committee of Life and Work and Faith and Order was formed, which in 1944 developed into The American Committee for the World Council of Churches. This American arm of the Provisional Committee carried on a tireless program of education and promotion, which was the main factor in leading the American churches into steadily increasing commitment to the ecumenical movement.

In the first Christmas season after the outbreak of war, President Franklin D. Roosevelt sent letters to Pope Pius XII, to George A. Buttrick as president of the Federal Council of Churches, and to Cyrus Adler, president of the Jewish Theological Seminary, inviting their "parallel endeavors for peace and the alleviation of suffering."[34] The letters were quickly followed by the President's announcement that he had appointed Myron C. Taylor as his "personal envoy to the Vatican" with the rank of ambassador.[35] This action precipitated a spirited controversy over the separation of church and state.

---

[33] Roswell P. Barnes (1901–   ), after a pastorate in New York in the University Heights Presbyterian Church, became associate secretary of the Federal Council's Department of International Justice and Goodwill, 1937. In 1938 he was appointed associate general secretary of the Council. When the National Council of Churches was formed in 1950, he became the executive of its Division of Christian Life and Work, and in 1954 associate general secretary. He was executive secretary of the U.S. Conference for the World Council of Churches, 1958–1964.

[34] George A. Buttrick (1892–   ) was pastor of Congregational Churches in Quincy, Ill., and Rutland, Vt., 1915–1921, pastor of First Presbyterian Church, Buffalo, 1921–1927, and of Madison Avenue Presbyterian Church, New York City, 1927–1954. He was preacher to Harvard University and professor of Christian Morals, 1954–1960.

[35] The facts in the case and a record of the reaction in Protestant circles are given in *Federal Council Bulletin* (January, February, March, and May, 1940).

In Protestant circles there was a swift reaction of questioning and misgiving. The Federal Council warned that if the President's appointment of a "personal envoy" should prove a stepping-stone to a continuing diplomatic relationship with the Vatican, it would be strongly resisted. The ground of opposition was that the historic separation of church and state in America would be breached by such an arrangement, since it would confer on one church a special status, not held by other churches, in relation to government. In the public debate that followed, an impressive united stance of the Protestant bodies appeared. The Southern Baptist churches, ordinarily aloof from movements of cooperation, found themselves informally associated with the Federal Council on this issue. On no public question had Protestants been so close to unanimity.

In the Protestant opposition to diplomatic relations with the Vatican there was doubtless a mixture of elements. The main one was a deep-rooted conviction that it violated a fundamental American tradition which had been a blessing to both political and religious life. There was a sincere, almost passionate, feeling that it would be contrary both to an American heritage and to sound public policy to give what would be, in effect, preferential treatment to a single church. In some degree, however, there was a less admirable attitude—a disposition to distrust the Roman Catholic Church and to fear that a recognition of the Vatican would strengthen its political influence. The gracious ecumenical temper which was to develop between Protestant and Catholic a few years later had not yet appeared.

10

A Second Wartime Testing

(1941–1945)

AFTER more than two years in which the United States held aloof from the war, the world situation was becoming more ominous with each passing month. Denmark and Norway had been occupied by Nazi forces. The Netherlands and Belgium had been overrun. The French had capitulated. The Balkans had been largely brought under Hitler's domination. The British, driven from the Continent at Dunkirk, were desperately defending their country against attack from the air. In the Far East there had been a full-scale invasion of China by Japan, which had made a military alliance with Germany and Italy.

Political isolationism received reinforcement from religious commitment to peace. There was, however, a growing sentiment in the churches that America should not avoid participation in the deepening struggle. One of the early indications of changing attitudes was the founding of a new publication, significantly called *Christianity and Crisis*, at the beginning of 1941. It was launched by a group of churchmen, with Reinhold Niebuhr as their chief spokesman, who were convinced that a neutral stance was morally irresponsible. In the first issue he summarized the situation in the churches:

> At the present moment a basic difference of conviction runs through the whole of American Protestantism and cuts across all denominational distinctions. There is, on the one hand, a school of thought that believes war could be eliminated if only Christians and other men of good will refused resolutely enough to have anything to do with conflict. Another school of thought, while conceding that war is one of the most vivid revelations of sin in human history, does not find the disavowal of war so simple a matter. The proponents of the latter position believe that there are historic situations in which refusal to defend the inheritance of a civilization, however imperfect, against tyranny and aggression may result in consequences even worse than war.[1]

The attack on Pearl Harbor on December 7, 1941, put an end to the

---

[1] *Christianity and Crisis*, February 10, 1941.

argument—both in the nation and in the churches—over America's participation in the war.

Trying to Avert War

A few months before the Japanese bombardment of Pearl Harbor, there was a dramatic sequence of events, involving the American and the Japanese churches, which was a striking illustration of the extent to which the missionary movement had begun to create a supra-national fellowship. A face-to-face meeting of representative Christian leaders of the two countries took place for the purpose of considering whether there was any way in which they could help avert the threatened conflict. The initial step was taken by 190 American missionaries in Japan, who on February 16, 1941, sent a cablegram to the Federal Council of Churches voicing their deep anxiety over rising political tensions. Two days later Ralph E. Diffendorfer, the executive of the Methodist Board of Foreign Missions, arriving in New York from Tokyo, brought a message from the National Christian Council of Japan proposing a deputation of friendship from the American to the Japanese churches.[2] On February 23 another cablegram from Japan suggested as an alternative that the conference be held on the Pacific coast of the U.S.A. The suggestion was warmly approved and the Japanese delegation arrived on April 12. The conference was in session in Riverside, California, from April 20 to 25.

The nine delegates from Japan were outstanding Christian leaders, including Toyohiko Kagawa, the widely known social worker, and Tsumejiro Matsuyama, a member of Parliament. The seventeen American delegates were trusted representatives of missionary and ecumenical interests, including Douglas Horton, Bishop James C. Baker, Roswell P. Barnes, Kenneth S. Latourette, John A. Mackay, Walter W. Van Kirk, and A. Livingston Warnshuis. The discussions were carried on in an atmosphere of complete frankness and mutual trust. They were focused primarily on the increasing danger of war, with consideration also of immediate problems of the Christian movement in Japan, such as patriotic participation in ceremonies at Shinto shrines. A message from the conference to the churches in both nations concluded, "We have committed ourselves before God to a ministry of love, forbearance and reconciliation with the people of all lands."[3]

The conference had no tangible results in preventing war. It could not reverse the current of political and economic forces that had long

---

[2] RALPH E. DIFFENDORFER (1879–1951), a Methodist minister, served the Methodist Board of Foreign Missions 1924–1949 and became its chief executive officer. He was one of the Americans most active in the International Missionary Council. After his retirement, he was the leading American in helping to develop Japan International Christian University.

[3] Federal Council of Churches, *Annual Report, 1941*, p. 51.

been gathering a fateful momentum. But the meeting of the American and the Japanese churchmen contributed decisively to the strengthening of a Christian fellowship that could survive the terrific strain that lay ahead.

For the second time within a single generation the American churches had to orient themselves to world-wide war. Their attitude, however, was markedly different from what it had been in 1917–1918. In the first war there had been an uncritical identification of Christianity with the cause of America and its Allies. The professed aims of the government had been baptized in wholesale fashion with the Christian name and given an unqualified Christian blessing. In the second war the churches were more independent in their judgments. There was, for example, a considerable criticism of the governmental policy of herding the Japanese of the West Coast into internment camps. Although support of the war was unquestioned, the churches did not picture it as a Christian crusade. Instead, they viewed it as a grim necessity which they could not avoid and which they would face resolutely. With rare exceptions, they did not use their pulpits as instruments of national propaganda and were careful not to fan fires of hatred. They concentrated their wartime efforts primarily on a religious ministry to men in the armed forces and on alleviation of the suffering caused by the war. They were at pains to defend the rights of the conscientious objector. They maintained a fellowship in prayer with Christian leaders of other lands, not excluding Germany and Japan.

The concern that even in wartime the church should not lose its ecumenical character was summarized in "A Message to Our Fellow-Christians," issued by the Federal Council on December 30, 1941:

> The host of young men who in this hour of crisis answer their country's call are a special concern of the Church. It encompasses with gratitude and prayer all now summoned to render sacrificial service, whether in the armed forces or other work of national importance. . . . It sends many of its ministers to serve as chaplains and seeks to create a wholesome environment in every camp community. . . . It be-friends loyal minorities, including those of alien birth or those descended from peoples with whose governments our country is now at war. . . . To the best of its ability it should care for refugees and prisoners of war and all others caught in the appalling suffering of the world. . . . In times of war Christians in different nations are still members of the one Body of Christ. They must pray not merely for their own national interest, but that God's will may be done in and through all nations.[4]

Cooperation in Serving Soldiers

The drafting of the nation's youth into the armed forces laid a heavy demand upon the churches for chaplains. A year before Pearl Harbor

---

[4] *Federal Council Bulletin* (January, 1942).

the General Committee on Army and Navy Chaplains had begun to meet its enlarging responsibility by securing the release of Paul D. Moody, president of Middlebury College, for several months' service in developing the effectiveness of the chaplaincy. Having been associated with Bishop Brent in the administration of the chaplains' work overseas in the First World War, he was especially qualified for the new emergency.[5] When the war began there were 1,342 chaplains in the army and navy. When the war ended, there were more than 11,000, of whom nearly three-quarters were Protestant. The General Committee on Army and Navy Chaplains, originated by the Federal Council, was granted autonomy in its operations in order to enable it to serve denominations which were not members of the Council. A Southern Baptist, Rufus W. Weaver, served as chairman of the Committee from 1935 to 1941.

A new development in the ministry to men in uniform at this time was the Service Men's Christian League. Initiated by the International Council of Religious Education, it was strongly supported during the war by the denominational organizations for work with youth. Since it was impossible for them to project their denominational structures into the armed forces, they welcomed the League as a way of demonstrating that the local church had not forgotten its young people. Within a year there were more than a thousand units of the League, carrying on their program under the leadership of the chaplains. Its most important project was the publication of a monthly magazine, *The Link*, for distribution in the armed forces. The name was designed to emphasize the continuing bond between the local church and the men. It provided popular religious reading, including material for discussion groups. At the peak of its circulation in 1945, nearly 500,000 copies were being printed monthly. It met such an obvious need that after the war it was continued by the General Commission on Army and Navy Chaplains on a permanent basis.

A publication which would serve the interests of the chaplains in their difficult ministry was also urgently needed. In October, 1944, the first issue of a monthly magazine, *The Chaplain*, appeared under the sponsorship of the General Commission, and has continued to be published ever since.

To help the chaplains in their preaching the Federal Council's Department of Evangelism sent special missions into the camps. There were eighty-six such deputations, each lasting several days, before the war was over. Another timely contribution was a series of retreats in different areas of the country for the spiritual refreshment of the chaplains. To assist them in their personal counseling the Council sent

---

[5] PAUL D. MOODY (1879–1947), son of the famous evangelist, was a Congregational minister in St. Johnsbury, Vt., 1912–1917. After his service overseas 1917–1919, he was associate minister of Madison Avenue Presbyterian Church, New York City, 1919–1921, and president of Middlebury College, 1921–1942.

clergymen experienced in this type of ministry to the camps to give guidance to the chaplains in dealing with men who were ill or in trouble or facing moral or spiritual difficulties. More than a hundred seminars of this kind were held.

When the chaplains went overseas, contacts with them were maintained through periodic visits by national church leaders. Bishop Adna W. Leonard lost his life on one of these missions in 1943, when the army plane on which he was traveling met with a tragic accident.[6] Others who made similar visitations to different overseas areas were Bishop G. Bromley Oxnam, Bishop Henry Knox Sherrill, and William B. Pugh.[7]

A different type of visitation of the camps in this country was conducted by the National Conference of Christians and Jews. A team of three—a Protestant minister, a Roman Catholic priest, and a Jewish rabbi—went together to three hundred different centers. Their message was broadly educational, emphasizing the need for mutual understanding among all religious groups and for cooperation among them in the postwar world.

Cooperation in Defense Communities

In addition to the millions of men in the military organization there were other millions who served in wartime industrial centers. When the expanded program of national defense began, boom towns sprang up almost overnight, in which there were either no churches or churches with wholly inadequate resources for their multiplied responsibilities. Even in well-established industrial areas the sudden spurt in population intensified many community problems. Families were transplanted to unfamiliar environments, children of working mothers were uncared for, recreational facilities were meagre, delinquency grew apace. To meet such emergency conditions, the denominational agencies of home missions erected new church buildings where necessary, provided funds for day nurseries and other enterprises of child welfare, supplied

---

[6] ADNA W. LEONARD (1874–1943) was a Methodist pastor from 1898 to 1916, when he was elected a bishop. He was chairman of the General Commission on Army and Navy Chaplains, 1941–1943.

[7] G. BROMLEY OXNAM (1891–1963), Methodist minister, was founder and pastor of the Church of All Nations in Los Angeles. From 1928 to 1936 he was president of DePauw University. In 1936 he was elected a bishop. He was president of the Federal Council of Churches, 1944–1946, and co-president of the World Council of Churches, 1948–1954.

HENRY KNOX SHERRILL (1890–   ), rector of the Church of our Savior in Brookline, Mass., and of Trinity Church, Boston, was elected bishop of Massachusetts in 1930. From 1947 to 1958 he was presiding bishop of the Episcopal Church. He was president of the National Council of Churches 1950–1952, and co-president of the World Council of Churches, 1954–1961.

WILLIAM B. PUGH (1889–1950), Presbyterian pastor in Philadelphia and Chester, Pa., was elected stated clerk of the Presbyterian (U.S.A.) General Assembly in 1938 and held the office until his death in 1950.

personnel for supplementary ministries in local churches or in housing units remote from churches. All this called for careful coordination, which was effected through the Christian Commission for Camp and Defense Communities, jointly created by the Home Missions Council and the Federal Council of Churches a few months before America entered the war. Through this channel there was a pooled financing of program and personnel in seventy-four different areas.[8]

The Commission was also concerned with the ministry of the churches to men of the armed forces when at leisure in the towns adjacent to military centers. One of its early problems was the working out of mutually helpful relations between the churches and U.S.O. (United Service Organizations for National Defense), a federation of six welfare agencies providing social and recreational activities. U.S.O. represented a pioneering type of cooperation in social work by national agencies—including the Y.M.C.A., Y.W.C.A., and Catholic and Jewish organizations—each local unit of U.S.O. being assigned to one of the agencies for a unified operation in behalf of all.

At the beginning there was considerable confusion as to whether or how representatives of local churches might use the U.S.O. building for pastoral contacts with the men. The Commission on Camp and Defense Communities gave early attention to the problem, in consultation with the governing board of U.S.O. A satisfactory definition of relationships was agreed upon, which included hearty support of U.S.O. by the churches and assurance by U.S.O. that each of its units would be "a base for contacts between the churches or other groups in the community and the men in the camps."

Another concern of the Commission was the just treatment of Negroes in wartime industrial centers. It added to its staff a Negro minister, experienced in community problems, to survey local situations and try to draw white and Negro groups together in working for better conditions for Negroes and preventing discrimination in employment and housing.

Still another function of the Commission was representation of the churches in relation to governmental controls when wartime regulations affecting their work were involved. The Office of Price Administration, for example, did not at first include pastors in its definition of those eligible to purchase automobile tires under the rationing system. When, however, it was pointed out how seriously this affected their ability to carry on pastoral ministrations at a time when they were more needed than ever, clergymen were placed on the same basis as physicians and nurses. At another time a preliminary ruling of O.P.A. limited fuel oil for churches to Sundays only, but consultations soon resulted in a recognition of the value of their weekday activities.

[8] Federal Council of Churches, *Biennial Report, 1944*, pp. 48–49.

Serving Unpopular Minorities

After the decision of the government to permit conscientious objectors to military service to do "work of national importance" under non-military auspices, a National Service Board for Religious Objectors was created. The so-called "Peace Churches"—Friends, Mennonites, Brethren—carried the main burden of its support. The Federal Council of Churches, however, held a continuous consultative relationship with it, since almost every denomination had some members whose religious convictions would not permit them to bear arms.

An unpopular group whom the churches did not overlook were interned aliens and prisoners of war, German for the most part. For these men behind the barbed wire on both sides of the conflict, War Prisoners' Aid of the Y.M.C.A. undertook the chief service, but the Home Missions Council and the Federal Council set up a special committee for the more specifically religious aspects of the program in 160 base camps in this country. Three pastors from neutral Sweden were enlisted for a systematic visitation of the prisoners, providing Christian literature and supplies for worship in their native tongues.[9]

A unique service was rendered by the churches on a cooperative basis in connection with the resettlement of Japanese Americans after their internment at the beginning of the war. Under the pressure of alleged military necessity, 100,000 Americans of Japanese ancestry—citizens and non-citizens alike—were evacuated from the West Coast and confined in several large camps. The decision of the government to intern them reflected a mood of fear and distrust which proved to be unjustified. When the War Relocation Authority later began to seek permanent homes for them in other parts of the country, the churches proved to be the major resource. A Committee on Resettlement of Japanese Americans, organized jointly by the Home Missions Council and the Federal Council, appealed to local churches, Young Men's Christian Associations, and other agencies to help secure housing and employment. Interchurch committees were formed in twenty-four of the larger cities to cooperate in the project, to accept responsibility for placement, and to foster a friendly atmosphere for the newcomers. The director of the War Relocation Authority voiced public appreciation of the work of these committees, sometimes carried on in the face of considerable local prejudice.[10] After two years of intensive service the Federal Council could say to critics who had been mistrustful of Japanese Americans:

> These are law-abiding people whose character and conduct have been exemplary under trying ordeals. . . . There has not been a single person

---

[9] Federal Council of Churches, *Annual Report, 1945,* p. 87.

[10] See Toru Matsumoto, *Beyond Prejudice: A Story of the Japanese Americans* (New York: Friendship Press, 1946).

of Japanese ancestry brought to trial in any U. S. court on charges of sabotage.[11]

Seeking a World Structure for Peace

Early in 1941 a Commission on a Just and Durable Peace was created by the churches, under the sponsorship of the Federal Council, and began a vigorous program of study and adult education. It had as its chairman a distinguished layman, John Foster Dulles, who a decade later was to become Secretary of State. A lawyer with wide international reputation, grandson of one former Secretary of State and nephew of another, he combined a deep religious commitment with a specialized knowledge of political affairs. He was deeply convinced that the churches had a distinctive and basic contribution to make to international relations. His point of view was expressed in the first address he made to the Federal Council when presenting a statement on the world situation:

> A few years ago, as a result of my thirty years of experience with international problems, I came to the conclusion that there was no hope of substantial progress toward peace unless there were in the world more people who would bring to bear upon international problems the type of Christian spirit which is reflected in the statement before you. . . . I have seen conference after conference fail because the participants felt that their only task was to promote the welfare of their particular nation without regard to the general welfare.[12]

Under Mr. Dulles's leadership a group of ministers, theologians, and professors of the social sciences worked together in a way that not only had great influence in the churches but also attracted wide public attention. After a year of preliminary work, it held a national study conference at Ohio Wesleyan University, March 3–5, 1942. Four sections produced findings on "Political Aspects of a Just and Durable Peace," "Economic Aspects of a Just and Durable Peace," "Social Aspects of a Just and Durable Peace," and "The Relation of the Churches to a Just and Durable Peace." A *Statement of Guiding Principles* was framed which was later made more simple and concrete in a declaration entitled *Six Pillars of Peace*. It dealt so tersely and pointedly with the main issues that it was constantly quoted. The "six pillars" were described as follows:

1. The peace must provide the political framework for a continuing collaboration of the United Nations, and, in due course, of neutral and enemy nations.[13]

---

[11] *Federal Council Bulletin* (June, 1944).

[12] *Federal Council Bulletin* (January, 1941), p. 6.

[13] "The United Nations" here refers to the powers allied in the war against Germany and Japan.

2. The peace must make provision for bringing within the scope of international agreement those economic and financial acts of national governments which have widespread national repercussions.
3. The peace must make provision for an organization to adapt the treaty structure of the world to changing underlying conditions.
4. The peace must proclaim the goal of autonomy for subject peoples, and it must establish international organization to assure and to supervise the realization of that end.
5. The peace must establish procedures for controlling military establishments everywhere.
6. The peace must establish in principle, and seek to achieve in practice, the right of individuals everywhere to religious and intellectual liberty.[14]

A study guide was prepared for use by groups in local churches in making the Six Pillars of Peace the subject of discussion. A careful historian says that "probably no report ever received more serious consideration·among church people."[15]

Six months after the issuance of *Six Pillars of Peace*, an "International Round Table of Christian Leaders" was convened at Princeton, N.J., attended by representative churchmen from several countries, including England, New Zealand, and Australia. They concluded that the Six Pillars afforded goals toward which they could all work. A little later an American interfaith *Declaration on World Peace*, initiated by the Church Peace Union, was issued by a large body of Catholic, Protestant, and Jewish spokesmen, following the same general line as the Six Pillars. To carry the campaign of education to the grass roots, the Federal Council, with the cooperation of the other interdenominational agencies, conducted "Christian Missions on World Order" in one hundred cities in November, 1942.

Early in 1944, the Commission on a Just and Durable Peace made a public plea that the postwar international structure should not be limited to preserving any *status quo*. "A basic choice must be made," it was urged, "between international organization to perpetuate by repression the particular structure of the world which will emerge from the war, and international organization which, in addition to such use of force under law as is a requisite of order, discharges tasks that are curative and creative."[16]

The activity of the Commission reached its zenith in the months immediately preceding the San Francisco Conference for the drafting of the Charter of the United Nations. From January 16 to 19, 1945, a national study conference was held in Cleveland, Ohio, chiefly focused on

[14] Federal Council of Churches, *Annual Report, 1943*, pp. 62–63.

[15] Winthrop S. Hudson, *Religion in America* (New York: Charles Scribner's Sons, 1965), p. 388.

[16] Federal Council, *Biennial Report, 1944*, pp. 135–137.

the provisional proposals which had been put forward in the previous fall by the Dumbarton Oaks consultation of four major powers. The churchmen at Cleveland warmly supported the Dumbarton Oaks outline for the United Nations but made nine concrete suggestions for amendment. These included a plea that the Charter clearly specify that all nations would be eligible for membership, that more adequate provision should be made for the protection of small nations, and that there should be greater stress on "human rights and fundamental freedom." The Sunday before the San Francisco Conference opened was designated as a Day of Prayer for its success.

During the San Francisco Conference, which convened on April 25, 1945, Walter W. Van Kirk served as a consultant to the American delegation, with Bishop Baker and O. Frederick Nolde as associate consultants.[17] They were in frequent touch with members of the delegation. Secretary of State Stettinius publicly acknowledged the debt of the emerging United Nations to the interest and activity of the consultants.[18]

Cooperation in Compassion

As the suffering caused by the war became greater and greater, the simple clearing house known as the Committee on Foreign Relief Appeals in the Churches, which had been functioning since 1939, was far from adequate. Toward the end of 1942, as the result of joint action by the Foreign Missions Conference and the Federal Council, it was succeeded by the Church Committee on Overseas Relief and Reconstruction. This furthered the work of nine church-related organizations, each with a defined area of concern, coordinating their appeals and representing them in their relations with governmental agencies. Among the projects which the nine organizations served were the following:

1. Help for struggling Christian institutions in Europe, through the Central Bureau of Interchurch Aid.[19] Initiated by the collaboration of the Federal Council and the Swiss Federation of Churches after the

---

[17] WALTER W. VAN KIRK (1891–1956), Methodist minister, was secretary of Federal Council's Department of International Justice and Goodwill, 1925–1950, and director of the Commission on a Just and Durable Peace throughout its existence. From 1950 until 1956 he was the executive of the National Council of Churches for International Affairs.

[17] JAMES C. BAKER (1879–   ), pastor of Trinity Church (Methodist), Urbana, Ill., 1907–1928, and organizer of Wesley Foundation at University of Illinois, was elected a bishop in 1928. He was chairman of the International Missionary Council, 1941–1947.

O. FREDERICK NOLDE (1899–   ), United Lutheran clergyman, became professor of religious education in the Lutheran Theological Seminary in Philadelphia in 1931 and dean of the graduate school, 1943–1962. After the creation of the World Council's Commission of the Churches on International Affairs in 1946, he was its executive director.

[18] *Federal Council Bulletin* (June, 1945).

[19] The original name was Central Bureau for the Relief of the Evangelical Churches of Europe. In 1945 its work was taken over by the Department of Reconstruction and Relief of the World Council of Churches' Provisional Committee.

First World War, the Bureau pioneered in relief in Europe and carried on a program of increasing ecumenical significance.

2. Resettlement of refugees, through the American Christian Committee for Refugees.[20] This found new homes for thousands who were forced by political circumstances to leave their native lands. It secured American sponsors for them chiefly through local councils of churches and councils of church women, raised funds for transportation, and supported legislation for the admission of refugees beyond the regular immigration quotas.

3. Aid for Chinese suffering from floods and famine or driven from their homes by the Sino-Japanese conflict. For this task the Church Committee for China Relief was responsible, with strong support from cooperating boards of foreign missions.[21]

4. Orphaned missions, deprived of their normal support from European churches by the vicissitudes of war. Foreign missions of German, French, Danish, Finnish, Norwegian, Dutch, and Belgian societies, which had been contributing about $4 million annually, were cut off from their former sources of aid. The International Missionary Council assumed the heavy burden of enabling these missions to carry on. More than $8 million were raised for this purpose, most of which came from the United States. The achievement took on special ecumenical meaning because the largest group of missionaries thus aided were connected with a country with which the United States was at war.[22]

But new needs kept appearing that no existing agency was prepared to meet. Something more than coordination of current appeals was called for. When, in August, 1944, the United Nations Relief and Rehabilitation Administration asked whether the churches could make a collection of clothing for the destitute in Europe, the Church Committee on Overseas Relief and Reconstruction itself undertook the task of securing the Protestant share. The response brought more than the suggested quota. In the following year the Committee embarked, somewhat experimentally, on a material aid program of its own, in reply to an urgent appeal from the World Council's Provisional Committee for clothing and bedding for war-devastated people. The Church of the Brethren, already deeply involved in an overseas ministry, put its ware-

---

[20] The original name was American Committee for Christian Refugees. It was changed in order to make it clear that it had a concern for all refugees, although by agreement with the Jewish agencies it concentrated on those who were non-Jewish or of mixed Jewish-Christian background.

[21] In 1944 the Church Committee for China Relief was expanded into the Church Committee for Relief in Asia.

[22] For a full account of the orphaned missions during the war see Kenneth S. Latourette and W. Richey Hogg, *World Christian Community in Action* (New York: International Missionary Council, 1949). Also W. Richey Hogg, *Ecumenical Foundations* (New York: Harper & Brothers, 1952), pp. 304–318.

houses in New Windsor, Md., and Modesto, Calif., at the service of the Committee. This new effort in material aid was soon to result in transforming what had been a coordinating committee into the central agency of unified administration known as Church World Service.

In the fall of 1941, while the United States was still a neutral in the war, the Federal Council of Churches decided that in the interest of maintaining contact with the churches of Europe it should send a representative to Geneva for as wide a consultation as possible. It fell to me to undertake the mission and I was scheduled to depart on December 9. Two days earlier came the attack on Pearl Harbor, immediately followed by the American participation in the war. The plan for a consultation in Geneva had to be postponed, but was taken up again a few months later. In September, 1942, a roundabout journey by way of Portugal, Spain, and the unoccupied part of France took me to Geneva. The little staff at the first headquarters of the World Council included a Dutchman (W. A. Visser 't Hooft), a German (Hans Schönfeld), and a Swede (Nils Ehrenstrom). In informal and unofficial ways, sometimes involving underground connections and the smuggling of messages across national boundaries, these ecumenical spirits were managing to keep some lines of communication open.[23] Switzerland was the one place in Europe where a measure of coming and going was possible for persons on both sides of the conflict. Dietrich Bonhoeffer, for example, before his imprisonment by the Nazis, was able to report to ecumenical friends in Geneva about developments in both church and state in Germany.

During our discussions in Geneva in the early fall of 1942 a memorandum was drafted setting forth the prospective need for postwar reconstruction and relief in Europe. This statement, which I brought back to America only a fortnight before the Nazi occupation of Southern France made further personal contacts with Geneva impossible for the next two years, forecast an organization of interchurch aid within the World Council and made it clear that the major responsibility for its support would fall upon the American churches.

In November, 1944, when the end of the war seemed not far away, A. Livingston Warnshuis was commissioned by the Church Committee on Overseas Relief and Reconstruction to explore the extent of postwar needs in Europe and ways in which the American churches should help.[24] In spite of the hazards of wartime travel, he visited London, Paris, and Geneva, for consultations with church leaders in each center. On

---

[23] See Rouse and Neill, *op. cit.*, pp. 709–711.

[24] A. LIVINGSTON WARNSHUIS (1877–1959), minister of the Reformed Church in America, was a missionary in China, 1900–1920. For the next twenty-two years he was one of the secretaries of the International Missionary Council. After his retirement, he was executive vice-president of Church World Service, 1946–1948. See Norman Goodall, *Christian Ambassador: A Life of A. Livingston Warnshuis* (New York: Channel Press, 1963).

his return he devoted his energies to forming an organization that would be adequate for the task ahead. Thus Church World Service began to take shape and was officially constituted in May, 1946, inheriting both the experience and the responsibilities of the earlier relief agencies.

The first American minister to volunteer for postwar service to the European churches under the plan that was being developed by the Provisional Committee of the World Council was a martyr to the cause, Theodore C. Hume. Appointed as a representative of the Congregational Churches, he was eager to get an early start in familiarizing himself with conditions in Europe without waiting for the war to end. On October 22, 1943, he lost his life when the neutral plane in which he was flying to neutral Sweden was shot down by a Nazi bomber.

Another dramatic incident, this time in connection with the Japanese, illustrated the alertness of the American churches to the first opportunity for postwar contacts with Christians in enemy countries. A delegation of four American churchmen—James C. Baker, Douglas Horton, Luman J. Shafer, and Walter W. Van Kirk—flew to Tokyo on October 12, 1945, to begin the process of reconciliation and renewed cooperation.[25] This was the first civilian group to go to Japan after the war for any purpose.

Unitive and Divisive Trends

While these developments were expanding the relations of the American churches around the world, wartime needs were contributing to an enlarging cooperation among themselves. In 1940 the Episcopal Church became a full-fledged member of the Federal Council. In 1944 the Southern Presbyterian Church voted to return to membership after an absence of a decade. In the same year the Church of the Brethren, although its pacifist position had tended to keep it somewhat separate in the past, joined the Council. In 1945 the Czech Moravian Brethren of North America applied for membership.

The spirit of unity was strengthened not only by the challenge of wartime responsibilities but also by the stimulus of wartime experience to reflection of more than usual spiritual depth. The Federal Council's report on "The State of the Church" at its biennial meeting in 1942 called attention to "a fresh interest in the sources of the Christian faith, in the Bible, and in the Christian tradition." It also noted "a definite re-

---

25 DOUGLAS HORTON (1891–   ) was pastor of Leyden Congregational Church, Brookline, Mass., and Hyde Park United Church, Chicago, 1925–1938; minister of General Council of Congregational Christian Churches, 1938–1955; dean of Harvard Divinity School, 1955–1959.

LUMAN J. SHAFER (1887–1958) was a missionary in Japan, 1912–1935, and secretary of the Board of Foreign Missions of the Reformed Church in America, 1935–1943. He was associate secretary of the Commission on a Just and Durable Peace, 1943–1945.

turn to theology and a marked turning toward worship as the center of the life of the church."[26] At the biennial meeting two years later the keynote message had a unifying evangelistic quality. After pointing to postwar social and international tasks, it said:

> Even if some Utopia were ushered in tomorrow, as a result of marvelous social engineering, it would be wrecked within a week if administered by men who are still narrowly self-seeking, still obsessed with materialistic standards of success, still cherishing a false pride in their own accomplishments, still lustful of power over others. . . . Repentance, conversion, and spiritual renewal are still the most indispensable words.[27]

There were decisive and disruptive influences also. In the Presbyterian Church in the U.S.A. the fundamentalist attack on Princeton Theological Seminary and the Board of Foreign Missions had led the General Assembly in 1936 to dismiss Carl McIntire from its ministry on grounds of "disapproval, defiance, and acts in contravention of the government and discipline" of the Church. With some of the most extreme and polemical fundamentalists, he organized in 1941 a small interdenominational group called the American Council of Christian Churches. He then launched a continuous barrage not only against the Presbyterian Church but also against other main-line denominations and their agencies of cooperation. Not succeeding in winning any significant support as a defender of Christianity against alleged "apostasy," he turned his guns on alleged "communism" in the churches, claiming that there was a subversive hand in their efforts in behalf of social welfare and world peace. By capitalizing on ignorance, prejudice, and fear, his organization became a fertile source of misunderstanding and discord.[28]

Another organization for common witness and action among theological conservatives, but different in temper from the combative and denunciatory American Council of Christian Churches, was formed in 1942—the National Association of Evangelicals. It was designed as a rallying center for Protestants who in varying degrees were unsympathetic with the ecumenical movement. The Association is not officially a council of denominations, since it includes in its membershp local congregations and associations concerned to defend doctrinal orthodoxy. Its purpose, as defined at the beginning, is "to represent all evangelical believers in all denominations and groups." Eligibility for membership is based on agreement with such specified points as the infallibility of Scripture, the Trinity, the virgin birth of Christ, His personal return to

---

[26] *Biennial Report, 1942,* p. 7.

[27] *Biennial Report, 1944,* pp. 18–19.

[28] See Ralph L. Roy, *Apostles of Discord* (Boston: Beacon Press, 1953), Chapters VIII, IX, X. Also his *Communism and the Churches* (New York: Harcourt, Brace & Co., 1960), pp. 228–234.

earth, regeneration by the Holy Spirit, and the resurrection of both the saved and the lost.[29]

The National Association of Evangelicals has maintained a critical attitude toward the interdenominational structures of main-stream Protestantism and has stimulated the establishment of parallel agencies such as the Evangelical Foreign Missions Association and the National Association of Christian Schools. The contrast which the N.A.E. has drawn between "evangelical" and "ecumenical," however, has tended to be confusing. There are many in the "evangelical" organizations who are truly "ecumenical" and the denominations of the National Council insist on their truly "evangelical" position. The only denomination which withdrew from the Federal Council during the period when the National Association of Evangelicals was getting under way was the small Reformed Episcopal Church, which in 1945 voted "to sever official relations . . . with fraternal greetings."

In the main stream of cooperative Protestantism the drawing together of the various interdenominational agencies moved gradually forward. At the local and state levels there were increasing instances of councils of churches and councils of religious education reorganizing their structures in some unified pattern. This trend reached a new stage in 1941 when the executives of both types of councils met together for the first time at Lake Geneva, Wis., as "The Association of Council Secretaries."[30] In some places a council of religious education or a home missions council expanded into a council of churches. In other places an existing council of religious education and a council of churches merged into an inclusive council responsible for all common tasks in the area. In 1945, however, there were still eleven states which had no council of churches, no council of religious education, no home missions council.[31]

The importance of cooperative survey and research in local situations was also receiving more recognition and a new method of providing a technical leadership for this type of service was tried. Denominational boards of home missions loaned members of their own staffs, the Federal Council provided general direction, and the communities which were surveyed covered expenses on the field. Five denominational boards

---

[29] See J. Marcellus Kik, *Ecumenism and the Evangelical* (Philadelphia: Presbyterian and Reformed Publishing Society, 1957); also James De Forest Murch, *Christianity Without Compromise* (Grand Rapids, Mich.: Wm. B. Eerdmans Publ. Co., 1956).

[30] The Association of Council Secretaries combined in a single professional group the Association of Executive Secretaries of Councils and Federations of Churches, dating from 1916, and the Employed Council Officers Association, made up of directors of Councils of Religious Education (or Sunday School Councils), which also had its origin in 1916.

[31] For statistics of local and state organizations for cooperation at this time, see Federal Council, *Biennial Report, 1945*, pp. 57–58.

(Northern Baptist, Congregational Christian, Episcopal, Methodist, Presbyterian, U.S.A.) participated in this arrangement beginning in 1945. There was sufficient pooling of financial resources to complete field studies of changing needs in ten areas in the first year and to begin studies in additional areas. The project was further significant as illustrative of the way in which the national interdenominational agencies were becoming increasingly involved in common projects, for the Committee on Cooperative Field Research was a joint enterprise of the Home Missions Council, the Federal Council, and the International Council of Religious Education.

At the national level the new trend toward merging the agencies of cooperation was gaining momentum and visibility. On December 9–11, 1941, there was a study conference at Atlantic City, N. J. on "the closer relationships of general interdenominational agencies," which recommended the creation of a single corporate structure combining the interests and functions of the Federal Council of Churches, the International Council of Religious Education, the Home Missions Council, the Foreign Missions Conference, the Missionary Education Movement, the Council of Church Boards of Education, the United Stewardship Council, and the United Council of Church Women.[32] A committee to continue the process of study and negotiation was formed, with Dean Luther A. Weigle as chairman and Hermann N. Morse as secretary.[33]

In the following year these eight agencies held meetings in the same week, December 9–11, 1942, in the same city (Cleveland, Ohio), with provision for several joint sessions and seminars. This gave a pronounced forward thrust to the movement of integration. Eight years would still be needed for completing it, since it involved official ratification not only by each of the interdenominational agencies but also by the denominational constituents of each.

A noteworthy feature of the Cleveland meetings was the common concern for religious liberty. This interest was stimulated in part by what was happening in totalitarian régimes and in part by reports that seemed to presage more restriction on missionary freedom in Latin American countries. A forthright affirmation and interpretation of religious liberty was issued, which attracted nationwide attention. A Joint Committee on Religious Liberty was established by the Federal Council

---

[32] The United Council of Church Women was organized in the same week in 1941 following an agreement between the National Council of Church Women and the women of the interdenominational mission agencies, for the purpose of providing leadership for church women in all their interests.

[33] HERMANN N. MORSE (1887–   ), an executive of the Presbyterian (U.S.A.) Board of Home Missions, 1914–1949, general secretary, 1949–1959; president of the Home Missions Council, 1945–1947; moderator of the Presbyterian General Assembly, 1952.

and the Foreign Missions Conference. Two years later it published a major book on the subject, surveying all parts of the world. Entitled *Religious Liberty: An Inquiry*, it proved to be a standard reference work and was translated into French, German, Italian, Spanish, Japanese, and Chinese.[34]

---

[34] M. Searle Bates, *Religious Liberty: An Inquiry* (New York: International Missionary Council and Harper & Brothers, 1945).

11

Postwar Ecumenical Advance

(1946–1950)

$\mathbf{F}$OR a few years after the Second World War there was something like a religious revival in the United States. Church membership increased substantially. In 1940, 49 per cent of the population had been members of a church; a decade later the figure was 57 per cent.[1] Contributions to the churches were mounting. A comparative study of fifteen major denominations showed an increase from $351 million in 1941 to more than a billion in 1952.[2] Unprecedented amounts of money were available for new church edifices. There was a conspicuous, though superficial, "surge of piety." Popularized versions of religious faith became best-sellers—like Rabbi Joshua L. Liebman's *Peace of Mind* (1946), Monsignor Fulton J. Sheen's *Peace of Soul* (1949), and Norman Vincent Peale's *The Power of Positive Thinking* (1952). "Youth for Christ" held Saturday night evangelistic rallies which drew considerable crowds. Prayer breakfasts in the national capital were attended by the highest public officials. The American Legion launched a "Back to God" movement which sanctified religious patriotism as contrasted with atheistic communism. An interfaith program called "Religion in American Life" was launched, with the cooperation of the Advertising Council of America, as an effort to capture nationwide attention by the use of newspapers, magazines, billboards, and radio in an annual campaign.

There were also more solid evidences of religious concern. Theological thinking manifested a renewed vitality in revived emphases on the transcendence of God, the authority of Biblical revelation, the centrality of Christ, and the mission of the church. The pastoral ministry received new attention and laid hold of modern psychological insights for personal counseling. There was a fresh vigor in Christian witness and

---

[1] See successive editions of *The Yearbook of American Churches,* ed. Benson Y. Landis (New York: National Council of Churches), especially the editions of 1952, pp. 234–267, and 1956, p. 236.

[2] *Ibid.,* edition of 1953.

action in social and international affairs, illustrated by ardent, but discriminating, support of the United Nations. The ecumenical movement was gaining strength, finding organizational expression in both the National Council and the World Council of Churches.

Still another indication of religious revival was the amazingly wide and favorable acceptance of the Revised Standard Version of the New Testament, which was published on February 11, 1946. In 1928 the International Council of Religious Education had acquired the copy-. right of the American Standard Version of the Bible and had appointed a committee of scholars to examine the question whether another revision was called for. After long discussion it had been decided that there was need for a thorough revision which would "embody the best results of modern scholarship as to the meaning of the Scriptures and express this meaning in English diction which is designed for use in public and private worship and preserves those qualities which have given to the King James Version a supreme place in English literature." Thirty-four distinguished Biblical scholars collaborated in the subsequent work, Luther A. Weigle serving as chairman and Roy G. Ross as secretary of the group.[3]

Racial and International Concerns

As a contribution to rallying the Christian forces for postwar responsibilities, the Federal Council met in a special session in Columbus, Ohio, March 5–7, 1946, to deal with new needs, "especially in the area of evangelism, world order, community tensions, foreign relief, and returning service personnel." One feature of the meeting marked it as clearly moving beyond previous commitments. This was an unqualified repudiation of racial segregation, on the ground that it "has always meant inferior service to the minority," is "always discriminatory," and subjects millions of people to "constant humiliation." The sharpest criticism was directed to the churches and church institutions for having so largely accepted segregation in their own life and practice. The heart of the declaration was this paragraph:

> The Federal Council of the Churches of Christ in America hereby renounces the pattern of segregation as unnecessary and undesirable and a violation of the Gospel of love and human brotherhood. Having taken this action, the Federal Council requests its constituent communions to do likewise. As proof of their sincerity in this renunciation they will work for a non-segregated church and a non-segregated society.[4]

---

[3] Roy G. Ross (1898–   ), minister of the Disciples of Christ; pastor in Carrollton, Ill., North Cornwall, Conn., and Milwaukee, Wis., 1920–1925; director of Young People's Work, 1926–1928, and executive secretary, 1928–1936, of the United Christian Missionary Society; general secretary, International Council of Religious Education, 1936–1950; associate general secretary, 1950–1953; general secretary, 1954–1963, of the National Council of Churches.

[4] For the full text, see *Biennial Report, 1946*, pp. 119–126.

The request to the denominations to take supporting action met with a prompt response. Within the next few months the General Council of the Congregational Christian Churches, the General Assembly of the Presbyterian Church in the U.S.A., the International Convention of the Disciples of Christ, and the Northern Baptist Convention made similar pronouncements, soon to be followed by still others.

A new procedure in translating opposition to segregation into concrete action came in 1949 when the Federal Council filed an *amicus curiae* brief with the Supreme Court of the United States in support of the petition of a Negro, Herman M. Sweatt, for a review of the case in which he had been denied admission to the University of Texas. This was the first time when cooperating churches had ever presented a brief to the Court.[5]

The international situation in the postwar years, dominated by a rising tension between the Soviet Union and the United States, was one which was less than war but also less than peace. In this crisis, the Commission on a Just and Durable Peace issued an analysis of Soviet-American relations, which received more than usual attention. There was a realistic recognition of the underlying conflicts between Marxist communism and Christianity, and it was forthrightly affirmed that "such differences will never be removed by compromise or surrender of faith by Christians." At the same time it was urged that "a new way of international accommodation" must be found which "will reckon with fundamental differences in outlook and practice." The conclusion emphasized the importance of "cooperation of the American and the Russian people at the scientific, economic, cultural and religious levels."[6]

The newly formed United Nations was an object of sustained concern in the churches. The Federal Council was represented by "accredited observers" at the Assembly, the Security Council, the Economic and Social Council, and the Commission on Human Rights. There was also a pronounced interest in aid to peoples suffering from war's aftermath. This took two major forms. One was a well-organized support for the European Recovery Program of the American government, illustrated by a public convocation in the Washington Cathedral, with President Truman and a group of members of Congress in attendance and with the Secretary of State, George C. Marshall, as one of the speakers. The other main thrust in foreign aid was assistance to refugees and displaced persons who were victims of totalitarian régimes. An appeal to Congress to enact special legislation to permit the United States to admit its "fair share" of them was followed by a long, continued program of resettlement by Church World Service. There were several years in which the average rate was a thousand resettlements a month.

---

[5] The text of the brief is given in the *Annual Report* of the Council for 1949, pp. 151–157.

[6] *Biennial Report, 1946,* pp. 240–249.

This was only one phase of the work of Church World Service. In the first three years of its operation (1946-1949) it sent funds and supplies to the extent of $40 million to forty countries.[7]

A project in which the foreign missionary agencies were especially involved was the founding of the International Christian University in Japan. This was stimulated in part by stirrings of conscience over the dropping of atomic bombs on Hiroshima and Nagasaki and in part by a realization of the strategic place that Japan could be expected to have in the future of Asia. At the first meeting of the Federal Council after the war, a proposal for the university was endorsed and steps taken which led to the establishment of a foundation for its support. By the end of 1949 the first $1 million had been contributed by American missionary boards and an interested group of Japanese had acquired a site for the University in a suburb of Tokyo. Four years later it conferred its first degree.[8]

The dropping of the atomic bombs on Japan in the last days of the war had raised an ethical problem which caused soul-searching among thoughtful leaders in the American Churches and raised the old issue of the Christian attitude toward war in a new form. In 1944 a group of scholars and theologians appointed by the Federal Council and headed by Professor Robert L. Calhoun of Yale University, made an extended report on "The relation of the Church to the war in the light of the Christian faith."[9] Issued several months before the attack on Hiroshima, it raised the question whether "total war," such as nuclear war would doubtless be, could ever be a "just war." The Commission concluded that "the church cannot acquiesce in the supremacy of military considerations even in war time, nor in the view that modern war may properly, even in the case of extreme peril to nation, church, or culture, become total war." They insisted that the United States should "under no circumstances be the first to use atomic weapons," but they were divided over the issue whether there might ever be circumstances in which their use would be justifiable. The most significant part of the report, however, was its penetrating analysis of the theological foundations on the basis of which the attitude of the churches should be determined.

At its postwar meeting in March, 1946, the Federal Council appealed to our nation, as the one which had first used the atomic bomb, to assume "a primary duty to reverse the trend which it began." Later, after

---

[7] See report in *Federal Council Bulletin* (February, 1949).

[8] An event which contributed in a popular way to ecumenical education at this time was an extended visit of Martin Niemöller, the outstanding symbol of Christian resistance to political totalitarianism. During three and a half months in the winter of 1946–1947 he spoke to overflowing audiences in seventy American cities.

[9] The theological section of the report is printed in J. H. Leith, editor, *Creeds of the Churches* (Chicago: Aldine Publ. Co., 1963), as a significant example of the "application of Christian faith to a specific situation in such a way as to illuminate and interpret it."

the development of atomic weapons by Russia had intensified the danger of catastrophe, the Council appointed a new study group of twenty leaders in Christian thought, headed by Bishop Angus Dun, to report on "The Christian conscience and weapons of mass destruction."[10] Like its predecessor, this group, although agreeing in its analysis of issues, was not unanimous at the point whether circumstances might arise—for example, an attack by a ruthless aggressor—which would warrant the use of atomic weapons and the building up of a stockpile against the possibility of such a crisis.[11]

New Areas of Cooperation

Several new fields of cooperation were entered in the early postwar years. In 1946 a Department of Pastoral Services was created, an expansion of the earlier Commission on Religion and Health, with a special interest in affording guidance in counseling both in parishes and in hospitals and other institutions. Its first concrete undertaking was a pioneering study of "Religious Ministry to Older People," based on extensive research into what the churches were doing and should do to provide a more adequate service to the elderly.[12]

Although a radio ministry had been an important field of the Federal Council's activity since 1929, the program had been centered primarily on messages of a sermonic or devotional type over national networks. The question was now being raised whether there ought not to be more originality in presenting programs that would appeal to diverse types of listeners. A desire was also arising in local councils of churches for guidance in establishing a radio ministry of their own. To meet these widening interests the Protestant Radio Commission was formed in 1948—an independent body representing several major denominations, national interdenominational agencies, and local councils of churches. Its field of concern included the network broadcasts already well established, the production of more specialized programs, experimenting with the new instrument of television, and holding of regional workshops on religious broadcasting.

New ground was broken in another field by the first National Conference on the Church and Economic Life, held in Pittsburgh, Pa., February 18–20, 1947. In contrast with most interdenominational gatherings, a majority of the delegates were laymen of experience in

---

[10] ANGUS DUN (1892–), Episcopal theologian and bishop, rector at Ayer, Mass., 1917–1918; associate secretary of Committee on the War and the Religious Outlook, 1919–1920, faculty member of Episcopal Theological School, 1920–1940, and dean, 1940–1944; elected bishop of Washington in 1944.

[11] *The Christian Conscience and Weapons of Mass Destruction* (New York: Federal Council of Churches, 1950).

[12] The results were published in J. Lennart Cedarleaf and Paul B. Maves, *Religious Ministry to Older People* (New York: Abingdon-Cokesbury, 1949).

business, industry, agriculture, and the professions. As was expected, the views of delegates were often far apart, but a report was produced which provided a sound base for further fruitful discussion in local or regional conferences of a similar type. A few months later the Federal Council established a permanent Commission on the Church and Economic Life, under the chairmanship of Charles P. Taft and the direction of Cameron P. Hall.[13] In 1949 the importance of its educational work was recognized by a grant of $100,000 from the Rockefeller Foundation for a long-term study of the ethical aspects of economic life. Before its work was completed, fifteen years later, it had published ten weighty volumes, including *Social Responsibilities of the Business Man, Social Responsibilities of Organized Labor,* and *Social Responsibilities in Farm Leadership.*[14]

A growing sense of need for cooperation in keeping in touch with developments in governmental circles led the General Council of the Presbyterian Church in the U.S.A. in 1944 to propose an interdenominational office in Washington to keep church administrators regularly and promptly informed on pending legislation and directives of Washington bureaus affecting their work. Several denominational boards agreed to make additional appropriations for this purpose. Accordingly, "the Washington Office of the Federal Council and Cooperating Bodies" was opened on October 1, 1945, under the direction of Benson Y. Landis.[15] A "Washington Memorandum" was inaugurated to provide weekly reports on a wide range of concerns, such as education, health, housing, social security, labor, agriculture, civil rights, child welfare, immigration, foreign aid, and international relations. Since 1947 the office has been housed in the Chaplains' Memorial Building, near the Capitol, which was acquired in that year as a headquarters for the General Commission on Army and Navy Chaplains.

There was occasional questioning whether this expansion of cooperative programs was altogether wise. Some friendly critics wondered whether it did not reflect too much of the same bureaucratic tendency

---

[13] CHARLES P. TAFT (1897–   ), Episcopal layman, lawyer, director of U.S. Community War Services, 1941–1943, and of Wartime Economic Affairs, U.S. Department of State, 1944; mayor of Cincinnati, 1955–1957; president of Federal Council of Churches, 1947–1948.

CAMERON P. HALL (1898–   ), Presbyterian minister, pastor of Christ Church, New York, and University Church, Madison, Wis., 1926–1939; secretary, Presbyterian Board of Christian Education, 1939–1946, and International Council of Religious Education, 1943–1946; executive secretary of Department of Church and Economic Life in the Federal Council and The National Council, 1946–1966.

[14] Published by Harper & Brothers, New York, at intervals between 1952 and 1965.

[15] BENSON Y. LANDIS (1897–1966), Moravian layman, trained in the social sciences, especially in rural sociology, in 1923 became associate secretary of the Federal Council's Department of Research and Education and continued to serve it and the National Council for forty-three years. He was the leading Protestant authority on religious statistics and edited sixteen successive editions of *The Yearbook of American Churches.*

which was becoming more and more characteristic of the secular world. But the new services that were being undertaken were clearly designed to meet needs of which forward-looking spirits in all denominations were aware, and often were supported just because they were pathfinders in new fields.

That ecumenical interest was widening was evidenced by six new applications for membership in the Federal Council at its biennial meeting in 1946. Since most of them were from very small bodies, the question arose whether there was a minimal strength that a denomination should have acquired in order to qualify for membership in the national federation. It was decided that a minimum of 5,000 communicants should be a normal criterion. In the case of the largest of the applicants, the Universalist Church, a different question was involved: would its membership in the Federal Council weaken the collective witness of the Council to Jesus Christ as "Divine Lord and Saviour"? By a divided vote, the application of the Universalists failed to receive the approval of two-thirds of the denominational delegations, as required by the constitution of the Council.

Anti-Ecumenical Reactions

While the ecumenical movement was gaining support, it was also meeting open opposition. This came partly from circles of extreme fundamentalism in theology, partly from circles of extreme conservatism in social and political outlook. The two groups tended to make common cause. Carl McIntire's *Christian Beacon*, Gerald B. Winrod's *Defender*, and Verne Kaub's output under the aegis of a so-called "American Council of Christian Laymen," constantly alleged the Federal Council was "pro-Communist." By playing on the fear of social change, and especially of "red infiltration" into the churches, these publications—together with various others that joined in the anvil chorus—created a considerable suspicion of and resistance to progressive leadership in both the larger denominations and their agencies of cooperation.[16]

The most serious attack at this time was in a book entitled *The Road Ahead,* by John T. Flynn, which appeared in 1949 and was reported to have a circulation of a million copies. It was primarily a political tract, directed against everything that savored of socialism, but one chapter was a slashing assault upon the Protestant churches for their support of the Federal Council. The Council, it was charged, was being used to "promote a social revolution." Among those singled out for special mention as having "seized upon the machinery of the churches" for this purpose were Bishop G. Bromley Oxnam and missionary E. Stanley Jones.[17]

---

[16] For a detailed and documented account of the attacks upon the leadership of the churches from the extreme right wing, see Ralph Lord Roy, *op. cit.*

[17] *The Road Ahead* (Chicago: Devin-Adair, 1949), p. 113.

Typical of the kind of misrepresentation which was involved was the condemnation of Bishop Oxnam for having been a sponsor of Soviet-American friendship rallies. What was carefully omitted was the fact that these rallies took place during the war, when America and Russia were Allies and when the highest government officials were similarly identified with Soviet-American collaboration.

Mr. Flynn's description of the Federal Council as "standing for State Socialism and tending toward Communism" was unqualifiedly disavowed by the whole group of denominational representatives in its executive committee. More important in public influence was a statement signed by fifty distinguished laymen in business, industry, and the professions, headed by John Foster Dulles, who declared, on the basis of their personal association with the Council, that the charges of socialism and pro-communism were "baseless." They concluded:

> We record our full confidence that the Federal Council functions with complete fidelity to Christian ideals. . . . We express our conviction that by providing the churches with a means of unified expression and action, it is performing an indispensable task.[18]

A Proposal for Union

In spite of the chilly blasts from quarters of theological and social conservatism, the ecumenical temperature continued to rise. It was felt not only in the strengthening of the agencies of cooperation but also in a quest for union. In June, 1946, the General Council of Congregational Christian Churches and the International Convention of the Disciples of Christ both proposed that the Federal Council convene "a plenary session of representatives of American churches to consider the possibility of closer unity" among communions already "in sufficient accord in essentials of Christian faith and order" to afford hope that union could be achieved.[19] The clear intent was to initiate a movement for organic union of churches which were not separated by serious differences over the ministry and the sacraments. The Federal Council responded by sending a communication to all its member denominations, inquiring whether they desired to participate in such a conference as had been proposed. The replies indicated that less than half of them were interested in doing so. It was accordingly decided that the conference ought to be developed as a project of the interested churches rather than of the Federal Council, although the Council might properly give assistance to any group of member churches desiring it.

On December 14–16, 1949, official representatives of seven denominations met at Seabury House in Greenwich, Conn., and organized them-

---

18 For the full text, see *Federal Council Bulletin* (March, 1950).
19 *Yearbook of Disciples of Christ, 1946*, pp. 19–20.

selves as an independent group, with consultants appointed by the Federal Council, the Home Missions Council, and the International Council of Religious Education. The seven were the Congregational Christian Churches, the Disciples of Christ, the Evangelical and Reformed Church, the Methodist Church, the Colored Methodist Episcopal Church, the African Methodist Episcopal Zion Church, and the Presbyterian Church in the U.S.A. Bishop Ivan Lee Holt was elected chairman of a continuing organization known as the American Conference on Church Union. Subsequent discussions were carried on from time to time, resulting in a preliminary sketch of a plan of union.

Since their differences in doctrine and sacramental practice were not serious, the crucial problem was to devise a polity that would be acceptable to churches of three types—episcopal, presbyterian, congregational. The structure proposed left the local church free to determine its mode of worship and to conduct baptism and the Lord's Supper according to its own tradition. At the presbytery or conference level there would be an administrator exercising the functions of a bishop. At a regional level there would be a synod, perhaps a dozen of them in the whole country. At the national level there would be a Council, which would be constituted as a federal structure of the regional synods. Within this new order the denominations might continue for a time but with the expectation that they would soon fade away.

Although the preliminary sketch of the plan was redrafted in 1953 and again in 1958, it never reached a stage of sufficient definition to be submitted to the denominations for their official consideration. The interest in both the World Council of Churches, which had recently been formed, and in the National Council, which was on the immediate horizon, was becoming so strong that the "Greenwich Plan," admittedly rather vague, was overshadowed.[20]

American Cooperation in Postwar Europe

Three days before the end of the war in Europe, three officials of the World Council's Provisional Committee—George K. A. Bell, Anglican Bishop of Chichester, Pastor Marc Boegner, president of the French Protestant Federation, and W. A. Visser 't Hooft, general secretary of the Provisional Committee—arrived in New York to confer with denominational officials about American participation in postwar reconstruction in Europe. Several denominations were already committed to such a program, and developed their plans in close coordination with the World Council's recently organized Department of Reconstruction and Interchurch Aid. Within a few weeks the National Lutheran Coun-

---

[20] Although the project of uniting seven denominations was too ambitious to succeed, unions within narrower limits occurred from time to time, fourteen of them in the first half of the twentieth century.

cil, the Presbyterian Church in the U.S.A., the Evangelical and Reformed Church, the Methodist Church, the Congregational Christians,
the Northern Baptists, and the Church of the Brethren all sent representatives to Europe, most of whom had offices at the headquarters of
the World Council and all of whom worked with it in warm accord.
Stewart W. Herman, an American Lutheran who had served as pastor
of the American Church in Berlin, became a member of the Council's
staff for Interchurch Aid. In the United States a Commission for World
Council Services, under the direction of Robbins W. Barstow, was
formed to further the securing of resources.[21]

While the representatives of the World Council's Provisional Committee were in America in the spring of 1945, they requested the Federal
Council to release its general secretary for six months' service in Geneva
in helping to complete the organization of the World Council in antici-
pation of its first assembly. The release was granted and I left for
Geneva at the begining of September. One of the early developments in
which it was my privilege to share was the initial reconciliation between
leaders of churches that had been on opposite sides of the battle line. On
October 18–19, 1945, the newly constituted Council of the Evangelical
Church of Germany was scheduled to hold its first session in Stuttgart.
An ecumenical delegation which included two Americans—Sylvester
C. Michelfelder, executive secretary of the Lutheran World Federation,
and myself—went to Stuttgart in the hope of working out arrangements for cooperation with the German Church. The delegation was
burdened with anxiety over the tension that might be expected between
them and the German churchmen. The tension disappeared at the very
first confrontation when the Germans, led by Pastor Martin Niemöller
and Bishop Otto Dibelius, voiced their penitence over what their nation
had done and over the failure of the church at large to present a stronger
resistance to Nazism.[22]

A few weeks later a deputation of three American churchmen—
Bishop G. Bromley Oxnam (Methodist), Bishop Henry Knox Sherrill
(Episcopal), and Franklin Clark Fry (Lutheran) made a survey tour
of Germany, looking into the needs of churches and people.[23] They
recommended that the American churches designate a representative to
work with the German churches during the years of reconstruction.

---

[21] ROBBINS W. BARSTOW (1890–1962), Congregational pastor in Woodstock, Vt., Concord,
N.H., and Madison, Wis., 1917–1930; president of Hartford Seminary Foundation, 1930–1944;
executive of Commission for World Council Services and Church World Service, 1945–1950;
an executive of National Council of Churches, 1951–1958.

[22] See Rouse and Neill, *op. cit.,* p. 715.

[23] FRANKLIN CLARK FRY (1900–   ), Lutheran pastor in Yonkers, N.Y., and Akron, Ohio,
1925–1944, became president of the United Lutheran Church of America in 1944. From 1954
to 1968 he was chairman of the Central Committee of the World Council of Churches, and
president of the Lutheran World Federation, 1957–1963.

In the following summer (1946) I spent several weeks in Germany developing the arrangements for such a liaison. An agreement was reached with General Lucius D. Clay, the Deputy Military Governor of the American Zone of Occupation, under which a representative of the American churches, to be appointed by the Federal Council, would have complete freedom of contact with German church leaders and be provided facilities for his work by the military governor. Julius Bodensieck, the president of Wartburg Theological Seminary, was duly appointed and served in Germany for the next two years. After his return, Roswell P. Barnes spent several weeks in Germany in 1949 as a counselor to the Religious Affairs branch of the American Military Government.

A timely impetus to Christian reconstruction in Europe came a few weeks after the end of the war by a gift of a million dollars by John D. Rockefeller, Jr., with the understanding that half of it would be used for the establishment of an ecumenical study and training center. It was this gift that made possible the opening of the Ecumenical Institute at Bossey, near Geneva, in the summer of 1946, a project which has had world-wide influence in ecumenical education and spiritual renewal. Another encouraging incident in the early postwar period was a contribution of $100,000 from the Lutheran Church-Missouri Synod to the World Council for relief and reconstruction, even though the denomination was not organizationally related to the ecumenical movement.

Bringing the World Council to Birth

Due to wartime restrictions, the World Council's Provisional Committee had not been able to meet since 1939. During the war years, however, the American members had kept up a continuous activity in its behalf, maintaining an office in New York and creating an American Committee for the World Council of Churches under the direction of Dr. Leiper. On February 21–23, 1946, the Provisional Committee was at last able to meet as a whole in Geneva and plan for official inauguration of the World Council. A committee on arrangements for the first assembly was appointed and a general theme, "Man's Disorder and God's Design," was chosen.[24]

At the invitation of the American members, the Provisional Committee met in the following April at Buck Hill Falls, Pa. At this session the decision was officially made to hold the assembly in Amsterdam in 1948. The Study Department, under the chairmanship of Henry P. Van Dusen,[25] had the responsibility for preparatory studies

---

[24] It fell to me to serve as chairman of the committee on arrangements.

[25] HENRY P. VAN DUSEN (1897-), Presbyterian minister, was a member of the faculty of Union Theological Seminary, New York, 1926–1963, and its president, 1945–1963. He served as chairman of the joint committee that outlined the basis for the merger of the International Missionary Council with the World Council of Churches in 1961.

in four areas: "The Universal Church in God's Design," "The Church's Witness to God's Design," "The Church and the Disorder of Society," and "The Church and International Disorder."[26] A budget of $110,000 for the expenses of the assembly was projected, of which 70 per cent was requested from American sources. As it turned out, during the whole decade while the World Council was "in process of formation," about 80 per cent of the financing came from America. As the Geneva office reported, it was "chiefly due to the consecration of those who raised the funds for the Council in America that it (the Provisional Committee) had been able to continue at all."[27]

The establishment of the United Nations created the need for a world-wide agency of the churches that could maintain continuous contacts with it and specialize on international problems. The work of the American Commission on a Just and Durable Peace had provided an example of such an agency on a national scale and stimulated a hope for something similar in an international dimension. The Commission was asked by the World Council's Provisional Committee and the International Missionary Council to take the major responsibility in helping to develop a plan. In August, 1946, a conference was convened in Cambridge, England, attended by representatives of churches in seventeen nations, to study the question. The outcome was the creation of the Commission of the Churches on International Affairs. An English layman, Sir Kenneth Grubb, became the first director, with the American O. Frederick Nolde as associate director.[28] The general purpose was defined as that of serving the churches as a "source of stimulus and knowledge in their approach to international problems, as a medium of common counsel and action, and as their organ in formulating the Christian mind on world issues and in bringing that mind effectively to bear upon such issues."

Another significant event in this period was the enlarged meeting of the International Missionary Council, held in Whitby, Canada, July 5–18, 1947. It marked a heightened solidarity between the missionary societies and the Younger Churches as "partners in obedience." Still another important ecumenical occasion was the second World Conference of Christian Youth in Oslo in the summer of 1947, attended by a large delegation from America.

In preparation for the inaugural assembly of the World Council of Churches, American churchmen played a leading role. Robert S. Bil-

---

[26] The four studies subsequently appeared in published form (New York: Harper & Brothers, 1949).

[27] See David P. Gaines, *The World Council of Churches: A Study of its Background and History* (Peterborough, N.H.; Richard R. Smith, 1966), p. 219.

[28] In 1948 Mr. Grubb became the chairman and Dr. Nolde the director.

heimer took responsibility for organizing an educational program for the large number of "accredited visitors" who would be at Amsterdam.[29] Dr. Van Dusen, as chairman of the Study Department, enlisted the co-operation of a group of scholars in the production of four preparatory volumes on the basic themes of the assembly.

A less publicized study had to do with "The life and work of women in the churches," the first international inquiry into this subject. This was carried on as a volunteer effort by Twila Lytton Cavert, first at the Geneva office of the Provisional Committee for several months in 1945–1946 and later in New York. It was brought to a focus in a conference of representative church women of seventeen countries at Baarn, in the Netherlands, on the eve of the Amsterdam assembly. This led to the setting up of a special committee in the World Council as a continuing center of study. In the United States the Federal Council cooperated by making an inquiry, published as *Women in American Church Life*, which concluded that although women had made a great contribution, notably in missions, the American churches were far from taking full advantage of their potential for leadership.[30]

On August 23, 1948, a full decade after the Provisional Committee had been formed, the World Council of Churches came into official existence at an inaugural assembly in Amsterdam. The date signalizes the beginning of a new era in church history. Hitherto there had been national structures of cooperation, and there had been international conferences of the churches for particular objectives from time to time. Henceforth there was to be a permanent fellowship of churches throughout the world, officially organized on a constitutional basis representing them in their corporate capacity, and provided with appropriate instruments for continuous consultation and cooperation. The Message of the Amsterdam Assembly to the churches summed up its significance in one terse sentence: "We intend to stay together."[31] Among the one hundred and fifty churches which were enrolled as charter members, twenty-eight were American.

In the leadership of the Assembly, representatives of the American churches took an important but by no means a dominating part. Their participation at Amsterdam was less extensive than it had been in the planning for the Council. John R. Mott was one of the seven presiding officers. John A. Mackay was chairman of the section on "The Church's

---

29 ROBERT S. BILHEIMER (1917–), Presbyterian minister, was executive secretary of the Inter-Seminary Movement, 1945–1948; North American program secretary of the World Council, 1948–1954; and director of the Council's Division of Studies, 1954–1963. In 1966 he became the executive for international affairs in the National Council of Churches.

30 Prepared by Inez M. Cavert (New York: Friendship Press, 1949).

31 *The First Assembly of the World Council of Churches,* ed. W. A. Visser 't Hooft (New York: Harper & Brothers, 1949), p. 9.

Witness to God's Design." John C. Bennett was secretary of the section on "The Church and the Disorder of Society," the group that developed the concept of "the responsible society," which was to be very influential in Christian social ethics during the next decade.[32] Frederick Nolde was secretary of the section on "The Church and the International Disorder." Bishop Oxnam was chairman of the committee on Program and Administration, whose report was crucial for the future activity of the Council.

The address which precipitated the greatest argument of the assembly was made by John Foster Dulles. His interpretation of the ethical basis of the economic structures of Western society was sharply challenged by Professor Joseph L. Hromadka of Czechoslovakia from the standpoint of the social revolution in the East. The report of the section that dealt with this controversial issue said, by way of summary:

> The churches should reject the ideologies of both Communism and laissez-faire capitalism and should draw men from the false assumption that these extremes are the only alternatives.[33]

The subsequent historical development of a more-or-less mixed economy in both East and West seems to have given validity to this balanced judgment.

In the official organization of the World Council for the next six years Bishop Oxnam was named as one of the six co-presidents. Dr. Fry became vice-chairman of the Central Committee, the body that was responsible for continuous oversight, and succeeded to the chairmanship in 1954.

The most creative contribution of the American churches to the formation of the World Council was neither their financial support nor their personnel, but their experience with the conciliar pattern of relationships—a pattern which they had developed during four decades prior to Amsterdam. The organizational structure of the World Council was essentially that which had been worked out on a national scale in the Federal Council of the Churches of Christ in America. In a gracious acknowledgment after the Amsterdam assembly, Dr. Visser 't Hooft wrote:

> Now that the World Council of Churches has been formed, it desires to use this opportunity to express its deep debt of gratitude to the Federal Council of the Churches of Christ in America. You have not

---

[32] A "responsible society" was defined as one in which "those who have political or economic power are responsible for its exercise to God, and to the men whose well-being depends on it," and in which "economic justice and provision of equality of opportunity" are established for all.

[33] *The First Assembly of the World Council of Churches,* p. 80. In the original draft the phrase "laissez-faire" did not appear. It was inserted as the result of an amendment offered by Charles P. Taft.

only been pioneers in ecumenical relationships between American churches, but have very early seen the vision of the wider fellowship and taken important initiatives to prepare the way for that fellowship. And you have done so with great disinterestedness, with the result that a great deal of the credit for the formation of the World Council really belongs to your officers, whom you allowed to give time and energy to this task.[34]

If the American churches contributed substantially to the development of the ecumenical movement as an embodied reality, they also received much in return. What they gained was not only a strong reinforcement to their own native trends toward cooperation and unity but also a more intangible influence in the form of a widening theological outlook. The contacts with European scholars did much to stimulate fresh basic thinking in America.

The Evolution of the National Council

During the same postwar years in which the American churches were helping to consummate the organization of the World Council, they were also remaking their own structure of cooperation in the U.S.A. They had several agencies for consultation and coordination in specified fields but none that fully represented the entire movement toward greater unity. Just as the Protestant stress on freedom and diversity had at an earlier period produced many different denominations, so also it had later given rise to different interdenominational channels. Each of these was serviceable in a particular area—such as religious education, higher education, home missions, foreign missions—but none was inclusive enough to manifest the totality of the life and mission of the American churches.

As a result, neither the rank and file of church members nor those outside saw cooperative Christianity in its true strength and significance. They saw only segments of it and did not even know the names of all of the agencies among which the program of cooperation was parceled out. The Federal Council of Churches, being officially constituted by denominations in their corporate capacity, in principle represented their total concern; but in practice, many of the important cooperative activities were the responsibility of other agencies, like the Home Missions Council, the Foreign Missions Conference, and the International Council of Religious Education, which were related only to denominational boards functioning in limited fields of interest. What was lacking was a structure which would express the essential interrelatedness of all the interests, provide for united planning among them, and make visible an organic wholeness as one Christian community.

As has become clear in many earlier pages, the interdenominational

---

[34] Quoted in the *Federal Council Biennial Report, 1948,* p. 251.

agencies found themselves involved again and again in common concerns for which they would create *ad hoc* joint committees. Sometimes they formed joint agencies of a continuing character—like the Town and Country Committee representing the Home Missions Council and the Federal Council, or the Committee on Religious Liberty representing the Foreign Missions Conference and the Federal Council. During the late thirties and the forties the number of projects related to more than one interdenominational agency multiplied so fast that in a single year there were twenty-four![35] The question began to be raised, Why not some form of ongoing interrelatedness instead of creating a new joint committee whenever another need emerges?

In the evolution from the stage of various joint committees to that of an over-all permanent structure, an important influence was the work of the Inter-Council Field Department which had been established in 1939. This experiment of several of the interdenominational agencies in pooling their approaches to local communities had proved so satisfactory that it encouraged the idea of restructuring all the national instruments of unification in one corporate body.

During the 1940's a protracted process of exploring the future connections of eight interdenominational agencies was under way. In December, 1941, the "study conference on closer relationships" had made this penetrating diagnosis:

> Existing interdenominational organizations on every level are limited in their effectiveness, first because they represent only a part of the churches; second, because they represent only a part of the interest of the churches included in their constituency; third, because in different degrees they are all inadequately supported; fourth, because their interrelations are such that each is not sufficiently reinforced by the strength of all.[36]

Three different possibilities of advance beyond this stage were canvassed: (a) a further development of joint action by the several agencies within the existing pattern; (b) a federation of the agencies; (c) a merger of the agencies in a new inclusive body. It was the third and more thoroughgoing proposal that was recommended as the way ahead.

At first a "North American Council of Churches," embracing Canadian denominations as well as those in the U.S.A., was contemplated, since at that time there was no Council north of the border. When, however, it appeared in 1943 that the Canadian churches were moving toward a cooperative organization of their own, a "National Council of the Churches of Christ in the United States of America" became the accepted goal of those who were concerned for a unified structure in this

---

[35] *Work Book for the Constituting Convention of the National Council of the Churches of Christ in the United States of America* (New York: Planning Committee, 1950), p. 3.
[36] *Ibid.*, p. 4.

country. A proposed constitution for the National Council, together with an outline of suggested by-laws, was presented to the eight interdenominational agencies on April 25, 1944, with the recommendation that they submit it to their constituent units for consideration and action.

The adoption of the plan required approval not only by each of the eight interdenominational agencies but also by the denominational boards related to each and, finally, by the denominations as corporate bodies. This process of ratification was long and tedious. It had, however, the compensating advantage that, when finally completed, the new structure had solid foundations.

Four years after the submission of the plan, only five of the eight interdenominational agencies had given official approval, and only twelve of the denominations. It was clear, however, that support for it was steadily gaining momentum. This justified the changing of the name of the negotiating group—which had at first been called "Committee on Closer Relationships" and later "Committee on Further Procedures"—to "The Planning Committee for the Proposed National Council of the Churches of Christ in the U.S.A." In 1948 an executive secretary was secured in the person of Earl F. Adams.[37]

By the end of 1949 all but one of the eight interdenominational agencies had voted in favor of the plan and all of the constituent denominations that were involved had done likewise. The one uncertainty was the attitude of the Foreign Missions Conference. In 1949 it voted against merging its interests in a National Council of Churches. The reasons were twofold. One was the fact that some of the constituent boards of the Conference were independent units, unrelated to any denomination, or belonged to denominations that would not be members of the National Council. The other was a misgiving that in a combined structure including many interests, the distinctive emphasis on foreign missions might be weakened. A few months later, however, at a special meeting held in April, 1950, the Foreign Missions Conference reconsidered its earlier action and gave approval to the plan. This made the decision for the National Council unanimous.

Additional support now came from other quarters. Three Lutheran bodies—the United Lutheran, the Augustana Lutheran, and the Danish Evangelical Lutheran—voted to become members of the proposed council. This meant that American Lutheranism would be officially committed to interdenominational federation to a much greater degree

---

[37] EARL F. ADAMS (1900–1957) was a Baptist pastor in Hillsdale, Mich., and Buffalo, N.Y., 1925–1939; general director of promotion for the Northern Baptist Convention, 1939–1945; executive director of the Protestant Council of the City of New York, 1945–1948; executive of the Planning Committee for the National Council, 1948–1950; director of the Washington Office of the Council, 1951–1957.

than in the past.[38] Moreover, four interdenominational agencies that had not been previously involved in the negotiations now decided to enter into the union. These were Church World Service, the Protestant Radio Commission, the Protestant Film Commission, and the Inter-Seminary Movement.[39]

The Birth of the National Council

The Constituting Convention of the National Council of the Churches of Christ in the United States of America was held in Cleveland's public auditorium, November 28 to December 1, 1950. It coincided both with one of the heaviest snowstorms in the city's history and with an international crisis in Korea, but neither of these untoward events dampened the spirit of the six hundred official delegates and two thousand other participants. They felt they were sharing in a creative moment, the climax of a half century of groping toward a greater unity. At the service of worship on the first evening, the keynote was thanksgiving for the unity in Christ that made the National Council possible. On the next morning the formal act of constituting the Council took place. In an impressive ceremony the representatives of twenty-nine denominations—twenty-five Protestant and four Eastern Orthodox—affixed their signatures to the constitution, and twelve interdenominational agencies certified the transfer of their several assets and responsibilities to the new inclusive body. They then joined in singing:

> God of grace and God of glory
> On Thy people pour Thy power.

During the next three days the delegates went patiently through the process of perfecting the constitution and by-laws, establishing organizational structures, appointing personnel, and formulating policies for the future. They also heard a score of addresses related to the integrating theme, "This Nation Under God." A message of congratulation from President Harry S. Truman voiced appreciation for "the work which has been done in recent years by the interdenominational agencies which now combine their forces." The inaugural date for the beginning of operations under the new charter was fixed as January 1, 1951—precisely the midpoint of the century.

The fundamental character of the Federal Council, as a body officially constituted by the highest authority of the cooperating denominations

---

[38] The only one of these three Lutheran bodies which was related to the Federal Council was the United Lutheran, and it designated that relationship as only "consultative."

[39] The Protestant Film Commission was a new organization, formed in 1947 by nineteen denominational agencies to aid in advancing all phases of Christian life and work through the medium of film. The Inter-Seminary Movement, going back in its beginnings to 1880, was an association of students in 125 theological schools, encouraging them in ecumenical interests.

and directly responsible to them, was carried over into the National Council. One half of each denomination's representatives in the National Council, however, would be nominated by the boards and agencies of that denomination. Through this proviso, assurance was given that each specialized interest would have its voice in policy-making and programming, but without compromising the basic principle that the churches as corporate bodies exercised an ultimate control. The chart of organization was very complicated but it had the merit of fully providing for all the diverse concerns of the uniting agencies.

At the closing session in Cleveland the newly elected president of the National Council, Bishop Henry Knox Sherrill, stressed the spiritual foundations without which its future work would be futile:

> We rightly speak of more efficient organization; we wisely use modern methods of publicity and of promotion. But we must be very certain that there is more than organization, promotion and activity. Without a deeper reality of the Spirit, all our plans and methods are but sounding brass and tinkling cymbals. This National Council in years to come will have pronouncements to make upon many matters of grave importance. We must never forget that the authority for these will not rest simply in the constitution of this assembly but far more in how sincerely and humbly testimony can be given out of the vital spirit and experience of the churches.[40]

Since the Federal Council was the only one of the twelve merging organizations which had its rootage in the denominations as corporate bodies, its representatives were reluctant to see its name disappear. They felt that the new Council's continuity with the past would be needlessly minimized by the adoption of a new name. For a time they argued strongly for carrying over the old name into the new body. But it soon became obvious that it would be obstructive for the Federal Council to insist on clinging to its symbol of the past while the other organizations were sacrificing theirs, and the Council concluded that giving up its name could contribute to the cause which its pioneers had in mind a half century earlier.

The creation of the National Council was more than the devising of a more effective organization for interdenominational activities. It was also an achievement of the Spirit. It reflected a willingness of established agencies to surrender their vested interests for the sake of a greater goal. Each of the agencies had a history of which it was justly proud. Each was doing good work in an important field. Each might easily have insisted that it ought not to sacrifice its institutional existence

---

[40] For a full account of the Cleveland Convention, see *Christian Faith in Action: The Founding of the National Council of the Churches of Christ in the United States of America* (New York: National Council of the Churches of Christ in the United States of America, 1951).

for an untried plan. The fact that these organizations were not thus resistant but, on the contrary, took the initiative in proposing and working for a larger unity was a mark of spiritual vitality.

What had taken place at Cleveland was not church union but the denominations were nearer to being, in effect, one Christian community with twenty-nine branches than at any other time in their history.

12

The First Decade of the National Council

(1951–1960)

WHEN the National Council of the Churches of Christ in the U.S.A. began its official life on January 1, 1951, it was composed of twenty-nine denominations with a combined membership of 33 million in 143,000 congregations. In addition, there were as many more denominations which, though not corporate members, participated in some part of the Council's program. Associated with the Council in its general objectives, although organizationally autonomous, were councils of churches in 40 states and 875 local communities.[1]

The twenty-nine charter members covered a wide spectrum of ecclesiastical life, ranging all the way from Quaker to Eastern Orthodox. Five belonged to the Presbyterian and Reformed family—Presbyterian in the U.S.A., Presbyterian in the U.S., United Presbyterian, Reformed in America, Evangelical and Reformed. There were four Methodist bodies —the Methodist Church, African Methodist Episcopal, African Methodist Episcopal Zion, Colored Methodist. Four shared the Baptist heritage —American Baptist Convention, National Baptist Convention of America, National Baptist Convention, U.S.A., Inc., Seventh Day Baptist. Three were of Lutheran lineage—United Lutheran, Augustana Lutheran, Danish Evangelical Lutheran. Two had a Moravian background—the Moravian Church in America and the Evangelical Unity of the Czech-Moravian Brethren. Two bore the Quaker witness—the Five Years Meeting of Friends and the Religious Society of Friends of Philadelphia and Vicinity. The Episcopal Church, the Congregational Christian Churches, the Christian Church (Disciples), the Church of the Brethren, and the Evangelical United Brethren brought the Protestant total to twenty-five. The remaining four charter members were of the ancient Eastern Orthodox family—Russian Orthodox of North America, Syrian Antio-

---

[1] The eight states that did not yet have councils of churches were Alabama, Arkansas, Georgia, Louisiana, Mississippi, Nevada, Texas, and Wyoming. There was a council of church women in every state and also 1,800 local councils of church women.

chian Orthodox, Roumanian Orthodox, and Ukrainian Orthodox.[2]

When the first General Assembly of the National Council met in Denver in 1952, the thirtieth denomination was received into membership, the Greek Orthodox Archdiocese of North and South America, largest branch of the Eastern Orthodox in the Western world. An application from the International Council of Community Churches raised the puzzling question whether it was eligible for membership as a "communion" in the sense in which the term was used in the National Council's constitution. The issue was resolved, for practical purposes, by receiving the group of community churches into a consultative relationship. The Student Volunteer Movement, long the main agency for interesting students in foreign missions, became at this time the Missionary Services Section of the Council's Joint Department of Christian Vocation. In the following year the United Student Christian Council, the interdenominational agency for work in colleges and universities, became officially related as a Department of Campus Christian Life.

A Complex Structure

The newly formed National Council was a highly complicated structure. An experienced observer even characterized it as "the most complex and intricate piece of ecclesiastical machinery this planet has ever witnessed."[3] This was the natural consequence of the multiplicity of interests, each with its own organizational pattern, which had been brought together. There was, in fact, no important program of cooperation among the member churches which was not related to the Council.

The complexity of the structure was obvious from a glance at the chart of organization. There was a General Assembly, meeting biennially, and a General Board meeting bi-monthly. There were four divisions—Home Missions, Foreign Missions, Christian Education, Christian Life and Work—and each of these had from a dozen to a score of departments, commissions, and committees dealing with special fields. There were General Departments of United Church Women and United Church Men. There were Joint Departments of Evangelism, Family Life, Religious Liberty, Stewardship and Benevolence, American Communities Overseas. There were also Central Departments of Church World Service, Ecumenical Relations, Field Administration, Public Relations, Research and Survey, Publication and Distribution, Treasury and Busi-

---

[2] Related to the Council as consultative bodies, with voice but not vote, were the American Bible Society, the National Council of the Young Men's Christian Association, the National Board of the Young Women's Christian Association, the U.S. Conference for the World Council of Churches, and the General Commission on Chaplains and Armed Forces Personnel.

[3] Henry P. Van Dusen, *One Great Ground of Hope* (Philadelphia: The Westminster Press, 1961), p. 101.

ness Management.[4] There were a Broadcasting and Film Commission and a Bureau of Church Building. Altogether there were more than sixty different units, each with its own supervisory group. Diffusion of responsibility among them resulted in a rather weak administrative structure.

Although there was a wide diffusion of responsibility, a complete union of agencies—not merely a federation—had taken place. This was plainly evidenced by the acceptance of a constitution which vested all final authority in a General Assembly and a General Board. The actual unification of program, however, was a process that extended over a decade. At the beginning there was so much decentralization that some wondered whether the National Council was more than a broad tent thrown over all of the cooperative programs. For some time there was considerable creaking of cumbersome machinery. A professional consultant in institutional administration, who made an intensive study of the Council's structure after the first two years of experience, expressed his surprise that it could actually be a going concern:

> Any review of the Council separate from consideration of the cooperative character of the enterprise and the motivation and spirit of the participants would lead to the conclusion that it could not possibly work. Given the compromises that had to be made in bringing diverse units together, and recognizing the fact that the executive staff of the Council have little authority, even over staff work, other than the influence of their ideas and presence at meetings, the achievements of the past two years have indeed been extraordinary.[5]

A Process of Unification

What happened on the organizational side could be tersely summarized by saying that a structure which was loose-jointed at the start became truly organic within a decade. Living and working together was the great unifier. The Division of Home Missions and the Division of Christian Life and Work, for example—both involved in different ways with racial minorities, underprivileged peoples, and the relation of the churches to the American culture—came to see values in combining under a unitary direction. Needless to say, the right balance between departmental freedom and a unified over-all policy was not easy to attain. An early illustration of this was a tension between United Church Women and the General Board of the Council involving a doctrinal

---

[4] The distinctions between Joint Departments, Central Departments, and General Departments were carefully drawn but had little significance for those not closely related to the structure. A "joint" department functioned in behalf of two or more divisions. A "central" department was responsible for serving the Council as a whole. A "general" department represented the broad interests of lay constituencies.

[5] This comment was made by Donald C. Stone in reporting to the National Council's Committee on Survey and Adjustment. The working papers and the minutes of the Committee are in the Council's archives.

issue. Four Unitarians and Universalists had been nominated by state councils of church women for membership in the Board of Managers of United Church Women, but the General Board of the National Council ruled that they were ineligible because of the constitutional requirement that all members of all units must belong to communions "in agreement with the Preamble." United Church Women were unhappy over the ruling but accepted it loyally.

On the assumption that the administrative structure would need to be critically reviewed in the light of experience, the Constituting Convention of 1950 had made provision for a committee of appraisal. Its report to the biennial Assembly of 1952 clearly set forth the goal of "a closely knit organization with a well-integrated program designed to make a unified impact upon the life of the churches." In keeping with this, the Assembly created a Committee on Survey and Adjustment to carry on a further process of organizational self-examination. Its main conclusion was that the processes of decision making were too complicated. The recommendations contributed to a gradual strengthening of the general secretariat, especially in relation to central administrative services. A more thorough reorganization was to take place a decade later.[6]

A Common Headquarters

A major handicap to becoming "a closely knit organization" was presented by the widely scattered locations of the agencies that had come together in the Council. They had been domiciled in eight different buildings, seven in New York and one, housing the International Council of Religious Education, in Chicago. There was urgent need for a common headquarters, but where? To this question there was no easy answer.

Although the offices of all but one of the uniting agencies were in New York, there was a strong feeling that a more central geographical location might be desirable. In the interest of reaching a democratic decision a representative committee on headquarters, headed by Harold E. Stassen, was created by the General Board of the Council at its first meeting, with instructions to study the problem and make recommendations.[7] When Mr. Stassen resigned because of his increasing involvement in national politics he was succeeded by Edwin T. Dahlberg.[8]

---

[6] See pp. 248–250.

[7] HAROLD E. STASSEN (1907–), Baptist layman; governor of Minnesota, 1938–1945; president of the University of Pennsylvania, 1948–1953; special assistant to the President of the U.S.A. for disarmament negotiations, 1953–1958; president of the International Council of Religious Education, 1942–1950; vice-president of National Council of Churches, 1950–1952.

[8] EDWIN T. DAHLBERG (1892–), Baptist pastor in Potsdam, N.Y., Buffalo, N.Y., St. Paul, Minn., and Syracuse, N.Y., 1918–1950; pastor of Delmar Baptist Church, St. Louis, Mo., 1950–1962; president of Northern Baptist Convention, 1946–1948; president of National Council of Churches, 1957–1960.

The Committee held eleven sessions in different parts of the country —New York, Atlanta, Detroit, Chicago, Denver, Cleveland—over a period of three years. It conducted extensive hearings at which spokesmen for New York, Chicago, St. Louis, Columbus, Cleveland, Kansas City, and Pittsburgh presented their respective cases. A decision in favor of New York as the permanent headquarters was finally reached in 1954. The chief consideration in favor of New York was the fact that more of the member denominations had offices there than in any other city. Provision was also made for continuing an office in Washington for the purpose of keeping the churches informed about developments in government that are of concern to the churches. The decision to locate the central headquarters in New York was accompanied by the adoption of a policy for holding meetings of the General Board, as well as of the General Assembly, in different cities across the nation.

In connection with these protracted discussions there arose a proposal that the Council invite the denominations which had offices in New York to join with it in establishing common headquarters under one roof. Some years earlier this possibility had been seriously discussed and in 1948 the prospect had been sufficiently hopeful to warrant obtaining a special charter for it from the Legislature of the State of New York. The project, however, failed to enlist enough cooperation from enough denominations to make it practicable at that time. The creation of the National Council in 1950 gave a fresh impetus to the plan. The decisive factor in reaching a favorable decision was the offer of John D. Rockefeller, Jr., to donate an attractive site on Morningside Heights, overlooking the Hudson River and in close proximity to a cluster of religious and educational institutions, including Union Theological Seminary, Columbia University, the Riverside Church, the Cathedral of St. John the Divine, and the Jewish Theological Seminary.

Under a charter which had been granted earlier by New York State, a non-profit corporation was organized for erecting and operating The Interchurch Center.[9] The National Council made the initial move in 1954 by authorizing an investment of $600,000 of its funds in the project, and invited similar participation by denominational bodies. Those which agreed to cooperate in financing the center were the United Presbyterian, American Baptist, Reformed Church in America, and United Lutheran. Other church agencies and religious organizations became tenants on long-term leases.

The official decision to proceed with the Center was reported to the National Council by Edmund F. Wagner, chairman of the newly formed board of trustees of the Center, on May 17, 1955. During the next three

---

[9] The original charter of March 29, 1948, had been granted to "the Protestant Center." A certificate of amendment was filed with the Secretary of State on July 9, 1956, changing the name to "The Interchurch Center."

years Francis S. Harmon, a lay volunteer, gave almost full-time service to overseeing the day-by-day development of the project. Dana S. Creel became chairman of an operating committee.[10] The cornerstone for an eighteen-story structure occupying an entire city block was laid by President Dwight D. Eisenhower on October 12, 1958, and the first occupants moved in late in 1959. The service of dedication took place on May 29, 1960.

The Center includes not only offices but a chapel, a social lounge, a hall for exhibits, a cafeteria, private dining rooms, and parking levels. More important than the modern facilities which it provides for efficient work, the Center is an impressive visible evidence of the growing solidarity among the churches.

An Issue of Church and State

From the very beginning of its life, developments in American politics catapulted the National Council into the arena of public affairs. The first major issue was precipitated by President Truman's announcement that he would nominate an ambassador to the Vatican. In March, 1948, he had given informal assurance to Protestant Church leaders that he did not intend to name a successor to Myron C. Taylor, who had been President Roosevelt's personal representative at the Vatican. In September, 1950, President Truman indicated that he was contemplating sending an official ambassador. The reaction was swift and sure. "A Brief in Support of Maintaining a Valuable American Tradition," drafted by the Federal Council of Churches in the last weeks of its existence as a separate organization, was officially approved by the General Board of the National Council at its first regular meeting in January, 1951.[11] The Council's action had important support also from many denominations that were not within its membership. On October 20, the President submitted the name of General Mark W. Clark to the Senate for approval as ambassador to the Vatican.

On October 31, the General Board met in special session to consider what further action was called for. Without a dissenting vote, a declaration of opposition to the proposal was adopted, and a special committee, under the chairmanship of Franklin Clark Fry, was appointed to mobil-

---

[10] EDMUND F. WAGNER (1898–), Lutheran layman; business and banking executive; treasurer of the Lutheran Church in America; president of the board of trustees of The Interchurch Center since its establishment.

FRANCIS S. HARMON (1895–), Baptist layman; editor and publisher, Hattiesburg (Miss.) *American*, 1926–1933; general secretary, International Committee of Y.M.C.A.'s of United States and Canada, 1932–1937; vice-president of Motion Picture Producers and Distributors of America, 1945–1951; vice-president, National Council of Churches, 1958–1960.

DANA S. CREEL (1912–), lawyer, secretary of Rockefeller Brothers Fund and the Sealantic Fund, 1947–1951; director of both funds since 1951.

[11] *Reference Manual on U.S. Diplomatic Relations at the Vatican*, National Council pamphlet, 1951.

ize public opinion. The main thrust of the brief, submitted to the President and the Secretary of State, was in these two sentences:

> Diplomatic relations with the Pope, or technically with the Vatican, are, in effect, diplomatic relations with the head of a church. . . . To give one church a preferential status in relation to the American government would set aside the principle of according all religious bodies the same status.[12]

The flood of protests that poured into Washington from all parts of the nation against the President's proposal was surprisingly large, and it soon became doubtful whether the nomination would be confirmed by the Senate. Within three months after his name had been sent to the Senate, General Clark requested the President to withdraw it. The President announced his reluctant consent and intimated that he might later submit another nomination, but he let the matter drop. The issue remained dormant until John F. Kennedy in his campaign for the presidency in 1960 declared that he was "flatly opposed" to sending an ambassador to the Vatican.[13] This forthright stand by a Roman Catholic who became President of the United States seems to have laid the controversy permanently to rest.

The Issue of "McCarthyism"

The early years of the National Council fell in the period which is often called "the McCarthy era." It was a time when the spread of communism in the world, and particularly the conflict in Korea, evoked reactions of suspicion and distrust. There was almost an obsession with the danger of communist infiltration into America. The atmosphere was one in which it was easy to make political capital by playing upon the fears of the people. Senator Joseph R. McCarthy charged that the Department of State was honeycombed with Communists. He also turned his guns on other agencies of government, including the army, and to a less extent on the universities. The churches were a target of attack from the Committee on Un-American Activities in the House of Representatives. In this situation the National Council became a rallying center of protest against witch-hunt methods, the imputation of guilt by association, the reliance on allegations by undisclosed informers, and the imposition of loyalty oaths as a means of thought control.

At its first biennial Assembly the Council took note of the suspicion and confusion that were being fostered by such irresponsible methods of anti-communism, especially by the tendency to identify concern with social welfare or world peace as pro-communism. A "Letter to the Chris-

---

12 *National Council Outlook* (November, 1951).

13 *Look,* March 3, 1959. For a fuller account of the events in connection with the nomination of General Clark, see Anson Phelps Stokes and Leo Pfeffer, *Church and State in the United States* (New York: Harper & Row, 1964), pp. 277–280.

tian People of America" declared that "the conscientious expression of ideas must not be dealt with by a dungeon, a boycott, or an Index, nor by arbitrary governmental action." When the atmosphere of suspicion became more noxious, the General Board, on March 11, 1953, created a special Committee on the Maintenance of American Freedom, under the chairmanship of Bishop Sherrill, who had just been succeeded in the presidency of the Council by Bishop William C. Martin.[14]

In announcing the appointment of the Committee Bishop Martin commented that "some people are so frightened about Communist infiltration that they pay no attention to the danger of fighting it in un-American ways." The Committee was under instruction "to watch developments which threaten the freedom of any of our people or their institutions, whether through denying the basic human right of freedom of thought, through Communist infiltration or through wrong methods of meeting that infiltration."[15] A few weeks later the General Board rebuked the House Committee on Un-American Activities for publicizing unverified charges that two esteemed Jewish rabbis, Stephen S. Wise and Judah L. Magnes, had been followers of the Communist Party line. This was characterized as an especially "reprehensible act" since it blackened the good name of a religious leader (Rabbi Wise) who, having died, was unable to defend himself.

The mood of near-hysteria became worse, illustrated by Senator McCarthy's reckless accusations against officers of the government and by J. B. Matthews' blanket indictment of the loyalty of the clergy. In a widely publicized article the latter asserted that "the largest single group supporting the Communist apparatus in the United States today is composed of Protestant clergymen."[16] The charge confused Christian interest in social justice with political alignment with communism. When it was later announced that Senator McCarthy had appointed Matthews as the research secretary of the Senate Permanent Sub-Committee on Investigations, a storm of protest arose which resulted in the withdrawal of the appointment.

Two contributions from denominational leadership at this time were especially effective in dispelling the miasma of confusion and distrust that identified an interest in social reform with support of communism. The first was the demand of Methodist bishop G. Bromley Oxnam for a hearing before the Committee on Un-American Activities as an opportunity to refute charges against him. On July 21, 1953, when he was

---

[14] WILLIAM C. MARTIN (1893–), Methodist minister; pastor in Houston, Tex., Port Arthur, Tex., Little Rock, Ark., and Dallas, Tex., 1921–1938; elected bishop, 1938; president of National Council of Churches, 1952–1954.

[15] *National Council Outlook* (September, 1953).

[16] *The American Mercury* (July, 1953).

on the witness stand for several hours, his testimony called nationwide attention to unsubstantiated allegations.[17] The second factor contributing to a healthier climate of opinion was a "Letter to Presbyterians," officially issued by the General Council of the Presbyterian Church in the U.S.A. on October 21, 1953. The major role in drafting the letter was taken by John A. Mackay, at that time moderator of the denomination's General Assembly.[18] It boldly declared that "some Congressional inquiries have revealed a distinct tendency to become inquisitions" and that "attacks are being made upon citizens of integrity and social passion which are utterly alien to our democratic tradition." The letter insisted that dissent should not be regarded as treason nor nonconformity as disloyalty.[19]

Early in 1954 the General Board of the National Council took official action, urging procedural reforms in the work of Congressional investigating committees. It pointed specifically to current abuses such as stigmatizing individuals and groups as disloyal on the basis of unsupported accusations, releasing unverified data from committee files, denying an opportunity for the accused to cross-examine accusers, and functioning as virtual courts to determine guilt or innocence instead of keeping within the proper limits of legislative inquiries.[20]

In the following year a Senate sub-committee on Constitutional Rights initiated an inquiry into the status of American freedom as guaranteed by the Bill of Rights. Eugene Carson Blake, the current president of the National Council of Churches, was invited to be one of the witnesses.[21] The general tenor of his testimony, summarizing the position which the Council defended, was indicated by his plea, "Let no government or branch thereof think of itself as the arbiter or controller of men's opinions, convictions, or faith."[22] By this time, the nation was recovering from its jittery state and there was a general recognition that the churches had given a good account of themselves in defending freedom and opposing communism at the same time.

Five years later, however, in 1960, an incidental case of revived

---

17 For a full description of the hearing as viewed by Bishop Oxnam, see his *I Protest* (New York: Harper & Brothers, 1954).

18 JOHN A. MACKAY (1889–   ), Presbyterian theologian; principal of Anglo-Peruvian College, Peru, 1916–1925; lecturer for South American Y.M.C.A.'s, 1926–1932; secretary of Presbyterian (U.S.A.) Board of Foreign Missions, 1932–1936; president of Princeton Theological Seminary, 1936–1959.

19 For the full text, see Smith, Handy, Loetscher, *op. cit.*, Vol. II, pp. 549–555.

20 *National Council Outlook* (April, 1954).

21 EUGENE CARSON BLAKE (1906–   ), Presbyterian clergyman; pastor of First Presbyterian Church, Albany, N.Y., 1935–1940, and of Pasadena, Calif., Presbyterian Church, 1940–1951; stated clerk, General Assembly of United Presbyterian Church, U.S.A., 1951–1966; general secretary, World Council of Churches, since December 1, 1966.

22 *National Council Outlook* (October, 1955).

McCarthyite procedures made the National Council of Churches the object of much public attention. The occasion involved only a minor matter but it became a vivid symbol of the church-state issue. The United States Air Force, in a routine manner, published a training manual which included the old charge that there was a grave "infiltration of fellow-travelers into churches and educational institutions." More specifically, the Manual made the egregious allegation that thirty of the translators of the Revised Standard Version of the Bible, which had recently been published by the National Council, were "affiliated with pro-communist fronts, projects and publications."[23] The thirty were almost a *Who's Who* of the distinguished Biblical scholars of America.

On February 11, 1960, a letter from the National Council to the Secretary of Defense, Thomas S. Gates, Jr., described the introduction of such material into an official governmental document as "a patent contradiction of the First Amendment of the Constitution." The letter also declared that to "aver by innuendo" that the National Council of Churches was "associated with or in any way influenced by the Communist party is an example of irresponsibility at its worst." On February 17 the Secretary wrote that he was "distressed" by the contents of the Manual and on the following day the Secretary of the Air Force, Dudley C. Sharpe, wrote that the Manual "has been withdrawn and action is being taken to prevent recurrence of the issuance of such material."

When the facts in the case were traced down, it was discovered that the material which precipitated the protest had been prepared by a civilian employee of the air force, and that he had taken it from pamphlets of fundamentalist intransigents who operated "The Christian Crusade" of Tulsa, Okla., and "The Circuit Riders" of Cincinnati, Ohio. The National Council took advantage of the incident not merely to defend its own reputation but to draw public attention again to the dangers in McCarthyite methods. At the meeting of its General Board later in February, it declared that its protest had been made primarily "to voice the conscience of the American people in behalf of true American freedom and responsible government."[24]

The Issue of Racial Segregation

At the time when the National Council came into existence in 1951, political decisions over racial segregation were moving toward a climax. In this situation the Council reinforced the position against segregation

---

[23] The document bore the technical title of "Air Reserve Center Training Manual, 45–0050, Increment V, Volume 7," issued by Continental Air Command. Copies of it and of the extensive correspondence and publicity which it occasioned are in the archives of the National Council of Churches.

[24] For further detail about the incident, see Ralph Lord Roy, *op. cit.*, pp. 418–421, 469–470.

that had been outlined earlier by the Federal Council and the missionary agencies. It reaffirmed that segregation is "a denial of the Christian faith and ethic" and urged the churches to address themselves to changing both current attitudes and public practices. It held that the church has a twofold function:

> To create new men with new motives.
> To create a new society wherein such men will find a favorable environment within which to live their Christian convictions.

The statement added that although the churches were clearly striving to fulfill the first function they were not grappling firmly with the second, and concluded, "This is imperative now."[25]

The strongest emphasis was on the elimination of segregation in the churches themselves and in their own institutions. Attention was sharply called to the fact that although nine denominations had officially gone on record as rejecting the pattern of segregation, it was still more common in local churches than in public schools. After the Supreme Court decision of May 17, 1954, banning segregation in the schools, the National Council called on the churches to help in bringing about prompt compliance with the verdict.

Beginning in 1955 the Council concentrated attention on the areas of greatest tension, leading in the sixties to a program of active public engagement in the legislative struggle for the civil rights of Negroes and to participation in mass demonstrations in support of those rights.[26] This was regarded by the Council as an extension of the basic educational task of the churches. In his presidential address to the Assembly in 1960, Dr. Dahlberg summarized the Council's position not only in race relations but also in the whole social program by stressing first "the primary importance of evangelism, Christian education, and home and foreign missions" and then concluding:

> If we do not transform the human heart—if there is no new birth of the spirit—no conversion of the soul—then there are not enough policemen or auditors in the nation to keep the books straight. We cannot stop, however, with the acceptance of Christ as our personal Lord and Savior alone. Salvation is corporate and institutional as well as personal. The Apostle Paul makes this perfectly clear in his Colossian letter. He tells us that Christ is Lord over the thrones, dominions, principalities and authorities. He was attributing to Christ a sovereignty that applied to every aspect of life. . . . The National Council of Churches stands squarely behind this interpretation of the Gospel.[27]

---

25 For the text of the statement see Smith, Handy, Loetscher, *op. cit.*, Vol. II, pp. 542–549.
26 See pp. 240–242.
27 *Triennial Report, 1960,* p. 8.

Issues in International Relations

Concern for international understanding and peace was a prominent feature of the National Council, inherited from the earlier activity of the Federal Council and the Foreign Missions Conference. The issues which commanded most continuous attention during the fifties were support of the United Nations, opposition to universal military training in peacetime, control of nuclear armaments, American aid to under-developed nations, and economic policies that would narrow the gap between the rich and the poor nations. A steady stream of bulletins of information, outlines for discussion groups, and other materials for adult education on international problems poured forth each year. Whether they had any significant influence on public policies is argu-able, but there was no doubt that the National Council took seriously its responsibility to give guidance to the thinking of Americans about their relation with other peoples of the world.

An event which created no little public stir was the Study Conference on World Order, the fifth in a series of this character, held in Cleveland, Ohio, November 18–21, 1958. It brought together 500 delegates from thirty-three communions, including a considerable number of political scientists and lay participants in international organizations as well as theologians and clergy. Preparatory studies had been carried on in six areas of concern—Theological and Moral Considerations in Interna-tional Affairs, the Power Struggle and Security in a Nuclear Age, Over-seas Areas of Rapid Social Change, the Changing Dimensions of Human Rights, International Institutions and Peaceful Change, and Missions and Service and International Relations.

The Conference discussed this whole range of interests, but one aspect of the program proved to be so controversial that in the journal-istic reports it overshadowed everything else. This was the discussion of the attitude which Americans should take toward the People's Re-public of China. The majority, though not unanimous, view of the delegates was that the United States should consider steps looking to-ward the diplomatic recognition of China, at the same time making it clear that recognition does not imply approval of a government but simply a method of dealing with it. Admission of China to the United Nations was also recommended.

Although the Conference had no authority to define policies for the National Council or its member churches, being specifically designated as a *study* conference, the findings were generally regarded as reflecting a National Council position. The result was a wave of criticism from those who dissented. A group describing itself as "The Committee of One Million Against Admission of Communist China to the United Nations" called upon the Council to repudiate the Cleveland statement. The Gen-eral Board of the Council made it clear that the study conference did not speak for the Council but nevertheless stoutly defended the propriety of exploring the issue. On February 25, 1959, meeting in Hartford, Conn., the General Board issued what came to be called "the Hartford Appeal." It urged that the churches

Uphold the right and duty of the churches and their councils to study and comment upon issues of human concern, however controversial. Encourage from within and without the churches and their councils full and open criticism of all positions taken by them. Resist all efforts to discourage full freedom of discussion.

Both in the churches and in the public mind there was a good deal of confusion about the nature of "statements" or "pronouncements" by the National Council. In an effort at clarification the General Assembly of 1960 officially defined a statement by the Assembly or its General Board as an expression of the judgment of a representative group appointed by the member denominations, but with no binding authority on any church and always with a recognition of the freedom of any church member to dissent.

An Issue of Internal Policy

This issue of policy in making public statements was nothing new. The National Council inherited it from the experience of both the Federal Council and the denominations. There had been a temporary crisis over it in the National Council before it was many months old. It took the form of a conflict of viewpoint between a group of laymen committed to very conservative policies in socioeconomic life and the main-line group who officially represented the denominations in the General Board.

When the constituting convention of the National Council was drawing near in the fall of 1950, its Planning Committee had become conscious of a prospective weakness due to the lack of any extensive participation by laymen from the world of everyday affairs. To offset the deficiency to some extent, a group of laymen who were influential in industry, business, and the professions had been invited to serve in a sponsoring capacity. J. Howard Pew, prominent Presbyterian industrialist, was the chairman. Though active in their local churches, most of the members of this National Laymen's Committee had not previously had any close identification with either denominational or interdenominational affairs at the national level.

The Committee was not a part of the constitutional structure of the Council, its role being advisory only, but four of its members, including its chairman, were also members of the General Board. After several decisions had been taken by the General Board in which they had constituted a small dissenting minority, they took the ground that the counsel of the Laymen's Committee should be secured on any concrete issue of public policy prior to action on it by the General Board. Since the constitution of the Council clearly lodged full authority in the General Board, made up of the designated representatives of the denominations, the idea did not meet with favor.

Tension approached the breaking point in the spring of 1954, when two lay members of the General Board registered formal objection to the policy of making pronouncements on social and international affairs. The immediate issue concerned a statement on "Basic Principles and Assumptions for Economic Life," a document drafted after two years of study in the Department of the Church and Economic Life. Affirming the right and duty of the churches to examine economic policy and practice in the light of the Christian faith and ethic, it set out thirteen "norms for guidance." It pointed out the error both of undue reliance on government for securing social justice and also of supposing that a maximum of individual economic freedom will in itself result in a good economic order.

The argument over the statement was by no means simply a line-up between clergy approving it and laymen opposing it. Among those who had shared in its preparation or strongly supported it were lawyer Charles P. Taft, economist Kenneth E. Boulding, and industrialist J. Irwin Miller. In any case, the point at issue was not so much the specific content of the document as the larger question whether the churches should enter the realm of economics at all.

The General Board firmly upheld its right and responsibility in this field. At its next meeting, in the fall of 1954, it authorized the issuance of the statement on economic Principles and Assumptions. The vote— seventy-four in favor, four opposed—left no doubt that the Council would be free to voice its judgment on public matters when it felt that spiritual and ethical issues were involved.[28]

The General Board also concluded that lay representatives ought not to be a separate unit within the Council but be integrated into all its structures. Accordingly the Laymen's Committee ceased to function as a group after June 30, 1955. Some of the ultra-conservatives in the Committee soon discontinued their association with the Council, but others continued to serve in various relationships. In the end, the painful tension served to strengthen rather than weaken the commitment of the churches to a vigorous program of social education and action. The necessity for a clear-cut decision had cleared the air. There would, of course, still be criticism, and sometimes open attack, but it was now plain that the leadership of the denominations, as represented in the Council, could be counted on to give strong support to cooperative efforts

---

[28] *National Council Outlook* (June, 1954, and October, 1954).

to make the Gospel relevant to the social order.[29]

Issues in Religious Education

As the issue of released time for religious education became more and more a matter of public concern and of legal decision, it fell to the National Council of Churches to carry the responsibility for its defense. In 1948 the Supreme Court of the United States, in the Mc-Collum case brought to it from Illinois, had ruled that the use of school properties for religious classes violated the First Amendment of the Constitution. In 1952 the question of released time came to the point of judicial determination in another form. Under the New York Plan public schools were permitted, when requested by parents, to release students for one hour a week for religious teaching off the premises. At this time, about two million children were enrolled in weekday classes of religious education under the New York arrangement or similar legislative provisions in other states.

The constitutionality of this Plan was tested in the Zorach case. The defense was in the hands of Charles H. Tuttle as legal counsel for the National Council of Churches. Mr. Tuttle had been a stalwart champion of this program from its beginning and had served as the chairman of the Greater New York Coordinating Committee on Released Time, which included Protestant, Catholic, and Jewish representatives. He successfully presented the case for the constitutionality of the Plan, first in the lower courts and later in the Supreme Court. On April 8, 1952, the Supreme Court upheld the view that the Plan was constitutional since it did not involve any use of school facilities, any expenditure of public funds, or any coercion of pupils.[30]

The Protestant churches warmly welcomed this decision. In general, they have given strong endorsement to weekday religious education, even though they have often failed to take full advantage of the opportunity for it. They have seen in it a way of offsetting, at least in part, the lack of religious education in the public school without adopting the Roman Catholic alternative of establishing parochial schools. In 1956 the National Council held a national conference on the future of weekday religious education in the interest of furthering the program and improving its quality.

A decade after the Supreme Court decision on released time, the constitutionality both of non-sectarian prayer and of devotional Bible

---

[29] An illustration of continuing tension was seen in a denominational setting in 1966 when a group called "The Presbyterian Lay Committee, Inc." inserted an advertisement in leading newspapers attacking the proposed "Confession of 1967" for its affirmation that the church should be concerned with such matters as employment, housing, racial discrimination, political rights, and economic affairs. See *The New York Times*, December 27, 1966.

[30] For an account of the legal procedures, see Stokes and Pfeffer, *Church and State in the United States*, pp. 131–135, 363–371.

reading in the public school also came to a judicial test. In this later development the National Council of Churches, as well as the United Presbyterian Church, the United Church of Christ, and the Baptists, publicly supported the view that in a society as pluralistic as the American, such practices were inappropriate and unwise. The Court's decisions in 1962 and 1963 that the practices were unconstitutional aroused a furor of protest from many who felt distressed over what they regarded as the abandonment of a valuable historic tradition.[31]

The position the churches should take toward federal aid to education was a kindred problem with which the National Council was called upon to wrestle. In 1953 the General Board went on record as supporting the principle of federal grants to help local communities strengthen their educational work, at the same time stressing the importance of safeguarding the schools against federal control. In 1954 a new Department of Religion and Public Education was established in the National Council to serve as a friendly liaison between the cooperating churches and the public schools. In 1961 the Council reaffirmed support of the system of public education, holding it to be "a major cohesive force in our pluralistic society."

Aid to parochial schools, insistently urged by Roman Catholic leaders, was opposed by Protestants generally and by the National Council.[32] A modification of this position began to take shape, however, in the early sixties. In testimony at the hearings in 1965 on the bill providing for federal aid the National Council, while continuing to oppose grants to parochial schools, offered no objection to the policy of "welfare services to all children, whatever school they may be attending." The Council further supported experimentation in "shared time" or "dual enrollment" at the high school level. Under this arrangement the Catholic child's school time is divided between the parochial school and the public school. The child goes to the public school for such clearly "neutral" subjects as languages, mathematics, physics, chemistry, and physical education, thus relieving the parochial school of expenses for salaries of teachers in these fields and for such facilities as laboratories and gymnasiums. The National Council has taken a sympathetic attitude toward this experiment. On June 4, 1964, the General Board voiced the hope that it "may prove to be a means of helping our nation to maintain the values of a general system of public education, yet at the same time meeting the needs of those who desire a system of church-related education."

---

31 *Ibid.,* pp. 371–382.

32 *National Council Outlook* (June, 1954). A more detailed analysis of the reasons for opposition to federal aid for parochial schools was adopted by the General Board of the Council in 1961.

Revised Standard Version of the Bible

Although the National Council often seemed to outsiders to be primarily a body through which Protestant churches made public· pronouncements, informed church members valued it as the instrument through which important specialized common tasks were carried on. Conspicuous among these was the production of the Revised Standard Version of the Bible.

The work of translation was done by a group of distinguished Biblical scholars who had been appointed by the International Council of Religious Education more than a decade prior to the establishment of the National Council. The first fruitage had been the appearance of the Revised Standard Version of the New Testament in 1946. The whole Bible was published by the National Council on September 30, 1952.

In spite of the fact that many people still felt that nothing could take the place of the King James Version, the response of both the churches and the public to the RSV was overwhelmingly favorable. It was recognized that the translators had been able to use older Biblical manuscripts than had been available in earlier generations, to take advantage of the increased knowledge of Biblical times made possible by archeological research, and to bring the English text into accord with contemporary idiom.

The acceptance of the Revised Standard Version was phenomenal. Within seventeen months after publication it had a circulation of 2,647,000 copies in addition to 2,500,000 copies of the New Testament. Its sales stood at the top of the list of all non-fiction books in 1952, 1953, and 1954.[33] Thereafter it steadily continued to have an average circulation of about a million copies a year. In 1962, on the tenth anniversary of its publication, it was reported that twelve million copies of the Version had been sold, in addition to five million copies of the New Testament. In the meantime the Apocrypha had also been translated, and was published in 1957.

Probably the Revised Standard Version of the Bible did more than any other single thing to commend the National Council to the rank-and-file of Christians. In the week in which it was presented to the public, local observances were held in 3,400 communities, celebrating the event and magnifying the place of the Word in the life of the churches. In the nation's capital the first copy of the new Version was presented to the President of the United States, and a great audience heard the testimony that "the Bible has entered as no other book into the making of America."

A remarkable tribute to the scholarship of the Revised Standard Version was its acceptance in Roman Catholic circles. After a decade of

---

[33] *The New York Times Book Review,* October 7, 1956.

consideration, due authorization was given by the Catholic Biblical Association of Great Britain for an edition for Catholic use. The Catholic edition of the RSV New Testament was published in 1965, and of the Old Testament and the Apocrypha a year later. Only a few minor changes were made in the New Testament and none at all in the Old. The Introduction to the Catholic edition commented that the RSV had been "acclaimed on all sides as a translation which combines accuracy and clarity of meaning with a beauty of language and traditional diction." There was also this significant observation:

> For four hundred years, following upon the great upheaval of the Reformation, Catholics and Protestants have gone their separate ways and suspected each other's translations of the Bible as having been in some way manipulated in the interest of doctrinal presuppositions. . . . With the improvement of interdenominational relations and the advance of biblical knowledge, the possibility of producing a Bible common to all Christians was mooted as far back as 1953. It was felt that if such a thing could be achieved . . . the Word of God would then not only be our common heritage and unifying link but be recognized as such, and those engaged in theological discussion could appeal to the same authoritative text. A decisive step toward this objective could be made by editing the Revised Standard Version for Catholic use.[34]

Influential Catholics voiced high appreciation of the RSV. Albert Cardinal Meyer of Chicago saw in it the augury of "a happier age when Christian men will no longer use the Word of God as a weapon, but . . . find the God and Father of our Lord Jesus Christ speaking to them within the covers of a single book." Richard Cardinal Cushing of Boston declared that "the fact that we have adopted their text is a high tribute to Protestant scholarship."[35] This was a far cry from the day when American Catholics had gone to court to keep the King James Version from being read to Catholic children in public schools.

Before the year 1966 was over, the Revised Standard Version had won the approval of Cardinal Cushing for Catholic use without any changes whatsoever. Footnotes were added in some instances to explain the Catholic interpretation of the text, but the text itself was unchanged from that which the Protestant scholars had produced.

Wider Ministries of Compassion

A program impressive in magnitude and involving far-flung relationships was the work of Church World Service, both in overseas relief and in ministry to displaced persons and refugees. At the time when it

---

[34] Introduction to *The Holy Bible: Revised Standard Version Catholic Edition* (Camden, N.J.: Thomas Nelson & Sons, 1966), pp. v–vi. Vatican Council II was undoubtedly an important influence leading to the favorable Catholic attitude toward the RSV.

[35] Quoted in Hiley Ward, *Documents of Dialogue* (Englewood Cliffs, N.J.: Prentice-Hall, 1966), pp. 233–234.

became an integral part of the National Council in 1950, it was passing through a serious crisis. The postwar enthusiasm for responsibility abroad had subsided and postwar emergency funds of the churches were dwindling. In several of the foreign missionary boards the question was being raised whether a continuing organization for relief in lands where they were at work was necessary. There was a brief period of trying to transfer some of the activities of Church World Service to area committees of the National Council's Division of Foreign Missions. By the end of 1952, however, it was becoming clear that a permanent agency for united administration in overseas relief was indispensable.

In 1952 Church World Service assumed the administrative responsibility for "One Great Hour of Sharing," which had been initiated three years earlier by a group of denominational agencies as a method of securing a concentrated attention to world-wide needs, especially through public relations media. In the same year it took over the full direction of the Christian Rural Overseas Program (CROP), which had at first been an independent organization through which farmers made contributions of their produce for the relief of needy peoples.

CROP was only part of a material relief program which included food, clothing, bedding, vitamins, medical supplies, soap, and other commodities for the most needy situations overseas. The volume of these contributed supplies, gathered in large part by local councils of churches, varied from year to year, sometimes reaching an estimated value of $10 million. The administration of the program made it necessary to operate an overseas shipping service comparable to that of a substantial export firm.

In 1954, after the churches and other voluntary agencies had successfully urged the government to release surplus foods from the overflowing storehouses of the Department of Agriculture for the benefit of the hungry overseas, Church World Service became one of the major administrators in the complicated task of distribution. Under this arrangement Church World Service during the following decade distributed in fifty countries foodstuffs contributed by the government whose value was estimated to be in the neighborhood of $250 million.

A continuous program of Church World Service during the fifties was the resettlement of displaced persons and refugees from Eastern Europe. Federal legislation had to be secured in order to permit them to enter the United States. The Displaced Persons Act of 1948, for which the churches had pressed strongly, expired on June 30, 1952. With much urging from the churches, a Refugee Resettlement Act was passed by Congress in 1953, which permitted the admission of 214,000 refugees outside of the regular immigration quotas, provided definite assurance of a job and housing for each refugee was given.

This meant that there had to be a dossier of responsible information about each prospective newcomer, and a guarantee that he would not become a public charge. The refugees, usually unable to speak English, had to be met at port of arrival. Transportation to place of settlement in America had to be arranged. Some of them were ill and required institutional care. In spite of all this onerous detail, the number of those resettled by Church World Service passed the one hundred thousand mark by 1957. In the twenty-two years of its ministry to displaced persons and refugees from 1946 to 1967, it established 160,000 victims of totalitarian oppression in new homes.[36]

In addition to this primary activity in resettlement, Church World Service in the same period also provided extensive temporary relief and welfare services to multitudes of refugees in other lands. These included Chinese refugees in Hong Kong, Tibetan and Pakistani refugees in India, Arab refugees in Palestine, North Korean refugees in South Korea, African refugees in the Congo, and Cuban refugees in the United States. In Hong Kong alone Church World Service spent about $100,000 annually on health services, housing, child care, and other forms of compassionate help.

The energy which Church World Service poured into its program and its swiftness in making decisions in the face of emergency needs created problems in relationships with the World Council's Division of Interchurch Aid. From the ecumenical standpoint it was important that the aid which came from American churches should be clearly seen as an expression of Christian love, not of American national interest. When an American agency like CWS distributed commodities provided by the American government, it could not altogether escape the criticism of having political significance. A distribution by an international body like the World Council was not exposed to the same suspicion. Moreover, Christians in many countries—Great Britain, Holland, Canada, Switzerland, and others—were giving help generously in proportion to their means, and it was essential that the whole enterprise should be effectively coordinated. This could only be done through the World Council. There were occasions during the fifties when the World Council felt that Church World Service, in its commendable enthusiasm, did not take sufficient account of these factors, but a *modus operandi* was gradually evolved which has resulted in Church World Service functioning increasingly as the American arm of the World Council's Division of Interchurch Aid, Refugee and World Service.

Another impressive illustration of united administration carried on by the National Council in behalf of the denominations is the ministry to migrant workers who harvest our nation's seasonal crops. The

---

[36] The story of Church World Service is told in considerable detail by Harold E. Fey, *Cooperation in Compassion* (New York: Friendship Press, 1966).

migrants, chiefly Negro and Spanish American, have probably been the most exploited of American workers. Moving from place to place, following the sun as vegetables and fruits ripen, they are hardly accepted as a real part of the communities in which they work for a time. The lack of medical care, of housing standards, of sanitation codes, of collective bargaining, often spells deplorable living conditions, and children are neglected while parents are in the fields. Into this situation the women's home missionary societies entered as early as 1920. When the National Council was formed it assumed over-all responsibility for the program and its expansion.[37]

The ministry to migrants includes child-care centers, primary schools in improvised quarters, welfare services, informal adult education, recreation, religious education, and worship. One ingenious method for carrying on the program is to provide a fleet of mobile units, with equipment and trained workers who follow the roving workers as they move on from area to area. This ministry has reached a stage at which it directly touches the lives of well over 100,000 migrants annually in thirty states. It is carried on by a permanent staff of forty, reinforced in the summer by several thousand volunteers, recruited largely through local and state councils of church women.

Beyond the personal service rendered directly to the workers, the representatives of the churches have been continuously active in persuading local public agencies to assume more responsibility for the health, education, and welfare of the migrants on whom so much of the economic life of agricultural communities depends. The church representatives have also at times been effective spokesmen, on the basis of their first-hand knowledge and experience, for protective legislation at both the state and federal levels.

The Impact of Evanston

The world-wide contacts and ecumenical outlook of the American churches were markedly reinforced by the holding of the Second Assembly of the World Council in Evanston, Illinois, August 15–31, 1954. The preparatory studies, extending over three years, followed two different lines. One had to do with what was designated as the main theme, "Christ—the Hope of the World." The other was concerned with six topics related to contemporary tasks of the churches.

In the study of the main theme there was a deliberate facing of the theological tension involved in divergent interpretation of the Kingdom of God and of Christian eschatology. In general, the European members of the preparatory committee put more emphasis on the final consummation, while the American members stressed the lordship of Christ

---

[37] A popular description of this ministry appeared in *Saturday Evening Post,* October 4, 1952, under the title, "The Ladies Had an Answer."

and the action of the Holy Spirit in the historical process. To interpret the Christian hope in terms that did justice to both viewponts was a knotty problem. Their report was discussed at Evanston for major periods during four days, and without being "adopted" was sent to the churches "for their study, prayer, and encouragement." There were sharply differing judgments as to how fruitful the long discussion had been, but at least it had contributed to mutual understanding.

The contemporary tasks with which preparatory studies dealt were "Our Oneness in Christ and Our Disunity as Churches," "The Mission of the Church to Those Outside Her Life," "The Responsible Society in a World Perspective," "Christians in the Struggle for World Community," "The Church Amid Racial and Ethnic Tensions," and "The Christian in His Vocation." An "ecumenical survey" of thought and activity in each of these areas was made by a representative group of scholars from different geographical areas and different confessional backgrounds.[38]

The subject of racial and ethnic tensions came strongly into the World Council's purview for the first time. The discussion of this theme at Evanston was intensified by the presence of representatives of the Dutch Reformed Church of South Africa, where the question of *apartheid* had become an all-absorbing issue. The report took a forthright stand against "the whole pattern of racial discrimination" as "an unutterable offense against God, to be endured no longer." A resolution urged the member churches of the World Council to "renounce all forms of segregation or discrimination and to work for their abolition within their own life and within society." This was directly in line with the earlier position of the National Council of the Churches of Christ in the U.S.A. The delegates from South Africa expressed serious misgivings about the wisdom of the resolution but refrained from voting against it since they desired to "keep the door open for further conversation."[39]

The contribution of the American churches to the Assembly was evident in many ways. Bishop Oxnam as chairman of the committee on arrangements, with Robert S. Bilheimer as secretary, carried the heavy end of all the practical planning. Henry P. Van Dusen, as head of the World Council's Study Department, bore the general responsibility for all the surveys. Roswell P. Barnes was chairman of the preparatory commission on racial and ethnic tensions, and Theodore O. Wedel of the preparatory committee on evangelism. John C. Bennett was co-chairman of the preparatory committee on social questions. Four preparatory commissions had American secretaries—J. Robert Nelson for

---

[38] The six surveys and the final report on the main theme were published under the title, *The Christian Hope and the Task of the Church* (New York: Harper & Brothers, 1954).

[39] *The Evanston Report: The Second Assembly of the World Council of Churches,* ed. W. A. Visser 't Hooft (New York: Harper & Brothers, 1955), pp. 151–160, 328–329.

Faith and Order Studies, Richard M. Fagley for international affairs, Robert S. Bilheimer for racial and ethnic tensions, Paul R. Abrecht for social questions. Bishop Oxnam was one of the presiding officers of the Assembly. Chairmen of sections or committees included Bishop Richard C. Raines on evangelism, Bishop Martin on general policy, Bishop Dun on ecumenical action, and Eugene Carson Blake on finance and administration.

Two public events commanded extraordinary interest. One was a colorful Festival of Faith, a musical and dramatic presentation of the Biblical story of creation, redemption, and the consummation of all things in Christ. More than a hundred thousand persons thronged the vast stadium in Soldier's Field for the occasion. The other event was an address by the President of the United States, Dwight D. Eisenhower, at an outdoor gathering in Deering Meadow attended by twenty thousand.

An important aspect of the Evanston Assembly was the presence of fifteen delegates from the churches of four countries within the communist orbit—Hungary, Czechoslovakia, Poland, and East Germany. They were accepted as loyal Christians who had been faithful to their calling under adverse circumstances. Their participation did much to strengthen the picture of the church as a world community owing its life to the Gospel and not to be identified with any historically conditioned political or social system. Some sectors of outside opinion, however, interpreted the attendance of the East European churchmen as an indication that the World Council was "soft toward communism."

After the Assembly correspondence began with the Russian Orthodox Church, which in due time led to its membership in the World Council. A strong contributing factor in this development was the action of the National Council of the Churches of Christ in the U.S.A. in sending a delegation to Moscow for a conference in 1956. Nine American Christian leaders spent ten days in Russia in March, in a series of consultations with high officials of the Russian Orthodox Church and also, more briefly, with representatives of the Baptists and the Lutherans.[40] In the following June a group of Russian churchmen paid a return visit to the United States, and visited several cities under arrangements made by the National Council. Their presence was not entirely free from unpleasant incidents of picketing, stirred up by members of the fundamentalist American Council of Christian Churches. An indirect result of the exchange of delegations was a more appreciative understanding in America of the significance of the survival of the church in the revolutionary situation of the Soviet Union.

---

[40] The Americans who constituted the delegation were Eugene C. Blake (Presbyterian), Franklin C. Fry (Lutheran), Herbert Gezork (Baptist), Charles Parlin (Methodist), Henry K. Sherrill (Episcopal), D. Ward Nichols (African Methodist), and Paul B. Anderson (Episcopal); with Roswell P. Barnes and Walter W. Van Kirk of the National Council staff.

Studies in the Unity of the Church

Although American churches had been related to the Faith and Order movement ever since its origin in the Protestant Episcopal Convention of 1910, the active participation had been confined chiefly to theologians and denominational leaders. Few pastors and still fewer laymen were involved. The three world conferences, all held in Europe (Lausanne, 1925; Edinburgh, 1937; Lund, 1952), had made little impact on local communities in America. In the mid-fifties, however, a trend developed which was to domesticate the concerns of Faith and Order in the program of both the National Council of Churches and of state and local councils. The trend became clearly visible in the "North American Study Conference on the Nature of the Unity We Seek," held in Oberlin, Ohio, September 3–10, 1957.

At the beginning of 1955, the United States Conference for the World Council of Churches began to plan for the gathering by initiating a program of studies designed to enlist interest in local communities. The National Council of Churches and the Canadian Council of Churches joined in the sponsorship. The committee on arrangements, under the chairmanship of Bishop Angus Dun, secured Paul S. Minear, professor of New Testament at Yale Divinity School, as a full-time director for a two-year period. In sixteen cities in different parts of the continent a selected group was assigned a special theme for exploration and drafting of a statement which would be used at Oberlin as an orientation paper. Less formal groups in other places also held discussions on the basis of an outline entitled "Ecumenical Conversations," and nearly fifty of them reported conclusions. In all this process the focus was on the local conditions in which the participants were involved.

At Oberlin the over-all theme was "The Nature of the Unity We Seek." The basic work was done in twelve sections. All of their reports came before plenary sessions of the Conference for discussion and criticism and subsequent rewritings but no official adoption was sought. The value of the reports was assumed to lie in their intrinsic usefulness for further study. The Eastern Orthodox delegates, not feeling quite at home in discussions that started with Protestant presuppositions, registered a statement of their traditional conception of unity as "embodied and realized in the age-long history of the Orthodox Church."[41]

The significance of the Oberlin Conference lay less in the content of the reports than in its impetus to a widening study of theological and ecclesiastical issues in America. The most important concrete result was the decision of the National Council of Churches in 1958 to incor-

---

[41] Paul S. Minear, ed., *The Nature of the Unity We Seek: Official Report of the North American Conference on Faith and Order* (St. Louis: Bethany Press, 1958).

porate Faith and Order studies into its program and help local and state councils to develop effective programs in this field. Up to this time the conciliar bodies in America—national, state, local—had given little attention to theological study. In fact, there had been some fear that to do so might be disruptive and make practical cooperation in areas of community concern more difficult. After Oberlin this point of view began to disappear.

Another influence of the Oberlin Conference was a stronger orientation of subsequent Faith and Order studies to the local community and the local church. Henceforth there would be less of a disposition to define unity in terms of overhead structures, and more of a realization that it is where congregations of Christian people exist side by side that the problem of unity is most urgent. The accent on the local community was clearly manifested in the declaration of the New Delhi Assembly of the World Council in 1961, that the unity which is God's will is one which is "made visible . . . in each place."

One other noteworthy feature of the Oberlin Conference was a breakthrough in the relations of Protestants and Roman Catholics. For the first time in America there were official observers of the Roman Catholic Church at a gathering under Protestant and Eastern Orthodox auspices. The observers were well-known representatives of their Church, Father Gustave Weigel, Jesuit scholar, and Father John B. Sheerin, of the Paulist order.[42]

Their participation in the Oberlin meeting was so pregnant for better understanding between Protestants and Catholics that the "inside story" of their appointment as observers should be more widely known. In extending the invitation to the Catholic Church the committee on arrangements did not depend on either official correspondence or official interview but found the way to make a very personal approach. It was known that Norman B. Nash, the Protestant Episcopal bishop of Massachusetts, was a warm personal friend of John J. Wright, at that time the Catholic bishop of Worcester, Mass. Bishop Nash was asked to make a personal interpretation of the nature of the Conference to Bishop Wright. The latter was so interested that he took the initiative in suggesting to the Archbishop of Cleveland, in whose jurisdiction Oberlin

---

[42] GUSTAVE WEIGEL (1906–1964), Jesuit theologian, was professor of dogmatic theology at the Universidad Catolica in Chile, 1938–1948. From 1948 until his death he was professor of ecclesiology at Woodstock College. A member of the secretariat of Vatican Council II, he died in Rome between the second and third sessions.

JOHN B. SHEERIN (1907–   ), trained for the law and admitted to the New York bar in 1932, was ordained to the priesthood in 1937 and became a member of the Paulist order. Since 1948 he has been editor-in-chief of *The Catholic World*. At Vatican Council II he served on the American Bishops' Press Panel during two sessions, and was a *peritus* at the final session.

lies, that he appoint official observers.[43] It seems altogether probable that except for these very personal procedures the invitation might not have been accepted, since only three years earlier the Archbishop of Chicago had forbidden Roman Catholics even to be visitors at sessions of the World Council at Evanston. Both Father Weigel and Father Sheerin became highly influential in the next few years in building bridges of understanding between Roman Catholics and Protestants in America.

---

[43] This information is based upon recollections of personal conversations with Bishop Nash.

13

The New Ecumenical Climate

(1961–1967)

IN the 1960's the ecumenical movement developed a much more dramatic character. Hitherto it had been something that was taking place among the Protestant churches, with an increasing participation of the Orthodox. The Roman Catholic Church had held aloof. In the encyclical *Mortalium Animos* in 1928 Pope Pius XI, warning against participation in ecumenical meetings and projects, had declared that it was not "lawful for Catholics to give to such enterprises their encouragement or support." The prohibition was only slightly relaxed in 1949 by the "Instruction on the Ecumenical Movement" issued by the Sacred Congregation of the Holy Office. Under the guidance of Pope John XXIII, this insulation gave way to friendly dialogue and collaboration.

Although Roman Catholics had been forbidden to attend the Evanston Assembly of the World Council of Churches in 1954, seven years later they were represented at the New Delhi Assembly by five official observers, appointed by ecclesiastical authority. One of them was an American priest, Father Edward J. Duff, S.J.[1]

The Impact of Vatican II

The date which most clearly pinpoints the change in Catholic attitude was December 25, 1961, when Pope John XXIII officially convoked Vatican Council II for the following year. He had announced his intention to do so three years earlier and had publicly intimated that non-Catholic bodies would be invited to send observers. He had also appointed a Secretariat for Christian Unity, under the chairmanship of Augustin Cardinal Bea, to facilitate friendly contacts. Cardinal Bea generously acknowledged the historical role that non-Catholics had played in initiating the ecumenical movement. "We Catholics," he said, "must recognize with sincere gratitude that it is our separated brethren, Ortho-

---

[1] Five years earlier Father Duff had made an intensive study of the World Council's work in the socio-ethical field, published under the title, *The Social Thought of the World Council of Churches* (New York: Association Press, 1956).

dox, Anglicans, and Protestants, who gave the first impulse to the modern unitive movement."[2]

An amazing change now began to take place in Protestant-Catholic relations in America. It was impressively evident in irenic books by American Catholic scholars, like Father Gustave Weigel and Father George H. Tavard, and in leading articles in such Catholic magazines as *The Catholic World* and *America*.[3] Even more remarkable were occasional volumes in which Protestant and Catholic shared in the authorship, like *An American Dialogue*, by Robert McAfee Brown and Father Weigel.[4]

In organizational leadership an extraordinary development was the creation of a continuous channel of consultation between the National Council of Churches and the Catholic Bishops' Commission on Ecumenical Affairs.[5] By joint agreement in 1966 they established a "Working Group," as an instrument for keeping each other informed about plans, for discussing common problems, and for recommending parallel action as occasion may arise.[6] Even at its first session such thorny issues as mixed marriages and the relation of parochial schools to public education were not avoided. Several other "working groups," oriented to more doctrinal matters, were established between the Catholic Bishops and major denominational bodies—Presbyterian, Lutheran, Episcopal, Methodist, Orthodox—between 1965 and 1967. All this was in keeping with the Vatican Council's Decree on Ecumenism, promulgated on November 21, 1964, which had recommended "cooperation among all Christians" in problems of church and society and "dialogue" in matters of Christian faith and practice.[7]

The points of contact and of cooperation multiplied rapidly. In fields of social action, like race and poverty and peace, coordinated efforts became almost a matter of course. Advanced ground was broken in

---

[2] Augustin Cardinal Bea, *Unity in Freedom* (New York: Harper & Row, 1964), p. 103.

[3] See Gustave Weigel, S.J., *A Catholic Primer on the Ecumenical Movement* (Westminster, Md.: Newman Press, 1957) and his *Faith and Understanding in America* (New York: The Macmillan Company, 1959), and George H. Tavard, *Two Centuries of Ecumenism* (Notre Dame, Ind.: Fides Publishers Association, 1960).

[4] Garden City, N.Y.: Doubleday & Co., 1960.

[5] The National Conference of Catholic Bishops is responsible for the United States Catholic Conference, which was established in 1921 as a continuation of the National Catholic War Council and formerly called the National Catholic Welfare Conference.

[6] At the international level a joint "working group" of the World Council of Churches and the Vatican's Secretariat for Christian Unity held its first session in 1965. In this group R. H. Edwin Espy, general secretary of the National Council of Churches, was one of the eight representatives of the World Council.

[7] Walter M. Abbott, S.J., gen. ed., *The Documents of Vatican II, with Notes and Comments by Catholic, Protestant and Orthodox Authorities* (New York: Guild Press, American Press, and Association Press, 1966).

1966 when the National Student Christian Federation, which was a body related to the National Council of Churches but autonomous in its decision making, was transformed into the University Christian Movement. This embraces the major Protestant groups and two Roman Catholic bodies, the National Newman Student Federation and the National Federation of Catholic College Students. By 1967 Church World Service and Catholic Relief Services had reached a point of collaboration that enabled them to make joint shipments of grain to relieve famine conditions in India. In the same year the National Council's Overseas Medical Council and Catholic foreign missionary agencies began to survey possibilities of integrating Protestant and Catholic hospitals. The National Council also opened the way for the participation of Roman Catholic representatives in all of its program units.

The most surprising step in national relationships was the action of the National Council in adding a Roman Catholic priest to its official staff. In July, 1966, Father David J. Bowman, S.J. became associate director of Faith and Order studies. The young Jesuit priest was the first Catholic to serve on the administrative staff of a Protestant-Orthodox body.

At local levels several Roman Catholic parishes, and even dioceses, became full members of councils of churches. By the end of 1967 there were thirty cities in which such a step had been taken, including Austin, Fort Worth, and Wichita Falls, Texas; Kansas City, Mo.; Chico and Riverside, Calif.; Oklahoma City and Tulsa, Okla.; Grand Rapids and Muskegon, Mich.; Decatur and Naperville, Ill.; Columbus, Ohio; Pueblo, Colo.; Lexington, Mass.; Portland, Ore.; Tacoma and Seattle, Wash. In several other communities in which Catholic parishes did not go so far as to become official members of a council of churches they appointed "observers" as a means of fraternal contact, and shared in certain common projects. A document entitled "Information on Relations between the Roman Catholic Church and Councils of Churches" was prepared by the national "working group" to provide advisory guidelines for local developments.

Typical of the basis on which Catholic and Protestant congregations entered into an official relationship is the form which an applicant for membership in the Fort Worth Council of Churches fills out. First, there is an explanation that membership "does not bind or obligate any church to any commitment or course of action contrary to the belief and policies of said church, and that any member church is free to participate in only those phases of the program in which it has interest." The document then goes on:

> With these understandings, our church pledges itself . . . to look upon the work of the Council as an important part of the work of this church, performed cooperatively with other churches, to seek to play a strong

role in these cooperative endeavors to advance Christ's Kingdom in the Fort Worth area, and to contribute financially to the support of the united endeavor as our church is able.[8]

The most extensive participation of Catholics in a council of churches thus far is in the State of New Mexico. In 1965 the entire archdiocese of Santa Fe joined the New Mexico Council of Churches. A little later a Catholic priest was elected vice-president, the second highest office in the organization. In 1967 the Catholic diocese of Nevada became a member of the Northern California-Nevada Council of Churches.

Most significant in the new ecclesiastical climate that followed Vatican Council II was a pervasive change in relationships at the "grass roots." In numerous communities Protestant pastors and Catholic priests who had aloofly ignored each other began to recognize themselves as colleagues. Acrimonious criticisms gave way to mutual respect and shared concern. Catholic priests were heard from time to time in Protestant pulpits and Protestant leaders were seen at Catholic gatherings. Catholic scholars lectured in Protestant theological seminaries and Protestant scholars in Catholic institutions.

A simple but effective measure for furthering ecumenical understanding in local communities was the "living room dialogue." This was planned wholly for lay people, outlining a series of discussions by neighborhood groups small enough to meet informally in a hospitable home. A manual for such groups, issued jointly by the National Council of Churches and the Paulist Press, had a circulation of 150,000 within three years.[9] In 1966 there was for the first time a joint publication for use in the Week of Prayer for Christian Unity.[10] In several cities the Reformation Day rallies, on the Sunday nearest the date on which Luther posted his theses in Wittenberg, became Festivals of Faith or Festivals of Unity, in which Protestants, Catholics, and Orthodox shared.[11]

The age-old differences between Catholics and Protestants, of course, remain—in reference to such issues as the papacy, the authority of the hierarchy, and the place of the Virgin Mary in the Church—but at last they can be faced in an atmosphere of mutual Christian concern. An objective indication of this was the launching of an ecumenical information service, *Trends in Unity*, in 1967 as a cooperative project of

---

[8] Hiley Ward, *Documents of Dialogue* (Englewood Cliffs, N.J.: Prentice-Hall, Inc., 1966), pp. 131–132. This is a valuable sourcebook on contemporary Protestant-Catholic relations.

[9] William P. Greenspun, C.S.P., and William A. Norgren, *Living Room Dialogues* (New York: National Council of Churches and Paulist Press, 1965). A second manual was published in 1967.

[10] Sponsored jointly by the World Council of Churches and the National Council of Churches and recommended for Catholic use by the Bishops' Committee for Ecumenical Affairs.

[11] Ward, *op. cit.*, pp. 350–353.

the National Council's Department of Faith and Order and Roman Catholic agencies.

Cooperation in a Pluralistic Society

In the more genial ecclesiastical climate of the sixties there was a much more sensitive awareness of the pluralistic character of American society and of the attitudes that are appropriate to it. All through the nineteenth century and the earlier decades of the twentieth, Protestants tended to think of America as a "Protestant country." They had given such a dominant tone to the national culture at its beginning and had continued to be so large a majority of the population that Protestantism had taken on some of the aspects of an establishment, unofficial yet real. This was reflected, for example, in the Sunday "blue laws" and in the widespread practice of Bible reading and devotional exercises in a Protestant mode in public schools. Until about mid-century, Catholics and Jews felt on the defensive in maintaining their own religious heritage.

The date which most conspicuously symbolizes a change and marks a new stage of American pluralism is 1960, when John F. Kennedy was elected the first Roman Catholic President of the United States. His unqualified commitment to the separation of church and state went far to dispel lingering fears of Catholic domination. No one who remembers the poisoned atmosphere of 1928, when another Catholic, Alfred E. Smith, had been a candidate for the presidency, can fail to realize how marked a shift in Protestant attitudes had taken place within a generation.

The change had not come easily. Protestants had operated for so long from a position of cultural prestige that they were slow in realizing all the implications of a radical pluralism. Pockets of resistance to the change still remain, especially in small rural communities, and in other quarters also there is sometimes a nostalgic looking back to the "good old days" of Protestant hegemony. It has, however, come to be generally understood and accepted that no religious group may expect to see its viewpoint adopted by the American community as a whole.

The religious pluralism of the American people not only makes mutual regard among religious bodies a social necessity but also impels each to be clear about its own identity and commitment. If it cannot be a church of the masses it can be something more significant, a church of the faithful. Instead of becoming attenuated to the point of being hardly more than a religious sanction for "the American way of life," it is challenged to bear a distinctive witness to vital convictions of its own. At the same time, there is an equal challenge for every church to join hands with others insofar as they stand on common ground.

This has led both Catholic and Protestant Churches belatedly to reach out toward closer relations with the Jews. In a civic organization, the National Conference of Christians and Jews, many individuals of the three groups had worked together in certain projects since the early 1920's, but in the sixties there was a growing feeling that church and synagogue as corporate bodies ought to be more actively associated in many common interests. This concern found substantial expression in a joint support of several important enterprises of social welfare and social justice. Noteworthy examples were the interfaith conference on Religion and Race in 1963, which led to continuing coordinated activities for civil rights, the interfaith conference on Marriage and Family Life in 1967, and the anti-poverty program begun in the same year.

Beyond such collaboration in social action, there is a growing recognition of the need for dialogue between Christians and Jews at the deepest levels of their faith. This has not yet taken place to any great extent. In spite of the fact that Jew and Christian share a common spiritual heritage in the Old Testament, they have seldom faced together the agreements and the differences within this heritage. This promises to be a main item on the future agenda of study and dialogue of Catholics, Protestants, and Jews.

Concerted Action on Civil Rights

In the 1960's American churches, Protestant and Catholic alike, became more directly involved in public affairs. During the earlier decades of the century the deepening sense of responsibility for society had found its main manifestations in social education and in social services.[12] Now there were to be more active engagements in the rough-and-tumble of the civic and political arena. The new mood was symbolized by the oft-quoted remark that the church should be "out where the action is."

An outstanding illustration of the trend was the work of the Commission on Religion and Race, formed by the National Council of Churches on June 7, 1963.[13] The Council had a long-standing record of educational efforts for interracial justice but these were now supplemented by a more aggressive approach, designed to bring the support of the churches directly to bear in the struggle for civil rights on the economic and political fronts. The new strategy was prompted by the belief that the struggle represented a national crisis of conscience which demanded both a priority of attention and sharply focused methods of exerting in-

---

[12] Early illustrations of this type of concern were the Protestant formulation of "The Social Ideals of the Churches" (1908 and 1932) and the Roman Catholic "Bishops' Program of Social Reconstruction" (1919).

[13] Its first chairman was Bishop Arthur C. Lichtenberger. When he had to resign on account of failing health, he was succeeded by Eugene Carson Blake. Its first executive was Robert W. Spike.

fluence at points of public decision. The Commission was authorized to "make commitments, call for actions, take risks," in pursuit of the goal of helping the nation "to see this crisis in its moral dimension." During the next few years the Commission was a vigorous participant, and sometimes a prime mover, in the major phases of a national campaign to eliminate racism in America. Its work was closely coordinated with parallel efforts by Catholic and Jewish agencies. The preliminary basis for this collaboration had been established in January, 1963, when leaders of the three groups met in Chicago for the first interfaith conference on Religion and Race.

Visible evidence that church organizations were moving together into the center of the struggle for equal opportunity for Negroes was not slow in coming. The denominations of the National Council, the Catholic Inter-Racial Council, and the Synagogue Council of America joined with civil rights organizations in the spectacular March on Washington on August 28, 1963. It was an amazing demonstration of concern, climaxed by Martin Luther King's keynote address, "I have a dream." It was generally estimated that more than 200,000 persons participated, including conspicuous numbers of clergymen, priests, nuns, and rabbis.

After this public demonstration the Commission—again with strong Catholic and Jewish collaboration—shared in a prolonged effort to mobilize support for the civil rights bill which was being considered in Congress. Spokesmen for the churches testified in its behalf at open hearings in committees of both the Senate and the House of Representatives. While a filibuster against it was under way, the religious groups organized a massive convocation in Washington to voice support of the bill. Daily services of intercession were held in the Church of the Reformation, on Capitol Hill, with leaders of the three faiths as preachers.

At the same time local councils of churches and councils of church women across the nation were holding similar gatherings and stimulating their members to let their representatives in Congress know of their concern. On the occasion of the tenth anniversary of the Supreme Court's decision on the desegregation of public schools, church delegations from forty-four states went to Washington to publicize the wide support for the civil rights bill. When it finally became law on July 2, 1964, political spokesmen on both sides of the legislative debate credited the churches with having made the difference between passage and failure.

More difficult and more persistent projects of direct action lay ahead. One of these was the effort to break down the barriers against Negroes' exercising their suffrage as citizens in the most resistant areas. In the summer of 1964 several hundred volunteers, many of them clergymen, participated in Mississippi in a program of assisting Negroes to register as voters. In the following summer the Commission on Religion and Race provided an orientation course on the campus of Western College for Women for six hundred college and university students who had enrolled with civil rights organizations for work in the voter registration project.

In September, 1964, the Commission launched a long-term project in Mississippi, called "the Delta Ministry," for working with impoverished Negroes, chiefly evicted plantation hands, in alleviating their economic, educational, and social condition. The area of the Delta Ministry is a rich cotton-growing section where the average wage of the workers who hoe and pick the cotton has been less than $500 a year. The chief emphasis of the Ministry has been on establishing a sound economic base. Four hundred acres were acquired where a new community, Freedom City, is being built, in which Negroes can become self-supporting in small industries and on little farms of their own. A center for training Negroes for community leadership is also being developed. The project has attracted interest among churches in other lands. Through the World Council's Department of Interchurch Aid, gifts for the Delta Ministry totaling more than $150,000 were received from Christians in twenty different countries during the first two years of operation.

In 1967 a wider program was initiated, focused on conditions in urban centers across the nation and aiming to give support to local groups seeking equal opportunity for Negroes in all phases of community life. The program is a decentralized one, which leaves the planning and directing of projects to the leadership in each area but provides stimulus and reinforcement from national experience. Inferior education and discrimination in housing and in employment are special targets of attack. Such goals as these, calling for long-continued effort, are likely to be a major testing of the capacity of the churches to be durable campaigners for social justice.

An allied engagement in social action was the commitment to a sustained voluntary effort for the elimination of poverty. In 1964 the National Council of Churches decided to make this one of its priorities. Instead of creating a separate structure for the purpose, it organized an "anti-poverty task force," recruited on a lend-lease and part-time basis, partly from denominational agencies and partly from departments of the Council, working under an over-all plan and a coordinating staff. United Church Women, for example, recruited volunteers to screen young women applicants for the Job Corps.

The major thrust of the program was giving stimulus and guidance to the churches in local communities, through both denominational channels and local and state councils of churches and councils of church women. The whole undertaking was conducted in basic accord with

Catholic and Jewish bodies through an Inter-Religious Committee against Poverty, organized early in 1966. A more experimental type of collaboration was the setting up of an Inter-Religious Foundation for Community Organization.[14] In it five Protestant denominations—American Baptist, Methodist, Episcopal, United Church of Christ, United Presbyterian—together with two Catholic agencies, the American Jewish Committee, and the Foundation for Voluntary Services, have joined in an effort to help mobilize poor communities for greater effectiveness in solving their own problems.

Concerted Action for Peace

The support of the American churches for the United Nations was greatly enhanced when the Methodist Church in 1963 erected "The Church Center for the United Nations" at United Nations Plaza and generously placed its facilities for an ecumenical program at the disposal of the National Council's Department of International Affairs. The program at the Center embraces two main interests, the education of American Christians in international affairs and friendly contacts with United Nations personnel. Since multitudes of visitors come to the United Nations every year, the major emphasis is on conducting brief seminars for them on international problems and the work of the U.N. An average of about a thousand persons a month have shared in these seminars, most of them for a period of two or three days. Some of them, however, extend for longer periods and are planned for classes from schools and colleges.[15]

In the fall of 1965 another Study Conference on World Order was held, the sixth in a series that began in 1942. Again, as at the similar gathering in 1958, a spotlight of national publicity played upon its recommendation that the United States re-examine its policy of non-recognition of the People's Republic of China and, under clear conditions, support its admission to the United Nations. In the same year a team of Japanese Christians, critical of the American military intervention in Vietnam, came to America for conference with American Christians, and a delegation from the National Council held a consultation in Bangkok with representatives of the East Asia Christian Conference. In the following year there was a consultation in Bogota with leaders of the Evangelical Churches of Latin America on the radical social changes taking place in the southern continent.

---

14 See *The New York Times,* May 11, 1967. The term "Inter-Religious" indicates a type of structure that is not officially ecclesiastical and may include organizations of either individuals or churches.

15 The establishment of the Church Center for the United Nations was soon followed by the development of a similar center for Roman Catholic activity, carried on in connection with the parish Church of the Holy Family.

At its Triennial Assembly in Miami at the end of 1966 the deepening concern over the world situation led the National Council to make an intensified "Program for Peace" a high priority for the next three years. Four specific issues were docketed for study and action: the growing gap between the affluent and the underdeveloped nations, the role of the United States in the world community, the international aspects of race relations, and the crisis in Vietnam.

The concern over world poverty was accentuated by the experience of American Christians who had participated in the international Conference on the Church and Society held in Geneva under the auspices of the World Council, July 12–26, 1966.[16] The note that was sounded there most strongly was that although mankind now possesses the technological capacity to lift the burden of poverty from the backs of every people, the gap between the rich nations and the poor is widening instead of narrowing. It was pointed out, for example, that although during the years of the Marshall Plan after World War II, 2 per cent of the gross national product of the United States had gone to European reconstruction, today our country is providing only three-tenths of 1 per cent for assistance in all of Asia, Africa, and Latin America. The Geneva Conference proved to be a moment of truth for American delegates about American responsibility for foreign policy which would enable the underdeveloped nations to share more equitably in the world's resources. It was a surprise for Americans to discover that in the eyes of Asians, Africans, and Latin Americans the great dividing line is no longer between the United States and Soviet Russia, as representing capitalist versus socialistic policies, but between affluent countries—whether in the American or the Russian orbit—and those that still lack modern industrial development. In making world peace a special priority the churches of the National Council committed themselves to a vigorous effort to overcome the apathy, indifference, and lack of imagination which block progress in a new deal for the poverty-stricken parts of our world.

All in the Day's Work

Although the National Council's activity in public affairs became well known, most of its program lay in realms that received no spotlight. It consisted of steady day-by-day services to the member denominations in their basic tasks of evangelism, education, missions, and social welfare. Since these were little recognized outside the churches, a distorted image of the Council was widely prevalent. As Bishop Reuben H.

---

[16] J. Brooke Moseley, Episcopal bishop of Delaware, was co-chairman of the Conference, serving with M. M. Thomas of India.

Mueller said in his presidential address to the Council in 1966, after speaking of its more publicized aspect:[17]

> Our problem is how to keep all this in proper relationship and balance. The tendency is for the new and unusual to become the center of interest on the part of the public to the almost total eclipse of the many fine, constructive programs that have been going on for decades in cooperative Christian enterprise and have kept step with a changing world at the same time.[18]

Viewed in long-range perspective, the most significant role of the National Council is in bringing together, and making available to all, the best experience and the best thinking of a wide variety of churches. In fulfilling this role it performs eight different types of function.

1. The Council provides a meeting ground for the generation and exchange of ideas through stimulating interdenominational conferences and consultations. Typical of a far larger number were the following in the 1960's:

North American Conference on Church and Family
National Convocation of Christian Colleges
North American Conference on the Ministry of the Laity in the World
Quadrennial Student Conference on the World Mission of the Church
Annual Convocation on the Urban Church
Annual Convocation on the Church in Town and Country
Annual Training Conference for Outgoing Missionaries
National Faculty Conference on Faith and Learning in the University
National Consultation on Legalized Gambling
National Study Conference on the Church and Economic Life
National Conference on the Church and Society

Many of these and similar gatherings are more inclusive than the National Council's own constituency.

2. The Council produces and publishes materials that meet a recognized need in the ongoing program of all denominations. An important illustration is the annual study courses for missionary education in the local church. In the years 1964 to 1967 these included "The Changing City Challenges the Church," "Spanish Americans," "Races and Reconciliation," "Affluence and Poverty: Dilemma for Christians," "The Chris-

---

[17] REUBEN H. MUELLER (1897–), Evangelical United Brethren minister and bishop; pastor in Minneapolis, South Bend, and Indianapolis, 1921–1937; superintendent of Indiana Conference of Evangelical Church, 1937–1941; general secretary, Board of Christian Education and Evangelism, 1941–1954; bishop since 1954; president of National Council of Churches, 1963–1966.

[18] *1966 Triennial Report*, p. 13.

tian Mission in Southern Asia," "The Church's Mission Among New Nations," "Mission: The Christian's Calling," and "Christ and the Faiths of Men." In these and many other cases the whole process of planning, writing, and distributing is completely interdenominational. There are also many periodicals for common use, such as *International Journal of Religious Education, Information Service, The Church Woman,* and *Town and Country Church.*

3. The Council is a center for study and research in major areas of common concern. A five-year undertaking of this kind was the pooling of resources by sixteen denominations in the early sixties for producing a comprehensive guide for curriculum building in religious education.[19] It covers essential groundwork in theology and educational philosophy and practice, which denominational agencies had previously developed separately. Among many other studies in specialized fields in the same period were "Ethics for an Industrial Age," "Human Values in a Society of Advancing Technology," "The Biblical Basis of the Role of Women in the Church," "The Audio-Visual Resource Guide," "Tax Exemption of the Churches," and "What Is a Christian College?" Of a different type are the semi-monthly bulletins on "Religion in Communist Dominated Areas" and a continuous service of supplying missionary boards with the latest information about conditions in crucial regions like China and Africa.

4. The Council is an instrument of joint administration in projects that clearly call for combined resources and unified direction. The translation of the Bible, emergency relief overseas, and the resettlement of refugees are obvious illustrations. Other operations which would be impracticable on a denominational basis are the service to more than a hundred American community churches overseas, the provision for worship in forty-seven national parks and recreation centers, and the initiation of radio and television programs every week over national networks.

5. The Council is a stimulus to experiment and pioneering in new types of work which involve more than one denomination. An original undertaking of this kind involves thirteen denominations in Columbia, Md., where a new city is being built from the ground up as a project in progressive urban development. The Council is a catalytic factor in the formation of a religious facilities corporation for the community which is to erect and maintain the physical resources for all the congregations, thus avoiding competitiveness in church building, and arrange for cooperative ministries. A different kind of pioneering is the launching of a movement to encourage courses in religion in the nation's

---

[19] Published in 1965 under the title, *The Church's Educational Ministry: A Curriculum Plan* (St. Louis: Bethany Press, 1965).

public schools. With strong support from the president of the Council, Arthur S. Flemming, himself a distinguished educator, workshops and seminars are beginning to explore the possibilities.[20] The assumption behind the experiment is that the churches should move out together in taking advantage of the Supreme Court's comment that its decision against prayer and devotional Bible reading in the schools does not forbid objective teaching about religion as a part of a secular program of education. A policy statement on the subject, adopted by the Council's General Board on June 7, 1963, holds that while "teaching for religious commitment is the responsibility of the home and the community of faith," the public schools "have an obligation to help individuals develop an intelligent understanding and appreciation of the role of religion in the life of the people of this nation."

6. The Council serves as a collective voice for the member denominations in areas of public concern. In the eyes of those not closely related to its work, this often appears to be its primary function. It is, however, a relatively secondary one. In the triennium 1963–1966, for example, there were only eleven "policy statements." In addition there were nineteen "resolutions," which had to do with the implementation of policies previously laid down.[21] While several of the policy statements dealt with issues as controversial as the war in Vietnam, others were concerned with less publicized matters like drug addiction and family life. Contrary to a widespread impression, the policy statements issued by the General Assembly or the General Board do not claim to "speak *for*" the members of the churches, but rather to speak *to* them in the way of guidance.

7. The Council serves as a common agent for Protestant and Orthodox Churches in maintaining continuous friendly connections with Roman Catholic and Jewish bodies. In a society as pluralistic as ours such relationships are a matter of strategic consequence, yet they cannot be adequately established and sustained by separate denominations acting individually. Numerous concrete cases of interreligious collaboration in areas of social and civic responsibility have been cited on earler pages.

8. The Council is the main point of contact in keeping the member denominations as a group in touch with secular organizations and movements that are actively concerned with human welfare. These are widely varied—educational, cultural, philanthropic, industrial, professional,

---

[20] ARTHUR S. FLEMMING (1905–), Methodist layman; director of the School of Public Affairs, American University, 1934–1939; U.S. Civil Service Commission, 1939–1948; president of Ohio Wesleyan University, 1948–1953; member of President Eisenhower's Advisory Committee on Governmental Reorganization, 1953–1961; Secretary for Health, Education and Welfare in the Cabinet, 1958–1961; president of the University of Oregon since 1961; president of National Council of Churches since 1966.

[21] The full list of both "policy statements" and "resolutions" is given in the *1966 Triennial Report,* pp. 144–146.

civic, governmental. Many of these relationships call for a greater measure of specialized knowledge and experience than smaller denominations can have. Moreover, most of the secular agencies are not prepared to deal with denominations one by one but are glad to sustain a friendly connection on an interdenominational basis.

Restructuring the National Council

A three-year process of rethinking the internal structure of the National Council of Churches in the light of its operational experience resulted in a reorganization that became effective on January 1, 1965. The loose-jointed pattern of the earlier years, when the merged agencies were learning how to function as one body, was succeeded by a more cohesive organization with more clearly defined lines of delegated authority.

All the units responsible for program (with a single exception) were consolidated into four divisions—Christian Life and Mission, Overseas Ministries, Christian Education, Christian Unity.[22] This development was more than an administrative reshuffling. Behind it lay a serious reconsideration of what the member churches should expect from the Council, and from this a more explicit philosophy of organization emerged. The Division of Christian Life and Mission was to be concerned with the witness and work of the church among the American people and in relation to their culture. The Division of Overseas Ministries was to function similarly in all parts of the world outside our national borders. The Division of Christian Education was to address itself to all phases of Christian nurture and the teaching responsibility of the church. The Division of Christian Unity, a new structure, was to concentrate on bringing into sharper focus all programs directed primarily to fostering understanding and fellowship among the American churches, including Faith and Order studies, work with particular lay constituencies (women, men, youth), and relations with state and local councils of churches across the country.

In this reorganization there were changes in administrative arrangements affecting all four divisions, such as the establishing of three central offices for Program and Planning, Communication, and Administration. A further basic change was the assignment of greater authority to the General Board and the general secretariat. The over-all result was a more unified and closely knit structure.[23] More significant than any

---

[22] "Christian Life and Mission" was a union of the previous Division of Christian Life and Work, the Division of Home Missions, and the Central Department of Evangelism. "Overseas Ministries" was a union of the Division of Foreign Missions and Church World Service. The one program unit which was not embraced within a division was the Broadcasting and Film Commission, which, in addition to having its own program, provides a central service to all other programs and to the Council as a whole.

[23] A chart of organization as of January 1, 1965, is reproduced as an Appendix.

of the concrete changes was the evidence that the Council was not committed to patterns inherited from the past but could face the future with the flexibility that changing situations called for.

A fundamental need which was stressed in the discussions attending reorganization was for more comprehensive long-range planning by the cooperating churches. Its crucial importance was especially urged by the Council's president at this time, J. Irwin Miller, in the light of his own extensive experience in the economic and industrial world.[24] Effective long-range planning, however, requires such extensive expenditures on social and religious research that it is one of the areas of responsibility in which less advance has been made.

With the internal reorganization of the Council went considerable revision of its constitution and by-laws. Two new clauses were added to the statement of purpose. One declared that the Council is "to assist the churches in self-examination of their life and witness."[25] This was obviously a recognition of the need for spiritual renewal, parallel to the mood of Vatican Council II. It is of more than incidental interest that the American churches were beginning to look to the National Council as not only practically useful but as having important meaning at the deeper levels of the spirit.

The other addition to the constitutional statement of purpose was this insertion:

> To study and to speak and act on conditions and issues in the nation and the world which involve moral, ethical and spiritual principles inherent in the Christian Gospel.[26]

Although this purpose was already implicit in the constitution, it had not previously been spelled out in specific terms. Its addition at this time was prompted, in part at least, by questioning in conservative quarters as to whether the Council had any "mandate" to "take a stand" on public issues. The new clause left no doubt that the member denominations expected the Council to serve them in this difficult area of study and witness and action.

An additional article of the constitution indicated a growing solidarity between the churches and their Council. This had to do with the obligations assumed by a denomination in becoming a member:

> Communions in assuming membership in the Council thereby accept

---

[24] J. IRWIN MILLER (1909–), Disciples of Christ layman, president of Cummins Engine Co., 1945–1951, and chairman of the board since 1951; director of industrial and financial corporations; trustee of National Industrial Conference Board and Committee on Economic Development; chairman of board of trustees of Christian Theological Seminary; president of National Council of Churches, 1960–1963.

[25] Article II: 6.

[26] Article II: 8.

responsibility for assisting in the furtherance of its purposes and work, for sharing in its financial support, and for reporting and interpreting the purpose and work of the Council to their constituencies.[27]

The reference to "reporting and interpreting" was new. It reflected a concern over attacks on some aspects of the Council's program and a conviction that they could best be met by more adequate procedures within each denomination.

The Interdenominational Line-Up

During the seventeen years following the inauguration of the National Council ten additional denominations became members:

> The Greek Orthodox Archdiocese of North and South America in 1952
>
> The Hungarian Reformed Church in America in 1957
>
> The Polish National Catholic Church in America in 1957
>
> The Armenian Apostolic Church of America in 1957
>
> The Serbian Eastern Orthodox Diocese for the U.S.A. and Canada in 1957
>
> The Syrian Orthodox Church of Antioch: Archdiocese of the U.S.A. and Canada in 1960
>
> The Church of the New Jerusalem in 1966
>
> The Progressive National Baptist Convention, Inc., in 1966
>
> The Exarchate of the Russian Orthodox Church in North and South America in 1966
>
> The Antiochian Orthodox Catholic Diocese of Toledo and Dependencies in 1966

Of these ten bodies seven were outside the Protestant tradition. Their presence in the Council clearly evidenced its widening ecumenical character. One small Protestant group, the Unity of the Brethren, withdrew in 1965.

During the same seventeen years there had been three mergers within the Council's circle—Congregational-Christian and Evangelical and Reformed in 1957; Presbyterian (U.S.A.) and United Presbyterian in 1958; United Lutheran, Augustana Lutheran, and American Evangelical Lutheran in 1962.

The thirty-four denominations constituting the National Council in 1967 had a combined membership of forty-two million.[28] It could fairly be described as the central stream of church life in America, other than Roman Catholic. The National Council, however, is not the only instrument of interchurch cooperation among American Protestants. Two other organizations provide rallying centers for certain groups.

---

[27] Article III: 3.
[28] *The Year Book of American Churches, 1967,* pp. 198–214.

The more important of the two is the National Association of Evangelicals, with a membership of about 2,500,000, including local conferences, local associations, and congregations, as well as thirty-four denominations. The larger ones are chiefly of the Pentecostal and Holiness type—the Assemblies of God, the Church of God (Cleveland, Tenn.), the Pentecostal Church of God, the International Church of the Foursquare Gospel, the Pentecostal Holiness Church, the Free Methodist Church, and the Pilgrim Holiness Church.[29] Through affiliated missionary societies the N.A.E. is sympathetically related to a wider circle. It appeals to those who are committed to very conservative doctrinal views and to more traditional social outlooks than are reflected in most of the denominations of the National Council.[30] Within the National Council's members there are considerable minorities that share the views of the N.A.E.

The other agency of Protestant cooperation is the American Council of Christian Churches, comprised of a very small group of the most extreme and militant fundamentalists. Of its fifteen denominations, seven have memberships of less than 5,000. Its only large constituent is the American Baptist Association (Landmark), with over 650,000 members. The American Council is better described as a reaction against the ecumenical movement than as an expression of it. It devotes much of its energy to public attacks on the National Council and the mainline denominations, which are frequently pilloried as "apostate." When, for example, the General Assembly of the Presbyterian Church in the U.S.A. adopted the Confession of Faith, 1967, the American Council promptly declared that this meant "the death of the church," and its president announced that he would send a hearse across the country as a symbol of the fact. Another continuous interest of the American Council is an indiscriminate anti-communist campaign.

Outside of the National Council of Churches, the National Association of Evangelicals, and the American Council of Christian Churches, there are several large denominations not aligned with any of them. Most of these are on the theological right—like the Southern Baptist Convention, the American Lutheran Church, the Lutheran Church-Missouri Synod, and the Churches of Christ. Some of the unaligned, however, participate in limited phases of the National Council's work. The Southern Baptists, for example, shared in the major project of its Division of Christian Education, which resulted in the curriculum guide, *The Church's Educational Ministry*. The American Lutheran Church cooperates in several

---

29 *Christianity Today,* January 29, 1965, and February 17, 1967.

30 The evangelist Billy Graham, although identified with no organization, is widely regarded as typical of what "conservative evangelicals" stand for. At the same time he has many ecumenical contacts and was a speaker at the Triennial Assembly of the National Council of Churches in 1966.

of the Council's programs. Outside of the cooperative structures on the theological left are the Unitarian-Universalist Association and the Church of Christ Scientist. The aggregate membership of the unaligned bodies with a Protestant background is not less than twenty million.

Unions as Well as Cooperation

While interdenominational cooperation and federation were increasingly becoming characteristic of the American scene, there were also an unusual number of negotiations for organic union. During the nineteenth century such unions had been exceedingly rare.[31] In the first half of the twentieth a process of uniting groups of the same confessional background made considerable headway, resulting in fourteen mergers within the fifty years. After mid-century there were twelve unions within a brief span of fifteen years, a marked acceleration of pace. In a few cases one of the uniting groups was so small that the union might be more accurately described as an absorption, but in other cases the bodies that came together represented substantial strength. With the single exception of the merger that resulted in the United Church of Christ, the unions of the nineteen-fifties and sixties took place within denominational families and so did not involve the reconciling of serious differences in doctrine or polity.

Within the Lutheran circle the process of knitting up many groups, separated by ethnic and other differences, was climaxed by two unions in the early sixties. In 1961 the American Lutheran Church came into existence through the union of the Evangelical Lutheran Church, the American Lutheran Church, and the Lutheran Free Churches. A year later the Lutheran Church in America was created by a fusion of the United Lutheran Church, the Augustana Evangelical Lutheran Church, the American Evangelical Lutheran Church, and the Finnish Evangelical Lutheran Church. In 1964 the very small National Lutheran Church was incorporated into the Lutheran Church-Missouri Synod.

In the Presbyterian family the United Presbyterian Church in the U.S.A. was formed in 1958 by the merging of the Presbyterian Church in the U.S.A. and the United Presbyterian Church of North America. Two other groups, both small, the Reformed Presbyterian Church in North America and the Evangelical Presbyterian Church, joined forces in the Reformed Presbyterian Church, Evangelical Synod.

Within the Wesleyan tradition two unions were consummated in 1968. The major one produced the United Methodist Church by the merger of the Methodist Church and the Evangelical United Brethren Church. The latter was itself the result of an earlier union, in two stages, of three bodies, the Evangelical Association, the United Evangelical

---

[31] The most significant was the reunion of Old School and New School Presbyterians in 1870, healing the schism of 1837.

Church, and the Church of the United Brethren in Christ. The other union was that of the Wesleyan Methodist Conference and the Pilgrim Holiness Church, both of which had maintained a stronger accent on sanctification than was characteristic of American Methodist's generally.

In the Baptist circle there was a decision in the small Danish Baptist General Conference to disband in 1958 in order to facilitate the coming of its congregations into the American Baptist Convention.

Among the Quakers, who tend to minimize the importance of organization, the Philadelphia Yearly Meeting of Friends and the Yearly Meeting of the Religious Society of Friends of Philadelphia and Vicinity joined in a common fellowship in 1955. Two very small groups of Mennonites, the Conference of Evangelical Mennonites and the Evangelical Mennonite Church, united in 1953.

At the more liberal end of the theological spectrum the American Unitarian Association and the Universalist Church of North America effected a combination of forces in 1961.

The creation of the United Church of Christ in 1957 meant a blending of more diverse denominational heritages than any other union that has taken place in America. It was, in effect, a four-way merger, since each of the uniting bodies was the product of an earlier union. In 1931 the Congregationalists had united with the General Convention of Christian Churches, both congregational in polity but having very different historical antecedents. In 1934 the Reformed Church in the United States had merged with the Evangelical Synod of North America, both German in background but representing different traditions.[32] After 1957 these four denominations constituted the United Church of Christ. In 1959 it adopted a Statement of Faith, described as a "testimony" rather than a "test," and in 1961 a constitution for the United Church was validated.

The road to this union, however, was decidedly rough. The chief obstacle was the fear of some Congregationalists that union with a denomination of presbyterian polity would mean too much limitation on the freedom of the local church. Legal action in the civil courts to block the merger was the final resort of the objectors. When the judicial decision sustained the union, more than two hundred local churches, still unreconciled, continued their separate existence, forming the National Association of Congregational Christian Churches.[33]

While these unions were being consummated, there were other negotiations and conversations that proved abortive. Among the more conspicuous dead ends were those of the Episcopalians and the Presbyterians (1946); the Presbyterians U.S.A., the Southern Presbyterians,

---

[32] See p. 147.

[33] A complete chronological list of all American church unions that have been consummated in the twentieth century is to appear in a forthcoming companion volume.

and the United Presbyterians (1952); and the American Baptists and the Disciples (1952). Some of the efforts at union failed because protracted discussions revealed that the distance between the negotiating bodies was still too great to be bridged. Others petered out for lack of sustained interest.

A General Plan for Organic Union

There has been no American union as yet which has resolved the difference between a church that stresses the significance of a ministry ordained in the historic succession of bishops and a church that regards this as unessential or undesirable. The most comprehensive and far-reaching effort to surmount this obstacle grows out of a proposal made by Eugene Carson Blake on December 4, 1960, in a sermon in Grace Cathedral (Episcopal) in San Francisco. He called for a serious discussion of union to bring about a church that would be "truly Catholic" and "truly Reformed." His proposal contemplated a continuation of the historic episcopate, although without requiring any particular interpretation of the nature of the succession. In his explanation of this crucial point he said:

> The reunited church must have visible and historical continuity with the Church of all ages before and after the Reformation. This will include a ministry which by its orders and ordination is recognized as widely as possible by all other Christian bodies. To this end I propose that, without adopting any particular theory of apostolic succession, the reunited church shall provide at its inception for the consecration of all its bishops by bishops and presbyters both in the apostolic succession and out of it from all over the world from all Christian churches which would authorize or permit them to take part.[34]

Although Dr. Blake's proposal was entirely unofficial, in the following May the United Presbyterian General Assembly adopted a resolution which invited the Protestant Episcopal Church to join with it in an invitation to the Methodist Church and the United Church of Christ "to explore the establishment of a United Church truly Catholic, truly Reformed and truly Evangelical." In September of the same year the General Convention of the Episcopal Church made a favorable response to the invitation.

A "Consultation on Church Union" was thereupon officially organized. It held its first meeting in the spring of 1962 and since then has met annually for sessions of several days. The number of participating denominations has increased from four to ten, the new additions being the African Methodist Church, the African Methodist Episcopal Zion Church, the Christian Methodist Church, the Evangelical United Breth-

---

[34] Hiley Ward, *op. cit.*, pp. 161–166.

ren Church, the International Convention of Churches of Christ (Disciples), and the Presbyterian Church in the U.S. Several other denominations are represented by "observer consultants." At the fifth session (1966) a preliminary "Outline for a Possible Plan of Union" was presented, with the expectation that several years would be spent in perfecting it, and perhaps a whole generation in evolving a constitution if the plan should be officially accepted. When published, the outline was modestly called "Principles of Church Union" in order to guard against the impression that conclusions about structure had already been reached.

What the Consultation is engaged in is no mere merging of existing organizations by adjustment and compromise but a complete examination of what a church should be in its faith, its mission, its structure, its worship, its witness, and its service in today's world. What is hoped for is not only a united but a uniting church and, perhaps, finally an embodied manifestation of the whole church in America.

The Preamble to *Principles of Church Union* outlines the aim in these words:

> We resolve to attempt, under God, a truer expression of the fullness of the Church of Christ than any of the constituting churches can suppose itself to be. This includes a fidelity to God's revelation in the Scriptures greater than when churches merely appealed to the Bible's words to justify their separate ways. . . . It includes a more adequate and credible confession of faith than can be the case where separate traditions obscure the common inheritance. It includes a public worship and sacramental life which will manifest more clearly and surely the high priesthood of Christ, and the part of all believers in that priesthood, than is possible behind walls of separation which exclude some of those whom Christ has welcomed. It includes an ordering of the ministry which will recognize a greater diversity of the Spirit's gifts, and release those gifts for wider and more effective service, than is the case where separated ministries in separated churches are expected to give priority to the institutional interests of those churches.[35]

The Consultation is careful to make it clear that everything which it has done thus far is open to revision, but as now set forth it appears that the united church which is envisioned would include the episcopacy, with the principle of historic succession as a symbol of continuity; use the Apostles' and Nicene Creeds as historic expressions of the faith; permit the option of infant or believer's baptism; provide for the celebration of the Holy Communion by ordained ministers; unify the existing ministries by a corporate act which would seek God's blessing and authority for a common ministry for the united church.

It will probably be several years before the outcome of the Consultation on Church Union will be known, but at least it can be said that

---

[35] Hiley Ward, *op. cit.*, pp. 167–168.

never before in America has there been such a thorough effort to think through the whole range of issues involved in a union of widely different traditions. Earlier proposals—like the Philadelphia Plan of 1918, the plan for federal union in the early forties, and the Greenwich Plan of 1949—offered only sketchy outlines. The Consultation on Church Union is committed to a patient study of all the basic problems, a continuous program of education about them, and the exploration of possibilities of unified action in several fields while the study is still going on.

14

Today and Tomorrow

THE contrast between the denominational system as it was at the beginning of this century and as it is two generations later is nothing less than phenomenal. Within this brief span of time the separated churches have developed a new conciliar pattern which fosters mutual understanding, assures continuous consultation, facilitates cooperation in common tasks, provides a united administration of selected projects, and promotes serious study of a more complete form of unity still to be achieved.

The conciliar structure is a reality at all geographical levels—local, statewide, national, world-wide. Beginning as a movement within Protestantism, it has expanded to embrace the churches of the ancient Eastern Orthodox family. In the most recent development, the Protestant and Orthodox bodies have come into a cooperative relationship, even if still undefined, with the Roman Catholic Church—something which no one could have foreseen before the 1960's. Surveying what has taken place in the twentieth century, one is impelled to say, "This is the Lord's doing and it is marvelous in our eyes."

More important than the new conciliar structures and ecclesiastical connections is the spirit of which they are the outward expression. The main-line denominations are no longer aloof from one another, no longer content to plan and act as if they had no responsibility for one another. Differences of doctrine and practice remain but the emphasis is clearly on what unites rather than on what separates. There is still much duplication of effort, much lack of harmonious operation, much uncritical adherence to outmoded denominational procedures, but in the midst of all this there is a greatly heightened sense of constituting one body with many members. The major denominations, with few exceptions, are thinking of themselves not as rivals building up institutional empires but as allies serving the Kingdom of God. As H. Richard Niebuhr summarized our situation, in connection with an intensive study of theological education in America:

The denominations make it evident that they think of themselves increasingly as branches or members of a single community, as orders and institutions with special duties or assignments to be carried out in partnership with other branches of one society. . . . There are exceptions; denominations, and even more frequently small parties in them, contend for the sole validity of a particular form of creed, organization, or liturgy. . . . But to the sympathetic observer the increasing unity of American Protestantism is more striking than its apparent diversity.[1]

Five Stages of a Developing Unity

Looking back on the relations of the American churches to one another during the course of the twentieth century, we can plainly discern five different stages through which they have passed.

1.   At the beginning of the century the prevailing pattern was one of denominational isolation, inherited from the nineteenth century. When Christians in one denomination felt it important to work with other Christians in behalf of some Christian objective (as they constantly did) they bypassed the churches and created a nondenominational organization for that specific purpose. The American Bible Society and the International Sunday School Association were notable illustrations.

2.   A new stage was reached when denominational boards began to create interboard agencies through which to join hands in meeting common problems in their specialized fields. The Foreign Missions Conference of North America and the Home Missions Council were the earliest examples of this procedure.

3.   A third stage appeared when the denominations as corporate bodies drew together in a federated association. This reflected a concern not only for cooperation in various practical tasks but also for the relation of church to church and for the manifestation of their basic oneness in Christ. This was the impulse that created the Federal Council of the Churches of Christ in America, the first structure of a fully interdenominational character.

4.   A fourth stage emerged in mid-century when the interdenominational body and the several interboard agencies combined to form the National Council of the Churches of Christ in the U.S.A. Now, for the first time, there was a federated structure comprehensive enough to represent the member churches in the whole range of their life and work.

5.   The fifth stage, into which we are now moving, was reached when, under the influence of Vatican Council II and its decree on ecumenism, the Roman Catholic Church began to enter into new relationships of fraternal dialogue and collaboration with Protestant and Orthodox

---

[1] *The Purpose of the Church and Its Ministry* (New York: Harper & Brothers, 1956), pp. 16–17.

Churches. This is the pregnant stage in which the churches are finding themselves today, the only stage to which the term "ecumenical" can be fully applied.

In this historical evolution of a little more than sixty years, there has been a clearly discernible growth in the church's consciousness of its wholeness. In the *undenominational* stage, a concert of individual Christians for some particular purpose was secured and the churches as institutions were left out of account. In the *interboard* stage, certain denominational agencies, functioning in parallel fields, worked together at various points for the sake of a more effective operation. In the *interdenominational,* or federated, stage, the churches officially related themselves to one another as corporate entities in a corporate witness. In the *fully federated* stage in the National Council the churches have an over-all body which represents them in the total range of their activity. In the *ecumenical* stage American churches of the most widely separated traditions—Roman Catholic, Orthodox, Protestant—are becoming conscious not only of having a common responsibility in America but of being parts of one Body of Christ throughout the world.

In this latest development the ecumenical movement has no organizational embodiment which represents the whole. The nearest approach to it is the kind of consultative structures that have recently been set up in the "working committees" between the National Council of Churches and the National Conference of Catholic Bishops and between the World Council of Churches and the Vatican's Secretariat for Christian Unity.

There is no reason to suppose that the stage at which we have arrived is as far as we can go in the direction of unity. The experience which we have already had frees us from the sense of confinement within a static framework of the past. The progress which has been made points the way to fresh advances. The question is not whether we are to move on beyond the present horizon but what form the further quest of unity is to take.

The Conciliar Structure of Today

There is every reason to assume that the conciliar movement which has developed during the first half of the twentieth century is crucial for whatever advance may be made in the second half. We can hardly exaggerate the assets that reside in the councils of churches at all geographical levels from the local to the global. Any local council standing alone might be of little moment but it is important as a link in a network that relates the churches of a community to interdenominational structures of national and world-wide outreach. The National Council and the World Council, in turn, derive much of their significance from their relationship to councils with the same ecumenical commitment which are much closer to the daily life of church members.

Even though many of the local councils are not yet deeply rooted in the consciousness of the churches, they afford an indispensable foundation on which to build. The ecumenical movement will continue to be top-heavy until it is solidly grounded in each place where Christians actually live and work. Thousands of congregations still have virtually no ecumenical experience. They carry on their programs as if they were unrelated both to other churches in the same community and to the wider Christian fellowship of the nation and the world. The strengthening of "local ecumenicity" is the most strategic point of advance.[2]

The relation of the councils of churches at the different geographical levels to one another is weak in theory but fairly effective in practice. Structurally, each council—local, statewide, national, world-wide—is wholly independent of the others, responsible only to the churches of its own area. In program and leadership, however, they are interdependent and this interdependence would seem, in principle, to call for an organic interconnection. But how can this be effected while at the same time the principle is maintained that in each area the council is wholly responsible to the member churches in that area? Although no simple solution of this complex problem of relationships has emerged, working arrangements have been established which result in a growing solidarity within the conciliar movement as a whole. In informal ways the experience of councils at the different levels is brought into the thinking and planning of the others, at least in considerable measure. This result is effected largely through the fellowship of staff members of all councils with one another. An Association of Secretaries of Councils of Churches (local, state, national) although having no ecclesiastical status, exercises a strong influence in developing a common conciliar philosophy and a common program. A New York office of the World Council of Churches, under the same roof with the National Council, contributes to keeping the operations of these two bodies in close rapport.

At the present time a council of churches—at whatever geographical level—has no administrative or executive authority. Its role is consultative and coordinative. It has influence, sometimes substantial influence, but complete ecclesiastical sovereignty is retained by the denominations. There are, indeed, a few examples of *de facto* authority in administration (although never formally delegated) such as the National Council's work with migrants and its program of overseas relief. These, however, have to do with relatively recent activities, not with well-estab-

---

[2] For convincing analyses of the present situation in local communities, see William B. Cate, *The Ecumenical Scandal on Main Street* (New York: Association Press, 1965), and Forrest L. Knapp, *Church Cooperation: Dead-End Street or Highway to Unity?* (Garden City, N.Y.: Doubleday and Co., 1966).

lished denominational functions. The key issue for any major advance is whether this is to continue to be the case or whether the churches are prepared to invest their councils with a new measure of responsibility. The question cannot be long evaded whether the denominations have now reached the point of being willing to transfer any major function—foreign missionary work, for example—from fragmented administration by scores of different denominational boards to a unified administration under the National Council.

It is, of course, entirely possible for a council of churches to go on operating in ways that call for only incidental changes in the denominational bureaucracies. It can engage merely in piecemeal and marginal activities that do not seriously affect denominational structure or practice. On the other hand, there is no reason why it may not be used for a more important role. It could, if the denominations should reach the point of desiring it, not only assume significant administrative functions but also more "churchly" functions such as the joint appointment of missionaries and the joint ordination of clergy. Granted a readiness for it on the part of the denominations, there could be a step-by-step transition from a loose federation of wholly independent units to a federal union in which important responsibilities are officially delegated to the central body. And such a federal union might, in due time, evoke the kind of over-arching loyalty which would make it truly organic.[3]

Outside the Conciliar Structure

Although most of the main-line denominations are associated with the ecumenical movement in its conciliar expression, there are other bodies that remain outside, including the great Southern Baptist Convention, the Lutheran Church-Missouri Synod, and the Pentecostal groups. The chief reason for their aloofness is a feeling that the maintenance of their distinctive denominational positions in a rigorous way is more important than to join with other churches in common undertakings.

In the case of the Southern Baptists their emphasis on the local congregation as the only authentic form of church is urged as a reason for keeping them from official association with other bodies. This viewpoint was clearly voiced in a resolution of the Southern Baptist Convention declining membership in the World Council. "Our Convention," it said, "has no ecclesiological authority. It is in no sense the Southern Baptist Church."[4] At the same time a dissenting minority, although opposing

---

[3] This, it is worth noting, is what happened in the political history of the United States.
[4] *Annual of the Southern Baptist Convention, 1940*, p. 99.

organic union, held that "the basic spiritual unity of all believers should have a channel through which to give united expression to the mind and message of Christ in a world in which all Christian ideals are challenged."[5]

In the case of the Lutheran Church-Missouri Synod it is a concern for doctrinal purity which is chiefly urged as the reason for non-association with other churches. Its general position has been that there must be agreement in formulated doctrine as a precondition of either cooperation or union. For a long time this kept the Missouri Synod from membership even in other Lutheran bodies, but on January 1, 1967, it became a member of the Lutheran Council in the U.S.A. Some Southern Baptists and some Missouri Synod Lutherans share in limited phases of the work of the National Council of Churches, even though their denominations are not members of the Council, and some of their congregations are related to local councils.

The Pentecostal churches, grouped in more than a score of loosely organized assemblies, have a common denominator in their insistence on "speaking in tongues" as the sign of baptism by the Holy Spirit. The extreme spontaneity and individualism of their earlier stage are gradually being modified by the development of a more ordered institutional life. Some of the Pentecostal groups have a contact with non-Pentecostalists in the National Association of Evangelicals.

The National Association of Evangelicals does not place itself in full opposition to the conciliar structures but an emphasis on doctrinal orthodoxy as more important than unity makes it very critical of the ecumenical movement. There is a tendency in some quarters of the Association to speak of a new "evangelical ecumenism" and to set it against "conciliar ecumenism."[6] This terminology seems to assume that the ecumenical movement as it is developing is not itself "evangelical," an inference which its leaders stoutly reject.

As a measure for encouraging friendly dialogue among all churches on an equal basis, whether related to the ecumenical movement or not, the National Council's Division of Christian Unity in 1966 initiated an annual Faith and Order Colloquium. This is an entirely free body, neither committing the Council nor committed by it. All who attend come not as representatives of any group but as interested individuals, whether Roman Catholic, Eastern Orthodox, Anglo-Catholic, liberal evangelical, conservative evangelical, or bearing no label at all. The give-and-take of discussion centers each year around some concrete concern, such as conversion, evangelism, or the mission of the church to the world.

---

[5] William Wright Brown, *History of the Southern Baptist Convention: 1854–1953* (Nashville, Tenn.: The Broadman Press, 1954), pp. 250–269.

[6] See Carl F. Henry, *Evangelicals at the Brink of Crisis* (Waco, Texas: Word Books, 1967).

A Critique of the National Council

The National Council of Churches is so young—still in its teens—that any judgment about it must be tentative. As a distinguished American historian has said, in a wholly different connection, "we are always in a zone of imperfect visibility so far as the history just over our shoulder is concerned."[7] In the case of the National Council our perspective is even more limited because it is immediately before our eyes. The Council, however, is such a strategic factor in the movement toward unity that we must attempt an objective appraisal.

That the National Council has been a remarkable achievement in integration there can be no doubt. There is ample evidence that the leadership of the member denominations think of it not as "another organization" but as an extension of their own life and service. This is much more true of the Council today than it was of the interdenominational and cooperative bodies of the first half of the century. In spite of some internal strain in the 1950's, the Council has not only held firmly together but has established itself in the trust and confidence of the churches that created it. And it has achieved this impressive integration without sacrificing the prophetic spirit. It has not been content to seek a cautious consensus and to settle down in established bureaucratic grooves. On the contrary, in several areas it has provided an imaginative and adventurous leadership in the engagement of the churches with urgent problems of secular society.

There are, of course, points of weakness in its program. A crucial one arises from the general confusion in the churches over the nature of evangelism in the world of today. What constitutes effective witness to the Christian Gospel in the conditions of our time? On the one hand, there are many who are still committed to the traditional type of evangelistic appeal to the individual. On the other hand, there is a growing conviction that the converting power of the Gospel is made known less by verbal proclamation than by action in society in the spirit of the Gospel. Those who espouse the latter view urge that the main strategy in evangelism today is the conversion of the churches to a fuller understanding of and commitment to their mission in the world. For the time being, the evangelistic concern tends to be exhausted in discussions of strategy. This probing is important but is not a substitute for a positive program of nurturing a deeper evangelistic spirit throughout the churches, whatever may be the forms in which it is manifested.

The criticism of the National Council most frequently heard is that when it speaks on controversial subjects it does not really "represent" the churches. Whether or not there is validity in the charge depends on

---

[7] Arthur M. Schlesinger, Jr., in *The Crisis of the Old Order: 1919–1933* (Boston: Houghton Mifflin Co., 1957).

an analysis of what is meant by being "representative." Representative of the national leadership of the denominations? Or representative of the members of local churches? A careful review will show that there is a consistent parallel between policies set forth by the National Council and those which are voiced by national agencies of member denominations. Statements of the Council do represent collective judgments of responsible denominational leaders. It does not necessarily follow that the rank and file in local churches agree with their national leadership. There is often a considerable gap between the two, which should not surprise us. The national leaders have had more specialized training and experience than the average member of a local congregation and have been assigned to their posts for that reason. It is a part of their national responsibility to give the best guidance they can and it is more important to do this than to be representative in a merely statistical sense.

In its statements of policy on public issues, therefore, the National Council does not presume to speak *for* the churches in the sense of reporting an existing consensus within its total constituency. It speaks *to* the churches for the sake of affording guidance in examining the issues in the context of the Christian faith and ethic. The distinction between speaking "for" and speaking "to" may not always be clear but it is a basic consideration in appraising the Council's procedure.

Perhaps more important guidance would be given if the Council concentrated more intensively on a limited number of public issues. The National Conference of Catholic Bishops, by comparison, speaks less often and is less likely to respond to headline crises. It tends to take a longer look and to let less official groups (like the Catholic Inter-racial Council, for example) be spokesman in the more immediate situations. But both the churches of the National Council and the Catholic Church recognize a clear responsibility for providing guidance on controversial issues, for it is precisely the controversial issues that are most in need of whatever light the collective leadership of the churches can give.

The leadership of the Council—like that of the denominations—is more representative of the clergy than of the laity of the churches. Laymen and women of experience in business and industry and the professions of the workaday world are a minority in the supervisory and governing groups of the churches. In the General Board of the Council, for example—which is its policy-making body—there are 181 ordained ministers and 76 lay men and women.[8] The position of the Council on public issues would undoubtedly be more influential if it involved a larger measure of participation by men and women of first-hand contact with secular affairs. It should not be forgotten, however, that the National Council's active leadership includes lay people of the stature of J. Irwin Miller, Arthur S. Flemming, Charles P. Taft, Charles C. Parlin,

---

[8] The figures apply to the situation as of October, 1967.

Francis S. Harmon, Ernest A. Gross, and Mrs. James M. Dolbey. It would be a great source of strength if there were more of them.

Another question, to which there is no easy answer, is how far the statements of the Council or of its member denominations can wisely go in recommending specific courses of action. The sound principle, of course, is that a statement in the name of the churches ought to be clearly based on considerations derived from the Christian faith and ethic, not on the pragmatic judgments of those who draft the statement. On the other hand, general principles and broad moralizations are of little or no value in affording guidance for a decision in a particular situation. There are surely occasions when the churches are called upon to speak in terms of concrete action in the given historical circumstances. When an inhumane twelve-hour day in steel was industrial policy in the 1920's, when Nazi anti-Semitism was political policy in the 1930's, when there was a struggle in the 1940's to establish the beginning of a structure for world community in the United Nations, when racial desegregation and civil rights for Negroes were a public issue in the 1950's and 1960's, churches that spoke only in terms of such general principles as brotherhood and justice would have failed to bear effective witness to the meaning of the Gospel. What is needed is guidance that is concrete enough to search the conscience and stir to definite action. In many cases the finding of the right course for the churches between being too vague and being too specific is a matter of delicately balanced judgment, but the complexity should not deter them from their best efforts to keep their members alertly aware of and sensitive to their Christian involvement in society.

The Widening Ecumenical Horizon

The presence of the Roman Catholic Church in the ecumenical picture is making a great difference in the ecumenical movement. What began as a Protestant enterprise and then enlarged to include the Eastern Orthodox now embraces great Christian communities of all the historic traditions. The movement is now far wider than any organization. During the coming years, therefore, we shall be writing a new chapter in ecumenical history and developing relationships for which we have no established pattern.

Thus far the new Catholic-Protestant encounter has been chiefly in terms of friendly dialogue and consultation, but almost every week brings gratifying evidence of readiness for active collaboration. There are already remarkable examples of concerted planning in fields of social concern, such as racial injustice, poverty, and war. The presence of Catholic observers at Protestant-Orthodox meetings of many types and of Protestant-Orthodox observers at Roman Catholic meetings has been so fruitful in furthering a common sense of direction that the "observer" category may become *passé* in the not-distant future and give way to more continuous and more official relationships.

The friendly contacts of Catholics and Protestants and their common efforts in social tasks do not directly touch the historic differences between them in the realm of faith and order. At least, however, the contacts help to create a situation in which the things that divide are seen in a different perspective and can now be discussed in a reconciling atmosphere. A long Catholic-Protestant dialogue on both basic agreements and differences undoubtedly lies ahead.[9]

In an increasing number of local and state areas Roman Catholic parishes or dioceses are becoming full members of councils of churches. If this experimental trend continues it will probably affect the conciliar movement in ways that we do not yet see. It would hardly be realistic to expect that at the national or world levels a similar development will take place in the foreseeable future, but it is reasonable to look forward to steadily increasing cooperation between the National Council of Churches and the National Conference of Catholic Bishops, and also between the World Council and the Vatican. The great desideratum at this stage is to maintain an openness to the future and a readiness to move in the direction in which the Holy Spirit leads.

While rejoicing in the new relationship with Roman Catholics, the Protestant churches should not overlook the opportunity for strengthening their ties with the Orthodox. The main bodies of the Eastern churches in America are now full members of the National Council, but their role is still limited. Out of their rich historic heritage they have a potential contribution to make to American Christianity much greater than is yet realized. This is especially true at the level of the local communities where Protestant and Orthodox congregations exist side by side.

The new relation between Catholics and Protestants heightens the issue of the relation of both of them to the Jews. Under a strict definition of terms this lies outside the ecumenical movement. In its ecclesiastical usage "ecumenical" is specifically a Christian word, not one that has to do with goodwill and friendliness in general.[10] But if the relation of Christian and Jew is outside ecumenical structure it is not outside the ecumenical spirit. The ecumenical spirit reaches out for closer links with men of goodwill everywhere, and seeks to overcome institutional rigidities that keep men walled off from one another.

---

[9] "Dialogue" is a word that has been worn thin by constant usage in recent years. In its authentic ecumenical sense it signifies more than discussion. It implies a mutuality of relationship at a deep personal level.

[10] In 1963 there was a so-called *agape* in New York in which Protestants, Orthodox, Roman Catholics, Jews, Muslims, and Buddhists participated and to which the press referred as an "ecumenical" occasion. It was significant in its own way, and commendable for its own purpose, but it was not "ecumenical." I am indebted to Roswell P. Barnes for this illustration.

In America a pattern of cooperation between Protestant, Catholic, and Jewish bodies in the realm of social responsibilities is fairly well established. It is concretely expressed in the National Conference on Religion and Race of 1963, and in the current National Inter-Religious Committee against Poverty and the National Interfaith Committee to Promote Community Organization. There is hardly any phase of the National Council's social outreach in which its staff is not in frequent consultation with Jewish as well as Roman Catholic agencies operating in the same area of concern.

Thus far the cooperation between Christian and Jew has hardly gone beyond humanitarian and social concern and the combating of anti-Semitism, but dialogue at a much deeper religious level is called for. The Christian faith has Judaic roots—historical, theological, ethical. The God of the New Testament and the God of the Old Testament are the same. In spite of deep difference in the interpretation of the Person of Jesus Christ, Christians are (as Pope Pius XII said) "spiritually Semites." We cannot, therefore, regard the Jewish people and Judaism in quite the same way as all other people and all other religions. There is a special basis for sympathetic understanding, as well as joint endeavors in many ways.

The Prospect for Church Union

The record of church unions in the United States, thus far in the twentieth century, has been much less impressive than the advance in cooperation. There has been enough progress, however, to offer a modest measure of encouragement. Between 1900 and 1968 there were twenty-six different cases of consummated union. Most of them were within the confines of denominational families and so did not bridge wide distances of doctrine or polity.

The one church union in the United States which represents a major transcending of denominational family lines is that which produced the United Church of Christ. When it came into existence in 1957, by a merger of the General Council of the Congregational Christian Churches and the Evangelical Reformed Church, it was a fusion of two different types of polity, presbyterian and congregational, which had often been regarded as irreconcilable. The persistence of a considerable minority of Congregationalists as a separate body indicates how difficult it is to secure anything like a unanimous decision to unite if conflicts of ecclesiastical tradition are involved. Some of the lesser unions also have been marred by dissenting minorities. When the Cumberland Presbyterians merged with the Presbyterian Church in the U.S.A. in 1906 about one-third of them continued as a separate denomination. When the Evangelical Church was formed in 1922 by a union of the United Evangelical Church and the Evangelical Association, a dissident group of the latter organized the Evangelical Congregational Church. In Canada, likewise, when the United Church was created in 1925 by a remarkable merger of Methodist, Presbyterian, and Congregational bodies, a substantial minority of Presbyterians maintained a continuing Presbyterian denomination.

The most stubborn obstacle to any union crossing denominational family lines is the tension between churches which cherish the historic episcopate, with a ministry ordained in the historic succession, and churches which regard this as either unimportant or undesirable. A major testing of the possibility of overcoming this long separation is now being faced in the Consultation on Church Union in its effort to formulate a plan for a united church which will be "truly catholic, truly reformed, and truly evangelical."

The movement for church union is reinforced today by the growing realization that most of the historical differences between the denominations, once important, are now of minor significance and irrelevant to the critical situation in which all find themselves. The great issues are no longer between Episcopalian, Lutheran, Presbyterian, Congregationalist, Baptist, and Methodist, but between Christians of whatever tradition and people indifferent to the Christian faith and the Christian church in any form. The contemporary situation is a warning to every denomination not to let a preoccupation with past controversies stand in the way of the most effective present testimony to the basic meaning of the Gospel for the world.

Although advocates of union are often superficially criticized as being too enamored of mere size and practical efficiency, the fundamental aspect of the matter lies at a deep spiritual level. The most serious weakness of the denominational system is that denominations, as denominations, testify to secondary considerations and thus divert attention from the essential purpose of the church. The church exists to draw men to Christ, not to some doctrinal system, some form of government, some special interpretation of Scripture, or some form of worship. If it becomes clear that these particularized emphases obscure the central mission of drawing men to Christ, which is the sole ground of the church's existence, they cannot be permanently accepted as valid reasons for separation within the Christian community.

In exploring the possibilities of a union which will surmount the historical differences, a crucial problem is how to achieve a unity that is consistent with a rightful liberty and diversity within the Christian fellowship. Hosts of sincere and intelligent church members shy away from a movement toward union lest it lead to a loss of freedom and the reduction of everything to standardized views and practices. If, by some miracle of grace, we were to achieve "one great church" tomorrow, it would not long remain one church if it did not make generous room for differences of theological insight, of interpretation of Scripture, of Christian experience and practice.

There is every reason to expect that in the years ahead the number of unions among closely related denominational groups will continue to increase. Although new divisions may still occur, the trend is no longer centrifugal but centripetal. Whether there is likely to be a strongly supported movement for bridging the wider distances that separate major denominational families—especially those cherishing their respective emphases on the Catholic and the Evangelical traditions—is not yet clear. In any realistic appraisal of our situation it has to be admitted that a serious quest for far-reaching union is still largely limited to theologians and thoughtful denominational leaders. Among the rank and file of main-line Protestants the interest in denominational distinctions is disappearing and there is a general longing for union but little intensive probing of the underlying problems.

Some of those who are most concerned about the renewal of the church in spiritual depth wonder how much connection there is between union and renewal. They see that all the crucial issues of today—religious, theological, social—are not between the denominations but within each of them. These differences have to do with the essential meaning of Christianity and the mission of the church in the world more than with ecclesiastical structure. Those who are committed to renewal may even feel that a concentration on problems of structure may divert attention from primary to secondary issues. Any great forward movement toward union will depend on a clear perception of its relation to the nature and purpose of the church.

How much, for example, would church union affect the pattern of racial relations within the churches? If white denominations and Negro denominations lose their separate existence within the same national body, would white and Negro Christians still be isolated from each other in separated congregations in the local community? If so, the united church of the nation would still be failing in its mission of breaking down what St. Paul calls "the dividing wall" between Christians. If, on the other hand, union resulted in a fellowship in which racial barriers are really transcended, this would mean a creative advance both in the unity of the church and in its reconciling influence in our divided society.

Even though a remarkable achievement in union should lie ahead, the need for the conciliar movement would continue. Even if all ten of the denominations now involved in the Consultation on Church Union eventually merge into one church, the problem of an over-all unity would be far from solved. There would still be many other Protestant bodies and some of them, at least, will probably not be prepared to consider union for many years to come. There is good reason, however, to expect that they will be increasingly open to consultation, cooperation, and fellowship. To facilitate such relations interdenominational instruments will be necessary.

As for the wider relations of Protestant, Orthodox, and Roman Catholic, it would be wholly romantic to expect anything like formal union in any near future. We may, however, confidently look forward to a growing intimacy in witness and worship and work. Again, to facilitate this development, some conciliar structure, perhaps in modified forms, will be indispensable.

The Road Ahead

Within the ecumenical movement of today there is general agreement that in some vital sense the church is a single reality given to us by Jesus Christ in and with the Gospel. There is, however, no agreement as to how that oneness is to be manifested in outer structure. At this point there are at least three different conceptions. One view is that we would have unity if denominations were working together in a continuous partnership and happy concord, with no sectarian spirit, functioning as fully cooperative units within the Christian fellowship. For others, unity means this practical cooperation and a *plus*. The *plus* is the complete mutuality and intercommunion that involve a ministry recognized by all and sacraments open to all. For still others, the goal of unity will not have been reached unless and until autonomous denominations are superseded by an inclusive church with at least some measure of central authority. In this view neither a closely knit federation nor intercommunion is a substitute for corporate union.

The ecumenical movement of our time thus has an open-end quality. It represents the beginning of a pilgrimage whose ultimate goal we do not yet discern. There is no reason to be troubled by this, provided our direction is clearly toward a greater unity. We can trust the Holy Spirit to guide if we are prepared to keep on moving forward together.

In the earlier stages of the conciliar development it sometimes received little or no support from those who were eager for a more direct approach to unity through negotiation of denominational differences. They feared that increasing cooperation among the denominations might induce a superficial satisfaction with the established denominational system. It is now evident that these fears were unwarranted. The experience of working together in fellowship has produced mutual understanding, a realization of oneness at a level deeper than the differences, and a growing desire to make that oneness manifest to the world. It is only on the basis of such experience that negotiations involving the difficult theological and ecclesiological issues have any prospect of being crowned with success.

If we are to see the ecumenical movement in true perspective, we must constantly bear in mind that its essential genius is a concern not for the unification of ecclesiastical institutions but for maximum fellow-ship and effectiveness in the witness and work and worship of Christians as one People of God. The movement is primarily mission-centered rather than organization-centered. This must become more and more clear to the rank and file of the members of the churches if it is to have a dynamic quality and command great loyalties. Far more than the re-fashioning of denominational structures is involved. The basic thrust is toward the spiritual renewal of the church for its mission in the world.

Perhaps the most important thing to be learned from the history re-viewed in these pages is that we should be less timid and cautious in our hopes and expectations for the future. What has actually taken place within the memory of living men represents such a marked ad-vance that there is no reason to set limits to the possibilities that lie ahead. Beyond question, there has been a remarkable unification of Protestant and Eastern Orthodox forces within the last sixty years, and within the last six years a wholly unanticipated *rapprochement* between them and the Roman Catholic Church. As recently as 1961 a seasoned observer of world-wide Christianity could write that there was "no real-istic prospect" that the Roman Catholic Church would become a partici-pant in ecumenical Christianity. Yet today Vatican Council II is prov-ing to be one of the most potent ecumenical influences. We may even discover that what we have thus far witnessed in the ecumenical de-velopments of the twentieth century is only a prologue to one of the most creative periods in Christian history.

Appendix

Chart of Organization of the National Council

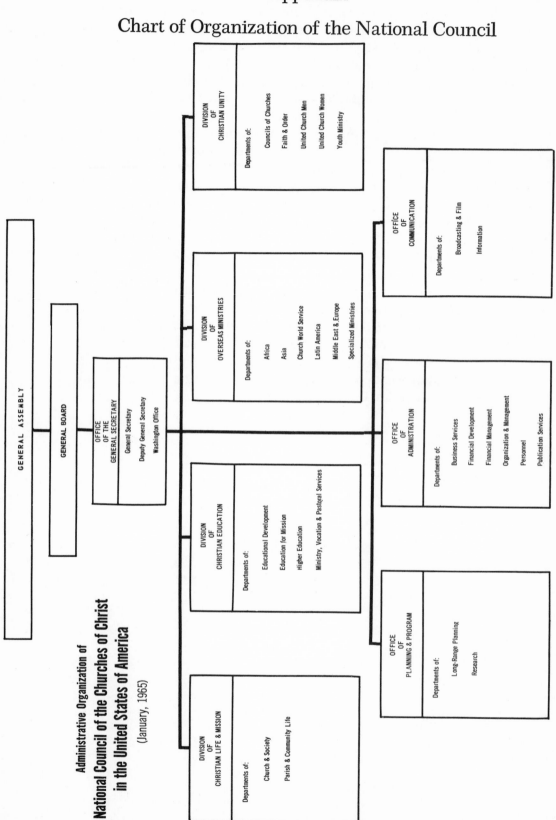

**Administrative Organization of
National Council of the Churches of Christ
in the United States of America**
(January, 1965)

GENERAL ASSEMBLY

GENERAL BOARD

OFFICE
OF THE
GENERAL SECRETARY

General Secretary
Deputy General Secretary
Washington Office

DIVISION
OF
CHRISTIAN UNITY

Departments of:

Councils of Churches
Faith & Order
United Church Men
United Church Women
Youth Ministry

DIVISION
OF
OVERSEAS MINISTRIES

Departments of:

Africa
Asia
Church World Service
Latin America
Middle East & Europe
Specialized Ministries

OFFICE
OF
COMMUNICATION

Departments of:

Broadcasting & Film
Information

DIVISION
OF
CHRISTIAN EDUCATION

Departments of:

Educational Development
Education for Mission
Higher Education
Ministry, Vocation & Pastoral Services

OFFICE
OF
ADMINISTRATION

Departments of:

Business Services
Financial Development
Financial Management
Organization & Management
Personnel
Publication Services

DIVISION
OF
CHRISTIAN LIFE & MISSION

Departments of:

Church & Society
Parish & Community Life

OFFICE
OF
PLANNING & PROGRAM

Departments of:

Long-Range Planning
Research

Selected Bibliography

by Erminie H. Lantero

I. PRINCIPAL LIBRARIES

National Council of Churches (Research Library; Archives of National Council and Predecessor Organizations), 475 Riverside Drive, New York, N. Y. 10027.

General Theological Seminary Library (Archives of World Conference on Faith and Order), Chelsea Square, New York, N. Y. 10011.

Union Theological Seminary Library (William Adams Brown Ecumenical Library; Missionary Research Library), Broadway at 120th Street, New York, N. Y. 10027.

Yale Divinity School Library (Day Historical Library of Foreign Missions), 409 Prospect Street, New Haven, Connecticut 06520.

II. BIBLIOGRAPHIES AND REFERENCE WORKS

Crow, Paul A., Jr. *The Ecumenical Movement in Bibliographical Outline.* New York: National Council of Churches, 1965. viii–80p.

Mead, Frank S. *Handbook of Denominations in the United States.* New York and Nashville, Tenn.: Abingdon Press, 2nd edn., 1961. 272p.

Rouse, Ruth, and Stephen C. Neill, eds. *A History of the Ecumenical Movement: 1517–1948.* Philadelphia: The Westminster Press (1954). 2nd edn. with revised bibliography, 1967. xxv–383p; bibliography, pp. 745–801.

Smith, James Ward, and A. Leland Jamison, eds. *Religion in American Life,* 4 vols. Vol. IV, *A Critical Bibliography of Religion in America,* by Nelson T. Burr. Princeton, N. J.: Princeton University Press, 1961. xv–545–1219p.

Yearbook of American Churches, The, 1934–1967, annual. Benson Y. Landis, ed. 1952–1966. Constant H. Jacquet, Jr., ed. 1967–   New York: National Council of Churches.

III. BACKGROUND IN AMERICAN CHURCH HISTORY

Abell, Aaron I. *The Urban Impact on American Protestantism: 1865–1900.* Cambridge, Mass.: Harvard University Press, 1943. x–275p.

Annals of the American Academy of Political and Social Science. "Organized Religion in the United States," ed. Ray H. Abrams. Philadelphia (March, 1948). v–271p.

Annals of the American Academy of Political and Social Science. "Religion in American Society," ed. Richard D. Lambert. Philadelphia (November, 1960). viii–220p.

Bacon, Leonard W. *A History of American Christianity.* New York: Charles Scribner's Sons, 1900. x–429p.

Brauer, Jerald C. *Protestantism in America: A Narrative History* (1953). Rev. edn. Philadelphia: The Westminster Press, 1965. 320p.

Gabriel, Ralph H. *The Course of American Democratic Thought: An Intellectual History Since 1815.* New York: The Ronald Press, 1940. xi-452 p.

Garrison, Winfred E. *The March of Faith: The Story of Religion in America Since 1865.* New York: Harper & Brothers, 1933. viii–332p.

Handy, Robert T. *The Protestant Quest for a Christian America: 1830–1930.* Philadelphia: Fortress Press, 1965. ix–254p.

Hopkins, Charles Howard. *The Rise of the Social Gospel in American Protestantism: 1865–1915.* New Haven: Yale University Press, 1940. xii–352p.

Hudson, Winthrop S. *The Great Tradition of the American Churches.* New York: Harper & Brothers, 1953. 282p.

————. *Religion in America.* New York: Charles Scribner's Sons, 1965. xii–447p.

Latourette, Kenneth S. *Christianity in a Revolutionary Age.* Vol. III, *The Nineteenth Century Outside Europe,* Chaps. I–IX. New York: Harper & Brothers, 1961. Vol. IV, *The Twentieth Century Outside Europe,* Chap. II. New York: Harper & Brothers, 1962.

————. *A History of the Expansion of Christianity.* Vol. IV, *The Great Century, A.D. 1800–A.D. 1914.* Vol. VII, *Advance Through Storm.* Chapters on the United States; full bibliographies. New York: Harper & Brothers, 1945.

Littell, Franklin H. *From State Church to Pluralism: A Protestant Interpretation of Religion in American History.* New York: Doubleday and Co. (Anchor Book), 1962. 174p.

Mead, Sidney E. *The Lively Experiment: The Shaping of Christianity in America.* New York: Harper & Row, 1963. xiii–220p.

Nash, Arnold S., ed. *Protestant Thought in the Twentieth Century: Whence and Whither?* New York: The Macmillan Company, 1951. xii–296p.

Nichols, James H. *Democracy and the Churches.* Philadelphia: The Westminster Press, 1951. 298p.

Niebuhr, H. Richard. *The Kingdom of God in America.* New York: Harper & Brothers, 1937 (Harper Torchbook, 1959). xxii–215p.

Schaff, Philip. *America: A Sketch of its Political, Social and Religious Character* (1885). John Harvard Library edn., intro. by Perry Miller. Cambridge, Mass.: Belknap Press, 1961. 241p.

Schlesinger, Arthur M., Sr. *A Critical Period in American Religion: 1875–1900.* Massachusetts Historical Society Proceedings, LXIV (October, 1930–June, 1932).

Schneider, Herbert W. *Religion in Twentieth Century America.* Cambridge, Mass.: Harvard University Press, 1952. 244p.

Smith, H. Shelton, Robert T. Handy, and Lefferts A. Loetscher. *American Christianity: An Historical Interpretation with Representative Documents.* Vol. II, *1820–1960.* New York: Charles Scribner's Sons, 1963. xv–634p.

Sweet, William W. *The American Churches: An Interpretation.* New York: Abingdon-Cokesbury Press, 1948. 153p.

————. *The Story of Religion in America* (1930). 2nd rev. edn. New York: Harper & Brothers, 1950. ix–492p.

Yoder, Donald W. "Christian Unity in Nineteenth Century America," in Ruth Rouse and Stephen C. Neill, eds. *A History of the Ecumenical Movement: 1517–1948.* Philadelphia: The Westminster Press (1954), 1967, pp. 221–262.

IV. AMERICAN INTERPRETATIONS OF THE ECUMENICAL MOVEMENT

Brent, Charles H. *Understanding: An Interpretation of the Universal Christian Conference on Life and Work . . . Stockholm, 1925.* New York: Longmans, Green, 1925. vi–64p.

Brown, William Adams. *Toward a United Church: Three Decades of Ecumenical Christianity.* New York: Charles Scribner's Sons, 1946. xvi–264p.

Cavert, Samuel McCrea. *On the Road to Christian Unity: An Appraisal of the Ecumenical Movement.* New York: Harper & Brothers, 1961. 192p.

————, and Henry P. Van Dusen, eds. *The Church Through Half a Century: Essays in Honor of William Adams Brown, by former students.* New York: Charles Scribner's Sons, 1936. xii–426p.

Ecumenical Review, The: A Quarterly. Geneva, Switzerland: World Council of Churches, 1948–

Gaines, David D. *The World Council of Churches: A Study of its Background and History.* Peterborough, N. H.: Richard R. Smith, 1966. xviii–1,302p.

Lee, Robert. *The Social Sources of Church Unity: An Interpretation of Unitive Movements in American Protestantism.* New York and Nashville, Tenn.: Abingdon Press, 1960. 238p.

Leiper, Henry S. *Christianity Today: A Survey of the State of the Churches.* New York: Morehouse-Gorham Company, 1947. xvii–452p.

————. *World Chaos or World Christianity.* Chicago: Willett, Clark & Co., 1937. viii–181p. (A popular interpretation of the Oxford and Edinburgh Conferences of 1937.)

Lunger, Harold L., ed. *Foundations of Ecumenical Social Thought: The Oxford Conference Report* (1937). Philadelphia: Fortress Press, 1966.

Mackay, John A. *Ecumenics: The Science of the Church Universal.* Englewood Cliffs, N. J.: Prentice-Hall, 1964. 294p.

Marty, Martin E. *Church Unity and Church Mission.* Grand Rapids, Mich.: Wm. B. Eerdmans Publ. Co., 1964. 139p.

McNeill, John T. *Unitive Protestantism: The Ecumenical Spirit in Its Persistent Expression* (1930). Rev. edn. Richmond, Va.: John Knox Press, 1964. 352p.

Minear, Paul S., ed. *The Nature of the Unity We Seek: Official Report of the North American Conference on Faith and Order, September 8–10, 1957, Oberlin, Ohio.* St. Louis: Bethany Press, 1958. (paperback, 1964). 208p.

Nelson, J. Robert, ed. *Christian Unity in North America: A Symposium.* St. Louis: Bethany Press, 1958. 208p.

Nichols, James H. *Evanston: An Interpretation.* New York: Harper & Brothers, 1954. 155p.

Skoglund, John E., and J. Robert Nelson. *Fifty Years of Faith and Order.* St. Louis: Bethany Press, 1963. 113p.

Soper, Edmund D. *Lausanne: The Will to Understand.* New York: Doubleday and Co., 1928. xiv–156p.

Van Dusen, Henry P. *One Great Ground of Hope.* Philadelphia: The Westminster Press, 1961. 206p. (Surveys cooperation of the last 165 years.)

V. HISTORY OF THE CONCILIAR MOVEMENT

Brown, William Adams. *The Church in America: A Study of the Present Condition and Future Prospects of American Protestantism.* New York: The Macmillan Company, 1922. xv–378p.

Calkins, Gladys G. *Follow Those Women: Church Women in the Ecumenical Movement.* New York: National Council of Churches, 1961. 108p. (Paperback. History of United Church Women and its antecedents.)

Christian Faith in Action: Commemorative Volume. The Founding of the National Council of Churches of Christ in the United States of America. New York: National Council of Churches, 1951. 272p.

Douglass, H. Paul. *Protestant Cooperation in American Cities.* New York: Institute of Social and Religious Research, 1930. xviii–514p.

Federal Council Bulletin, monthly. New York, 1918–1950.

Federal Council of the Churches of Christ in America. *Annual, Biennial,* and *Quadrennial Meeting Reports.* New York, 1908–1950.

Hutchison, John A. *We Are Not Divided: A Critical and Historical Study of the Federal Council of the Churches of Christ in America.* New York: Round Table Press, 1941. 336p.

Knapp, Forrest L. *Church Cooperation: Dead-End Street or Highway to Unity?* New York: Doubleday and Co., 1966. xi–249p.

Lacy, Creighton. *Frank Mason North: His Social and Ecumenical Mission.* Nashville, Tenn.: Abingdon Press, 1967. 300p. (Chapters vi–viii.)

Macfarland, Charles S. *Across the Years.* New York: The Macmillan Company, 1936. xi–367p.

————. *Christian Unity in Practice and Prophecy.* New York: The Macmillan Company, 1933. xvii–396p.

————. *Christian Unity in the Making: The First Twenty-five Years of the Federal Council of Churches of Christ in America, 1905–1930.* New York: Federal Council of Churches, 1948. 376p.

National Council of the Churches of Christ in the United States of America. *Biennial* and *Triennial Reports.* Annual Division Reports. New York: National Council of Churches, 1952–

National Council Outlook, monthly, 1950–1959. *Interchurch News,* monthly, 1959–   . New York: National Council of Churches.

Piper, John F., Jr. "The Social Policy of the Federal Council of the Churches of Christ in America during World War I." Unpublished doctoral thesis at Duke University, 1964. Microfilm at Union Theological Seminary.

Roy, Ralph Lord. *Communism and the Churches.* New York: Harcourt, Brace & Co., 1960. 495p. (Treats opposition from the radical right.)

Sanderson, Ross W. *Church Cooperation in the United States: The Nationwide Backgrounds and Ecumenical Significance of State and Local Councils of Churches in their Historical Perspective.* Hartford, Conn.: Association of Council Secretaries, 1960. 272p.

Sanford, Elias B., ed. *Church Federation: Inter-Church Conference on Federation, New York, November 15–21, 1905.* New York: Fleming H. Revell Co., 1906. 601p.

————. *Origin and History of the Federal Council of the Churches of Christ in America.* Hartford, Conn.: The S. S. Scranton Co., 1916. 528p.

VI. Cooperation in Christian Education

Bower, William C., and Percy R. Hayward. *Protestantism Faces Its Educational Task Together* (1949). 2nd edn. New York: National Council of Churches, 1950. xi–292p.

Brown, Arlo A. *A History of Religious Education in Recent Times.* New York: Abingdon Press, 1923. (Protestant religious education to the formation of the International Council of Religious Education in 1922.)

Christian Scholar, The, quarterly. New York: National Council of Churches, 1960–1967.

Church's Educational Ministry, The: A Curriculum Plan. St. Louis: Bethany Press, 1965. 848p. (Cooperative Curriculum Project of the National Council's Division of Christian Education.)

Cuninggim, Merrimon. *The Protestant Stake in Higher Education.* Washington, D. C.: Council of Protestant Colleges and Universities, 1962.

Dendy, Marshall C. *Changing Patterns in Christian Education.* Richmond, Va.: John Knox Press, 1965. 96p. (On the Covenant Life Curriculum, adopted by Presbyterian Church in the U.S. and four other denominations.)

Division of Christian Education, *Official Reports, Yearbooks.* New York: National Council of Churches, 1951–

Earnshaw, George L., ed. *The Campus Ministry.* Valley Forge, Pa.: Judson Press, 1964. 329p.

International Journal of Religious Education, monthly. Chicago: International Council of Religious Education, 1923–1951. New York: National Council of Churches, 1951–

Lynn, Robert W. *Protestant Strategies in Education.* New York: Association Press, 1964. 96p. (Paperback. Covers the history since 1800.)

Religious Education, bimonthly. New York: The Religious Education Association, 1906– . (Interfaith.)

Shedd, Clarence P. *The Church Follows its Students.* New Haven: Yale University Press, 1938. xvii–327p.

Smith, Seymour A. *Religious Cooperation in State Universities: An Historical Sketch.* Ann Arbor, Mich.: Office of Religious Affairs, The University of Michigan, 1957. 109p. (paperback).

Walter, Erich A., ed. *Religion and the State University.* Ann Arbor, Mich.: University of Michigan Press, 1958. vi–321p. (Symposium of Catholics, Jews, Protestants.)

Williams, George H. *The Theological Idea of the University.* New York: National Council of Churches, 1958. Reprinted as Part II in his *Wilderness and Paradise in Christian Thought.* New York: Harper & Brothers, 1962. 245p.

VII. Cooperation in Home Missions and Comity

Cate, William B. *The Ecumenical Scandal on Main Street.* New York: Association Press, 1965. 126p.

Douglass, H. Paul. *Church Comity: A Study of Cooperative Church Extension in American Cities.* New York: Doubleday & Co., 1929. vii–181p.

————, and Edmund deS. Brunner. *The Protestant Church as a Social Institution.* New York: Harper & Brothers (for Institute of Social and Religious Research), 1935. xv–368p. (Summarizes eighty field studies done by the Institute.)

Handy, Robert T. *We Witness Together: A History of Cooperative Home Missions*. New York: Friendship Press, 1956. 273p. (The definitive history to 1950.)

Home Missions Council, *Annual Reports*. New York, 1912–1950. Council of Women for Home Missions, *Annual Reports*. New York, 1912–1940.

Hooker, Elizabeth R. *United Churches*. New York: George H. Doran Co. (for Institute of Social and Religious Research), 1926. 306p.

King, William R. *History of the Home Missions Council, with Introductory Outline History of Home Missions*. New York: Home Missions Council, [1930]. 64p. (paperback).

Lindquist, Gustavus E. E., and E. Russell Carter. *Indians in Transition: A Study of Protestant Missions to Indians in the United States*. New York: National Council of Churches, 1951. 120p.

Lowry, Edith E., ed. *They Starve That We May Eat: Migrants of the Crops*. New York: Council of Women for Home Missions and Missionary Education Movement, 1937. 72p. (paperback).

Matsumoto, Toru. *Beyond Prejudice: A Story of the Church and Japanese Americans*. New York: Friendship Press, 1946. xii–145p.

Morse, Hermann N., ed. *Home Missions Today and Tomorrow: A Review and Forecast*. New York: Home Missions Council, 1934. xvi–419p. (Study by a Joint Committee of Home Missions Council and Federal Council.)

Piper, David R. *Community Churches: The Community Church Movement*. Chicago: Willett, Clark, & Co., 1928. 4–158p.

Rich, Mark. *The Rural Church Movement*. Columbia, Mo.: Juniper Knoll Press, 1957. vi–251p.

Shotwell, Louisa R. *The Harvesters: The Story of the Migrant People*. Garden City, N. Y.: Doubleday & Co., 1961. 242p.

VIII. Cooperation in World Mission and Service

Barton, James L. *The Story of Near East Relief (1915–1930): An Interpretation*. New York: The Macmillan Company, 1930. xxii–479p.

Bates, M. Searle, and Wilhelm Pauck, eds. *The Prospects of Christianity Throughout the World*. New York: Charles Scribner's Sons, 1964. 286p.

Beaver, R. Pierce. *Ecumenical Beginnings in Protestant World Mission: A History of Comity*. New York: Thomas Nelson & Sons, 1962. 366p.

Ecumenical Missionary Conference, New York, 1900. 2 vols. New York: American Tract Society, 1900. 558p., iv–484p.

Edinburgh, 1910. World Missionary Conference. 9 vols. New York: Fleming H. Revell Co., 1910.

Fey, Harold E. *Cooperation in Compassion: The Story of Church World Service*. New York: Friendship Press, 1966. 175p. (paperback).

Foreign Missions Conference of North America, Annual Reports. New York, 1893–1950.

Hogg, William Richey. *Ecumenical Foundations: A History of the International Missionary Council and Its Nineteenth-Century Background*. New York: International Missionary Council, 1949. 466p.

Jerusalem Meeting of the International Missionary Council, The, 1928. 8 vols. London: International Missionary Council, 1928.

Mott, John R. *Cooperation and the World Mission*. New York: International Missionary Council, 1935. 79p. (paperback).

Re-Thinking Missions: A Laymen's Inquiry After One Hundred Years. By the Commission of Appraisal, William Ernest Hocking, chairman. New York: Harper & Brothers, 1932. xv–349p. (A report that caused much controversy.)

Van Dusen, Henry P. *World Christianity: Yesterday—Today—Tomorrow.* New York: Abingdon-Cokesbury Press, 1947. 7–302p.

IX. COOPERATION IN SOCIAL, RACIAL, AND INTERNATIONAL AFFAIRS

Bennett, John C., ed. *Christian Social Ethics in a Changing World: An Ecumenical Theological Inquiry.* New York: Association Press, 1966. 381p. (Preparatory volume for World Council's Conference on Church and Society, Geneva, Switzerland, July, 1966.)

————. *Foreign Policy in Christian Perspective.* New York: Charles Scribner's Sons, 1966. 160p.

Campbell, Will D. *Race and the Renewal of the Church.* Philadelphia: The Westminster Press, 1963. 90p.

Carter, Paul A. *The Decline and Revival of the Social Gospel: Political and Social Liberalism in American Protestant Churches, 1920–1940.* Ithaca, N. Y.: Cornell University Press, 1956. 265p.

Gulick, Sidney L. *The Christian Crusade for a Warless World.* New York: Federal Council of Churches, 1923. 197p.

Handy, Robert T. *The Social Gospel in America: Gladden, Ely, Rauschenbusch.* New York: Oxford University Press, 1966. 399p.

Haynes, George E. *The Trend of the Races.* New York: Council of Women for Home Missions and Missionary Education Movement, 1922. 205p. (paperback).

Interracial News Service, bimonthly. New York: National Council of Churches, 1929–

Johnson, F. Ernest. *The Social Gospel Re-examined.* New York: Harper & Brothers, 1940. 6–261p.

Kelsey, George D. *Racism and the Christian Understanding of Man.* New York: Charles Scribner's Sons, 1965. 178p.

Kramer, Leonard J., ed. *Man Amid Change in World Affairs.* New York: Friendship Press, 1964. 175p. (Paperback. Originating in discussions of five study commissions convened by the National Council's Department of International Affairs.)

Lacy, Creighton, ed. *Christianity Amid Rising Men and Nations.* New York: Association Press, 1965. 192p. (Interdisciplinary symposium at Duke University, on the church's role in social revolution, sponsored by the National Council's Department of International Affairs.)

Loescher, Frank. *The Protestant Church and the Negro: A Pattern of Segregation.* New York: Association Press, 1948. 159p.

May, Henry F. *Protestant Churches and Industrial America.* New York: Harper & Brothers, 1949. x–297p. (Octagon, 1963).

Meyer, Donald B. *The Protestant Search for Political Realism, 1919–1941.* Berkeley and Los Angeles: University of California Press, 1960. 482p.

Miller, Robert Moats. *American Protestantism and Social Issues, 1919–1939.* Chapel Hill, N. C.: University of North Carolina Press, 1958. xiv–385p.

Moseley, J. Brooke. *Christians in the Technical and Social Revolutions of Our Time.* Cincinnati: Forward Movement Publications, 1966. 141p.

Niebuhr, H. Richard. *The Social Sources of Denominationalism.* New York: Henry Holt and Co., 1929. viii–304p. (Meridian Books, 1957).

Nolde, O. Frederick, ed. *Christian Messages to the Peoples of the World*. New York: Federal Council of Churches, 1943. 86p. (From documents of different communions, sponsored by Commission on a Just and Durable Peace.)

Obenhaus, Victor. *Ethics for an Industrial Era: A Christian Inquiry*. New York: Harper & Row, 1965. 338p. (Final volume in a 12-volume, 15-year project, *Series on Ethics and Economic Life*, authorized by Federal Council in 1949. "Afterword" by F. Ernest Johnson.)

Rauschenbusch, Walter. *Christianity and the Social Crisis*. New York: The Macmillan Company, 1907. xv–429p. (Harper Torchbook, Robert D. Cross, ed., 1964).

Reimers, David M. *White Protestantism and the Negro*. New York: Oxford University Press, 1965. 236p.

Relation of the Church to the War in the Light of the Christian Faith, The. Prepared by a special committee headed by Robert L. Calhoun. New York: Federal Council of Churches, 1943.

Spike, Robert W. *The Freedom Revolution and the Churches*. New York: Association Press, 1965. 128p.

Vines, K. N. "The Role of the Federal Council of the Churches of Christ in America in the Formation of American National Policy." Unpublished Ph.D. dissertation, University of Minnesota, 1953. (From standpoint of a political scientist.)

Visser 't Hooft, W. A. *The Background of the Social Gospel in America*. London and New York: Oxford University Press, 1929. 192p.

X. Interfaith Relations: Catholic-Protestant Dialogue

Abbott, Walter M., S.J., gen. ed. *The Documents of Vatican II* (with Notes and Comments by Catholic, Protestant, and Orthodox Authorities). New York: Guild Press, America Press, Association Press, 1966. xxi–794p. (paperback).

Ashworth, Robert A. "The Story of the National Conference of Christians and Jews." New York: National Conference of Christians and Jews, 1950 (mimeographed).

Brown, Robert McAfee. *The Ecumenical Revolution: An Interpretation of the Catholic-Protestant Dialogue*. Garden City, N. Y.: Doubleday and Co., 1967. 388p.

————, and Gustave Weigel, S.J. *An American Dialogue: A Protestant Looks at Catholicism and a Catholic Looks at Protestantism*. Garden City, N. Y.: Doubleday and Co., 1960. 216p.

Greenspun, William B., C.S.P., and William A. Norgren, eds. *Living Room Dialogues*. New York: National Council of Churches and The Paulist Press, 1965. 256p. (Paperback).

Herberg, Will. *Protestant, Catholic, Jew: An Essay in American Religious Sociology*. New York: Doubleday and Co., 1955. 320p.

Horton, Douglas. *Toward an Undivided Church*. New York: Association Press, 1967. 96p.

Knight, George A. F. *Jews and Christians: Preparation for Dialogue*. Philadelphia: The Westminster Press, 1965. 191p. (Paperback).

Landis, Benson Y. *The Roman Catholic Church in the United States: A Guide to Recent Developments*. New York: E. P. Dutton and Co., 1966. 192p.

Miller, John H., ed. *Vatican II: An Interfaith Appraisal*. New York: Association Press and University of Notre Dame Press, 1966. xii–656p.

Silcox, Claris E., and G. M. Fisher. *Catholics, Jews and Protestants: A Study of Relationships in the United States and Canada.* New York: Harper & Brothers (for Institute of Social and Religious Research), 1934. xvi–369p.

Stuber, Stanley I., and Claud D. Nelson. *Implementing Vatican II in Your Community.* New York: Guild Press and Association Press, 1967. 239p.

Tavard, George H. *The Catholic Approach to Protestantism.* New York: Harper & Brothers, 1955. 160p.

————. *Two Centuries of Ecumenism: The Search for Unity.* Notre Dame, Ind.: Fides Publishers Association, 1960 (paperback, 1962). 239p.

Ward, Hiley. *Documents of Dialogue: A Source Reference Book of Catholic-Protestant Relations Today.* Englewood Cliffs, N. J.: Prentice-Hall, 1966. xvi–525p.

XI. CHURCH UNION IN THE UNITED STATES

Brown, Robert McAfee, and David H. Scott, eds. *The Challenge to Reunion: The Blake Proposal Under Scrutiny.* New York: McGraw-Hill, 1963. 292p.

Consultation on Church Union: *Principles of Church Union, Guidelines for Structure: A Study Guide.* Cincinnati: Forward Movement Miniature Book, 1967. 144p.

Digest of the Proceedings of the Consultation on Church Union, 1962–1967, compiled by George L. Hunt. P.O. Box 69, Fanwood, N. J., 1967.

Douglass, H. Paul. *Church Unity Movements in the United States.* New York: Institute of Social and Religious Research, 1934. xxxviii–576p.

Dun, Angus. *Prospecting for a United Church.* New York: Harper & Brothers, 1948. xi–115p.

Ehrenstrom, Nils, and Walter G. Muelder. *Institutionalism and Church Unity.* New York: Association Press, 1963. 378p. (Chapters xii-xv. Symposium prepared under Commission on Faith and Order. Includes eight case studies of successful or unsuccessful union efforts.)

Garrison, Winfred E. *The Quest and Character of a United Church.* New York: Abingdon Press, 1957. 238p.

Hunt, George L., and Paul A. Crow, eds. *Where We Are in Church Union.* New York: Association Press, 1965. 126p.

Mudge, Lewis S. *One Church: Catholic and Reformed—Toward a Theology for Ecumenical Decision.* Philadelphia: The Westminster Press, 1963. 96p. (paperback).

Nelson, J. Robert. *Overcoming Christian Divisions.* New York: Association Press, 1962. 128p.

Outler, Albert C. *The Christian Tradition and the Unity We Seek.* New York: Oxford University Press, 1957. 165p. (Following Oberlin.)

Index